Historical Culture

Historical Culture

On the Recoding of an Academic Discipline

SANDE COHEN

UNIVERSITY OF CALIFORNIA PRESS
Berkeley · Los Angeles · London

University of California Press
Berkeley and Los Angeles, California
University of California Press, Ltd.
London, England
Copyright © 1986 by
The Regents of the University of California
First Paperback Printing 1988

Library of Congress Cataloging in Publication Data

Cohen, Sande
      Historical culture.

      Bibliography: p.
      Includes index.
      1. Historiography.   2. History - Philosophy.
I. Title.
D13.C59 1986   907.2   85-8672
ISBN 0-520-06453-4

Printed in the United States of America
1 2 3 4 5 6 7 8 9

For Max

Contents

Acknowledgments

I thank John Johnston, Howard Singerman, and Scott Waugh who generously criticized chapters one and two; I am especially grateful to Jeremy Gilbert-Rolfe for his assiduous comments on chapters one through three, as well as for the many intellectual discussions of the past two years. I also thank Hans Rogger, Hunter Dupree, and Arnold Springer for their many kindnesses. And without the support of Donna Cowan, I would not have had the time to write at all.

Permission has been granted for approximately 2,000 words from *Capitalism and Material Life: 1400–1800* by Fernand Braudel, translated by Miriam Kochan, copyright © 1967 by Librarie Armand Colin; English translation copyright © 1973 by George Weidenfeld and Nicolson Ltd. Permission has also been granted for approximately 1,000 words from the Appendix, pp. 147–164 in *Weimar Culture: The Outside as Insider* by Peter Gay. Copyright © 1968 by Peter Gay, reprinted by permission of Harper & Row, Publishers, Inc.

I wish to thank Merlin Press for permission to reprint from E. P. Thompson's *The Poverty of Theory*. London: Merlin, 1978.

S. C.

Ocean Park-Venice, Ca. 1981–1984

The longing to make the spook comprehensible,
or to realize non-sense, has brought about a
corporeal ghost, a ghost or spirit with a real body,
an embodied ghost.

Caspar Schmidt, nineteenth century

We want nothing whatever to do with
those . . . who use their minds as they would a
savings bank . . . all proud partisans of leveling via
the head.

André Breton

History is always written from a sedentary point of
view, and in the name of a unitary State apparatus.

Gilles Deleuze

The bourgeois sign is a metonymic confusion.

Roland Barthes

Introduction

The academy recodes our reactive culture. A culture is reactive when it continues to narrativize itself despite, at any moment, being six minutes away (by missile) from its own nonnarrative obliteration. The dissemination of models of "history" promotes cultural subjects who are encouraged to think about nonnarrative relations—capitalism, justice, and contradictions—in a narrative manner. Narrating screens the mind from the nonnarrative forces of power in the present, insofar as "historical" narration reduces present semantic and pragmatic thought (connotation) to forms of story, repetition, and model, all of which service cultural redundancy. Historical thought is a manifestation of reactive thinking-about, which blocks the act of thinking-to. The "perplexity of History" (Arendt's term), a Liberal projection which also includes, unhappily, most of Western Marxism, arises, I argue, from the ill-conceived act of trying to make "history" relevant to critical thinking. What actually occurs by means of "historical thought" is the destruction of a fully semanticized present.

This introduction draws the reader into a consideration of assumptions, hypotheses, and reasonings concerning my starting point, the nonaccessibility of the presence of the present once narrative thinking dominates semantics, where an obligation to history generates the illusion of the autonomy of historical culture, which in turn reinforces the cultural debilitation of radical thought. This introduction is an interpretation of the present in which I argue that critical thinking is not possible when connected to academic historical thinking.

Preliminary Considerations

Initial readers of this text isolated a contradiction: how can this academically based critique, founded on unfamiliar terminologies and strategies of thinking, in good faith critique a particular academic sector, the discourse of historians? Does one not perpetuate the very status of the academia one criticizes in offering a critique so distant from the significations of even everyday academic life?

The charge of bad faith is serious and legitimate because it raises some political-semantic aspects of the privileges, purposes, functions, roles, and social effects of writing, most of which are at best latent. So at the outset I acknowledge that my use of interpretants—terms and concepts that name and analyze meanings—is radically unfamiliar. But I argue that this must be so: in the present cultural-economic conjunctions, academic discourse, in its presumed everydayness (its empiricism and abstractions, its once "progressive" genres like psychoanalysis and Marxism) leads the intellectual evasion of what is specific to the present; academia absorbs contradictions even when it is critical. From this assessment, instead of assuming the normalcy of academia, I try to alter the intellectual acceptance of academia as a just player in the overall organization of knowledge. I argue that the high university's cultural functions can be decoded by analysis of its intellectual texts, which should, of course, parallel social-political critiques as well. To do this, I must then resort to a discourse that slows reading, that refuses to convince a reader by its cadence or even rightness, and that is no longer academic in its effects, even if its presentation must necessarily appear academic.

The unfamiliarity of some of the terminology and modelings I perform on historical discourse should be seen as an attempt to present the internal discursive cultural operations of an academic sector, the utterances of historians. My hypothesis is that academia can be examined as to its elementary intellectual effects by starting with its textual products, which are to be understood as context-producing renderings, not texts that respond to reality. One must not let the idea of academia as a responsive writing intrude on understanding what it does: academia is not a reactive subjectivity whose writings result in paradigms that objectify reality. I argue that academic writing is immersed in the creation of reactive thinking, and if one works through the textual arrangements of academic history, its "disposition is going to reveal all of its mythifying context" (Lyotard 1984:29–30). If this commits me to the analytic-Structuralist position of myth-critique, it is because I am interested in showing how academic historical texts perform their own "mute jurisdiction," how they release their built-in intellectual and cultural effects, the latter consumed by readers who, to use De Certeau's phrase, become "renters and not the owners of their own know-how."

In stressing "disposition" or immanent critique set against academic practices, I thus do not pretend to have transcended existing semantic and implicative systems; as Barthes reminds us, "discourse moves . . . by clashes . . . as the paradox which goes against the surrounding or preceding doxa" (1977:200). This text is bound to a kind of academic intelligibility, but it no longer academizes: it offers no transcendence of anything. It cannot: because of the division of thinking, it is already an overdetermined object. Of course, the only complete alternative to an academic critique of academia would be a discourse that really transcended writing, but this cannot be imagined without relapsing into the belief of being "outside" language. The comforting notion of "outside" (including opposition), a mode of belief in transcendence, still sustains artists and writers: it offers the mind the illusion of intellectual gratification. I do not think it is the function of an intellectual to gratify the mind by writing, since it is an open question as to what form of signifier (word, image, gesture) is best capable of conveying different contents. I reject the new-left position that advances the idea that writing "in the name of" (the poor, etc.) can "lift repression" or "help us to remember" (Eagleton 1983:viii), because such propositions are still subjective resolutions that do not transfer except to other academics. In short, I do not treat writing as a cultural universal.

Academia tries to stand outside—transcend—the law of the equivalence of all value. But since education, learning, and knowledge cannot be said actually to transcend—give rise to a future significantly different from the present—only immanent transcendence exists—the multiplication of nonconnecting contexts. Real transcendence has been made immanent in actual cultural-economic relations. The division of thinking is so intensive that only one's exchange-functions are relevant to a context; nothing can close the gaps between the context of writing (research, grants, and the like) and the context of exploitation (unpaid labor, boring labor) or between aesthetic skill and discovery, and repetition, redundancy, and monotony. As Baudrillard has put it, "in place of the reflexive transcendence of mirror and scene" where one could subjectively project, that is, believe, that one's language, habits, customs, beliefs, and behavior were aligned with the tendencies of a collective context, today it is one's connections, contacts, and feedback that matter: these latter terms designate that intellectual activity is part of a "nonreflecting surface . . . where operations unfold" (1983c:127). Here contradictions, the site where reality itself is to appear, according to both liberalism and Marxism, do not disclose and announce to society what it must recognize. Instead, contradictions are fully embedded in incommensurable contexts, no longer (if they ever were) indicators of temporal direction and thus transcendence (resolution, fulfillment). In this sense, what divides academic Marxism and liberalism, dialectics or nondialectics, are impoverished signs, since both share as their real context the sixty-five million or so semiliterates in this country.

For example, the Marxist law of expanding value certainly defines a permanent level of capitalist practice, with a virtual infinity of implications; but the current Marxist academic activity that promotes aesthetic works as a transcendence of the division of labor is no longer part of a "critical distance." The dialectic imputed to be in history and thus manifested in cultural works (or texts) does not exist and is simply mystical. Indeed, Jameson, the leading academic Marxist in literary criticism, has recently attempted to synthesize the 1960s as a collective progressive "moment," yet he still protects academia as a cultural zone; he treats it as a "minute configuration" of multiple contradictions (1984:208), not as itself a contradictory player. Academic Marxism has actively followed the path of expanding Capital: to many it appears to be engaged in trying to evade the flattening of its own value—it promotes means discontinuous with the contradictions it isolates, it presupposes as necessary for its own activities exactly what is blocked in society as a whole, transcendence from contradictions. From this angle, its academization ought to create some internal criticism/exposure of academic practices, but such is not the case.

Another way of putting this is simply to state, for now, that the liberal incapacity to articulate a nonideological discourse on the future has been partially filled by academic Marxism, yet both groups refuse to acknowledge the cultural nihilism of the present. Science has absolutely triumphed, as Nietzsche predicted, but so has illiteracy in the capitalist West, to the point where the Chief Justice of the Supreme Court can today suggest that some juries should be directly based on expertise and knowledge: anyone who occupies a post of knowledge should be judged by doubles, those who know what academics know. Neither liberal nor Marxist academics will deluge Burger with intellectual critiques, just as academia as a whole remains silent on the connections between the Chicago School of economics and the current mass detentions in Chile. I no longer project academic writing as a transcendence (resolution) at all; its products are not part of any dialectic whatsoever, regardless of the fate of any specific academic text.

For in the face of the dissolve of all notions of collective transcendence (God, History, Language, Technology, Utopia), in the impasse of both liberalism and Marxism, I believe one cannot sustain the notion that writing can be projected as the constitution of a significant difference within culture.

I am not going to deny the extreme intellectualism of this text. Nor do I deny that such intellectualism might only be another way of arriving at a dead end, that writing against academia only reinforces the critic's notorious "narrow limits with which he is allowed to suffer without upsetting the world" (Barthes 1972:155). I am convinced only that the strange familiarity of academic discourse, its promotion of "need and right" by means of language, can be rendered as distorting insofar as such language sustains the autonomization of thought and society. After all, given the investments academia makes in its written performances, its writings can then hardly be considered anecdotal evidence.

Overdetermination of Transcendence and Criticism

In what follows, the term *transcendence* means any semantic-intellectual figuration (presented to thought) which produces the effect that cultural-intellectual contradictions, within texts and between texts and something else (institutions, functions), are resolved by any *closure of thinking*. Transcendence promises what can be called symbolic gratification, where experience or consciousness or literature are projected as more than partial values (see Baudrillard 1975:149–150).

Transcendence is a type of utterance designed for maximum distance from reality and intimate appropriateness to reality—a discourse that simulates the objectification of cultural contents and activities by wrapping them in "can" and "must," truth and belief (modals and their combinations). Obligative thought is generally its characteristic mode. I propose that transcendence is manifested by a sign-system that aims at the control of immanence, in which the semantic explosions of the latter, at the level of perception, are reduced and diffused. Regarded negatively, the idea of contradiction, for example, fails as a transcendent category for use in analysis, as its ideational force generates the "evenness" of categories. Can one reason from contradiction to "must" (have-to) with any effectivity today? (Contradictions make academics happy, being intrinsic to the circulation of irony.) The anarcho-semiologist can say that transcendent discourse is frequently "an egg white emptied, then volatilized in the gas of the holy ghost" (Artaud), a sarcastic rendering of Habermas's "scientized" contention that apex-propositions or utterances that evoke transcendent obligation "have the double function of proving that validity claims of norm systems are legitimate and of avoiding thematization and testing of discursive-validity claims" (1973:112–113). As applied to academia, there is layer upon layer of linguistic-intellectual evasion and displacement of explicit discourse, which would manifest the wanting, knowing, and being of academic writing as it transcendentalizes. I would like to supplement Habermas's recognition that bourgeois society avoids "rational discourse" as long as it can with the notion that it must prevent "rationality" from "breaking out." Imperative, vocative, and narrative modes, for example, are combined in the academic system with the effect that commands, namings, and stories sustain the real transcendence of immanent contradictions (for example, academics in the State Department say that President Reagan cannot say what he knows about the Soviets; in hearing this story, defense contractors know their subsidies are commanded to continue—no one's "wantings" need be mentioned).

Such present irrationality is embalmed by analogy, enthymemes, classemes, and so on. The linguistic relay, all of the ways in which signifiers acquire use and exchange value (and lose it), is simultaneously the form and content of this layer of bourgeois culture, where internal competition over the means of making acceptable and unacceptable a language attached to programs of stabilization drives much of the academy forward. The difference between an academic-bourgeois text about positive transcendence ("need," for example, society needs to modernize the subject) and an academic new-left critique of negative transcendence, the subjective side of culture (for example, the continuing "loss of self"), is the insubstantial one of calibrating signification to the iteration of "problems." Neither are intensifications of exposing the language-moves of pacifying discourse. The future, in both cases, is the projected manifestation of those who determine the language and signs of "need, necessity, requirements, conditions" in accordance with defensive signications, a tactic just as common among radicals as not (for example, Adorno's protective-reactive "subject" or Kristeva's unleashing of a "subjective polytopia"). It seems that it is difficult for many to accept that

> Writing is a blind alley . . . because society is a blind alley. . . . there can be no universal language outside a concrete and no longer a mystical or merely nominal universality of society (Barthes 1967*b*:87).

In the deployment of transcendence, there is the power to expel from institutional situations unacceptable cognitions; in this sense, the linguistic relay—as a general mode of transmission—is seldomly founded on truth but more frequently on pseudo-law, where the pseudo-lawful is only mythically the scene of periodic "innovations" of "public discourse." (The special case of how new codings are introduced will be taken up in chapters three through five.) In short, what is continuous in bourgeois society is the recoding of sedentary nondisruptive significations, which includes the vast significations of the modern Left (see Deleuze and Guattari 1983:52–58). I think there is an academic linguistic code and in chapter one I try to isolate it by focusing on the construction of "transcendence," a task continuous with the current French critique of the performance of ideological writing, academic writing treated as a mode of bureaucratic-ideological organization, an intensification of Althusser's ideological state apparatus (see Deleuze 1977:143).

I focus on the cultural transcendence of history considered as an academic practice because today transcendence is the sole category of capitalist society which determines, intellectually, modalities of distance between thought and the social: not only does a transcendent content (money, the novel, research) require obligative thought but transcendence also positivizes—intellectually, it subsidizes "need and right" as legitimations of discourse. As both content and thought, transcendence can be understood as the category of contemporary *cultural value*, by means of which the myth of the will to culture is protected from dissolution. The positive semantic charges of cultural transcendence are rendered as the "long-term," the necessary, the un-alterable, the obligative, and so on. But such significations of transcendence are immersed in sign-forms or distortion devices which encourage subjects to gravitate to what Deleuze has called "a fictitious voice from on high that functions as a signifier" (1977:240), where culture—as the fusion of thought and con-tent—generates reactive subjects, not unrestrained criticism. The historian who narrates by means of the cultural voices of nostalgia or realism or a celebration of, say, the inventive spirit thereby encodes those voices as full positions, symbolic roles of presence, as intrinsic components of what it means to be "cul-tural" in the first place. In this regard, I agree with Baudrillard's contention that academic "discourse" has, as its trajectory of fulfillment, the redefinition of all serviceable connotations so as to stabilize denotation, thereby bringing signification and lan-guage to a halt insofar as subjects are encouraged to not chal-lenge simulations of culture. Our culture manufactures "resurrections of difference," like the belief that we live in an Age of Information, which, at the least, recodes the temporal illusion of the idea of an "age," and encodes an entire "philos-ophy" of acceptance (see Baudrillard 1983c:16).

Since the cultural function of academic historiography is ma-terially based on its linguistic performance, criticism can seek to dissolve cultural familiarity—transcendencies within imma-nence—in order to think through the strangeness of our cultural systems from their semantic nucleus on up (if that is indeed the direction involved). In saying this, I echo the Russian Formalist emphasis on isolating devices of enculturation, linked to Nietzsche's insight that cultural criticism is initiated by stressing the functions of transcendence; one can try to "think to" where academic language presents the mind with closure, resolution, answer, an activity that replaces the passive "thinking of." Rev-olutionary criticism may be over, as one often hears; but the Russian Constructivist energization of criticism—"A picture must be active, it must do something in the world" (Tiege)—at least stresses writing as the negation of "reproduction, patching, imitation, restoration, idealization, [and] sentimentalism." In fo-cusing on both the functions and strangeness of "historical thought," this quagmire of cultural stagings, criticism as the "activization of differences" (Lyotard) cannot stop at the level of isolating contradictions. It should try to dismantle the machinery and apparatus of the "cultural languages" through concrete knowledge of whether or not they promote anticapitalism, the latter the intellectual ethic I consider the basis for a rejection of historical thinking. Anticapitalism, I argue, is not compatible with any form of historicism, especially at the level of semantic thinking. Criticism can demonstrate what cultural dominance is all about in the present without providing alternate schemes of transcendence (models of desire, positive forms, necessities). Narrative functions, like those singled out by Greimas's theory of actantial roles (sender, receiver, victim, and so on) can be presented as transcendent and autonomous relations (for example, there are always victims) only because language can enact this performance *and* Western capitalism can integrate its cultural effects, the cultural surplus from narrative worlds that conform to the laws of our society. Exploitation is easier to send and receive when a transcendent history is presented as the very form of exploitation (for example, the myth that current wages are acceptable by comparison to past inequities).

Accordingly, I present this work as a modified version of deconstruction theory, wishing to avoid its mega-announcements ("freedom is only a dream" says Derrida) but utilizing some of its terminology. This work is a *pragmatographia* of the narrative culture circulated by contemporary historians, an analysis of the written actions whereby readers gain belief (resolve to act) and habit (rules of action) so as to be reactive subjects. On this view, the delegitimization of narrative knowledge releases one's mind from the reproduction of narrative exchange.

Historiographical Transcendence (Objections)

Historians are obligated to present the past as somehow transcendent, whereby all kinds of cultural pairs—rich and poor, victors and victims, winners and losers, city and countryside, capital and labor—are linked to some third entity, the one that shapes, unites, and determines the narratability of such pairs: class, capital, repression, human nature, technology, and so on. This third entity—the transcendent thing—fills a blank: classically it answers a question according to models of inquiry, and so satisfies conditions of interpretation, description, and explanation, thus providing history with continuity and discourse with meaning. But I will stress that history texts provide such answers (for example, isolating a transformation) only in reading time; and when such answers are carried over from past to present-now and locate present-now within the answer about time-then, the reader is actually subject to a past futural to his time and thus contained by such thoughts. In effect, there is no language of the present, which vanishes in its specificity, contained, as it were, in narrated repetition. The intellectual effect is that the present is unknowable, unreachable, unnameable and remote until attached to transcendence (here, continuity); once known this way, the present dissolves into a jumble of results and consequences—an unenacted undoing—propped up by a transcendental relation. The neo-Marxist historians, the Genoveses, tell me why this is so in the most serious of idioms; enriched by psychoanalysis, historical thought is a form of transcendent cognition, indispensable to thought in the first place because one is brought to

> the irreconcilable antagonisms inherent in the human condition and, therefore, to that tragedy of historical process once addressed so eloquently by Christian theology. . . . psychoanalysis encourages a sensibility capable of mastering a disordered world and . . . addresses the historical problem of mediating the contrary claims of order, authority, freedom, and rebellion (Genovese 1976:218).

Such investments in an identity between psychoanalytic discourse treated as a conveyor to this transcendence and history provokes a plethora of wonderings: Who is to "master" such "disorder"? How is the historian attached to "mastery"? Why "irreconcilable"? What is a "sensibility"? (One knows that historians have never found a plausible argument to demonstrate an embodied historical sense, an organ akin to Freud's placement of the mental agencies in the neurones.) What, in fact, is a "disordered" world? Notions like "human condition" violate even historical thought. More importantly, one sees the non-narrative ideation—"human condition"—directly smuggled into thought, which is thus a narrativized thought. From a perspective where the Genoveses use "irreconcilable antagonisms," a nonnarrative discursive unit (the postulate of opposition) to situate history in transcendence, how is, say, the "disordered" fact of 1982's forty million infant deaths worldwide by starvation, made historical by reference to tragedy?

I will stress that the collapse of the bourgeois-liberal contents of transcendence—progress, knowledge, value, and so on—have been rerouted by much of neo-Marxian historiography into the ethical aspect of transcendence, the obligation to "think historically." Unlike either group, my analysis isolates those history functions that, as with any discourse that closes gaps (Lévi-Strauss), promote the myth that history is a condition of knowledge. Concepts such as change and transformation do not belong in the category of "history." My combination of semiotic theory, existential-anarchist attitudes toward cultural passivity, and the original Marxist focus on unpaid labor instead leads to such questions as, "How much history is required to produce the ordinary educated public in the first place?" Where does historical thought itself begin and end when viewed as a cultural supply system, a way of generating what Lyotard (1984:48) calls "the pragmatic posts of institutional life?" The actual history problem itself is to be found in the textualizing of this enculturation.

To the issue of writing history at all, I want to say this for now: neither the historian's presentation of extraordinarily strange past materials nor specific tactics for representing it (the essay, thick description, and the like) annuls the negative intellectual effects of narrative history. This is what I try to prove in chapters three through five. I can imagine the idea of history as an intellectually valid activity; but as I read such works I am immediately plunged into multiple semantic, logical, psychological, theoretical, and other such ideations. These relations of intellectuality, nonnarrative, are now far more interesting to specify than is continuing to promote ways of energizing or renewing the writing of history. To put this another way: at the end of his *Idea of Nature* (1933), Collingwood argued that scientific thought about nature showed the former's dependence upon the Idea of History, which Collingwood believed to be a sufficient or nondependent mode of thought (another mode of transcendence) (Collingwood 1967:176). In rejecting the Idea of History as autonomous, sufficient, and so on, it seems to me that I can postulate more important discursive frames: abstract semantics, paralogy, the theoretical plateau itself, each of which is far more useful for learning how to think in a nonreactive manner. There are lots of stories to tell; they are unavoidable. But historians do not really tell stories: stories are embedded in histories. I think I can argue that there is no way the historian's narrative can acknowledge—and remain a narrative—the gaps and codings of gaps between their utterances and some "collective subject of narration," the latter conferring on the mind that one is incorporated in society as one is narrated some collective history. Western culture is, in my opinion, not a subject—and without that, or until it is created, history can only try to simulate for the mind some transcendent obligation.

Historiographical Transcendence (Its Common Myth)

This project has nothing to do with the writings of the so-called new philosophers, such as Levy, who have proclaimed that "history does not exist." Such formulations are regressions. They try to slip language behind thought, bypassing arguments such as Danto's that history is what "historians say it is." Danto's statement itself, however, is insufficient: it does not isolate the history effects as they pertain to an audience, the manufacturing of public life, and, most of all, it keeps alive the illusion that historians can transmit a cultural common history, one ideological kernel frequently shared by bourgeois and neo-Marxist historians. A cultural common history is revealed in any of the forms of belief in one world, common problems, universal issues, or necessary structures. Mink (1978:142–145) has shown, brilliantly, that such suppositions are always related to belief in the untold story, a belief so dominant it occurs within acts of historical research as well as narrative presentation, and which can neither be validated nor abandoned by historians. As soon as one focuses on the incompatibility between truth and coherence claims raised by every narrative (for example, that a specific narrative's dates, types, existents, occurrences, and outcomes are not arbitrary), there is no longer the possibility of conceiving a singular narrative history as the container and completion of each and every narrative text. Each text crowds out the intellectual space of the other. Mink, in fact, has reworked Lévi-Strauss's argument that each historical narrative is related by a disjunctive inclusion of what it sets before itself as the "analogically given past"—some central subject coded as a continuous quantity, but which is uninsertable with other such subjects. Only the last-written, all-subsuming historical narrative could find for itself enough room to locate perfectly within itself the correct place of all that has happened and has been already narrated. Such a last narrative would also be the point at which historical thought internally collapsed and became a bible. To critique common history is necessarily to critique the historian's recoding of all possible modes of existence into told stories.

Yet Mink does not push his own analysis far enough. He neglects to qualify "historical thought and representation" with the rider "academic"; and more seriously, he fails to recognize that bourgeois-academic discourse must occlude recognition that there is *no uncoded common language,* which it promotes even as the referential dimension has become difficult to model under "realism." Common language is today a pure fantasy, one of those real illusions of the mind. Simply, linguistic practice has exploded "language." It is now impossible to believe that metaphor or double articulation or "poetic aporia" or communicative models or notions of intention characterize anything but a metalinguistic practical strategy in one's dealing with language and its possible fields of performance. Yet within capitalist society language is heavily coded: it requires, for example, discursive functions to exclude what can be uttered and written in relation to social *topoi.* At a foreclosure sale, dispossessed owners usually shed tears in relation to emotional loss and monetary ruination,

but such expressions do not transfer—they are not translatable—
to the bemoaning performed before the cameras by public officials about such human tragedy. Everyone speaks his or her
function, an idea discomforting to the ideology that language is
a way out of contradictions, a way in to value. Even the second
articulation of language (phonemes) is subject to law and ownership (for example, Apple Computer Company won an injunction in 1983 against another company's use of the sounds
"pine-apple" in computer games).

Hypotheses of Historiographical Transcendence

With all that in mind, as a prose culture, academic discourse
does not promote forms of knowing that threaten the accumulation of surplus value, the constant of capitalist exploitation.
From this angle, it is an open issue whether academia has been
a disaster upon culture, projecting upon the social endless ideal-
izations of literature, technology (expertise), and so on, while
mass illiteracy has speeded up. The function of most systematic
academic codes of signification is to muffle and contain, displace
and reduce, pseudosynthesize and thereby recode multiple
social-intellectual contradictions, dispelling the latter's intellectual force. Academia's role is to stabilize contradictions by producing   pseudocollective   meanings—"painlessness"   for   the
mind, as Nietzsche put it. Exploitation of labor is ceaselessly
remade the most universal content of society and appears in
innumerable academic formulations as normal. Yet it is a strange
relation where the hypercoded economic level and thought
meet, where the permanent shock of exploitation receives a constant, instant normalization by one or more discourses. Today
Western society is clogged by its indigestible accumulated surplus value, and federal officials use the phrase "snuggle up"—
coined by academic economists—when calling for increases in
interest rates. "Snuggle up" reduces interest functions to an
imaginary story context (the intimacy of money?), the intellectual
effect of which is to further the transcendence of economic codes
from criticism. Academic culture—that which makes "snuggle

up" acceptable—organizes intellectual atrophy at a faster pace than it generates intellectual breakthroughs. My initial hypothesis concerning academic history is this: by imposing the form of story, academic history reproduces a culture of common language, common society, or common reality in the face of uncommon language (codes), class society, and uncommon realities (chasms between cultural worlds).

I propose to analyze the uncommon presence of academic historiography, viewing it as a force of what Lyotard (1984:23–37) has called the Grand Narrative tradition. I do not start by presuming the normalcy of its social status or allegorical functions, what professional historiography has included as part of its self-definition. Unlike Lévi-Strauss, I do not presume history texts to be related to deep structures of mind or self, nor do I think it useful to assume such texts arise out of a cognitive need, today stressed so much by Jameson and others, unwilling to suspend a demand for historical totality in the face of capitalist permutations. The masses never know the discourses of culture or society so as to be able to clash with academic sign usage; the masses have nothing to say about their subjection to intellectual programs in advance of the latter's production, so it would be too much of a leap to start with existing narrativized designations of history, for example, that historical thinking arises from the history of the West since, say, the French Revolution. Within historiography, the masses are held to be open to the transformations of historical thought, that is, to the relinearization of thought, a perpetual revisionism in which thinking is reduced to story. Both academic liberals and leftists agree on the need for more history, for perspective and understanding. Reaffirmed are acceptable distances, negative and positive, between criticism and existing social practices, insofar as story blunts one's thinking about the nonrepeatable, the specificity of what is.

An aestheticism of thought always grips historiography: contact between its texts and nonacademic readers supports balance, equilibrium, and resolution as prevailing forms of reality, even when it is acknowledged that negativity dominates society. My second hypothesis is this: academic historiography is part of the overall requirement for cultural stability and sustains a future organized, in advance, as the neutralization of existing contradictions, these dismissed as necessary means or moments of mediation (on neutralization, see Greimas 1984:246). Present-now is articulated by historians as positive-negative combinations of what must be. As a discourse, history can thus be considered one of the forms of mythic speech, since it is structurally a closure of thought, as Barthes showed; but as a text, it generates cultural reproduction in the advanced societies. In this latter sense, I propose to read its significations as practices: What provisions for the intellect are conveyed through the reading consumption of history? What strategies for action upon advanced capitalist society are transmitted by high academic narrative history?

Here I focus on devices of telling in which the appearance of the cultural modals—must, need, certitude, necessity, and so on—are grafted to historical thought and legitimated by the telling. I analyze documents ranging from White's defense of history as a form of poetics to the covert political positions of the leaders of the historical profession. How do historiographers embed the transcendence of historical knowledge in nonknowledge (for example, truisms), in textual devices (for example, the shifter *I*, performative onsets that ground utterances in an "outside"); how are passive readers presumed (for example, the reader systematically precluded from critical thought); and how is the pseudotheatricality of time (for example, drama) accomplished? I argue that such thought is always tied to implicit definitions of the expelled thought form, the antihistorical. If historical thought is a genre of thought, where does it begin and end by comparison to, say, a grammar of action or narrative voice? If a narrated past can reach into its future readers' intellect by means of semantic analogies of experience, how can such a text be called historical as opposed to, say, programmatic? How is the past made acceptable to emit its message and be read? How is the past made present-able so that it is neither too present (which cancels past) nor too past (which annuls its readability)? If there is no present-able past apart from the means of presentation (textual devices), which aspects of a historical text convey the informational channel as opposed to the enculturation channel? How can such textual levels even be characterized? Here I should say that I believe historical discourse presupposes as its material context the academic legitimation of narrative culture as such: life is a story and nonlife equals unnarratability, the equation manifesting the former as positive, a position that reclaims negativity as meaningful, while to nonstory or unnarratability belongs mere positivity, an ethnological degree zero of existence because many accept that narrative culture is already a transcendence of nonstory. Since I think such a presumption is a great intellectual disaster, I analyze claims for a narrative culture without protecting any connection between historical thought and need, just as one must reject any unmotivated (natural) thread between such thought and society. I analyze written connections, imaginary relations, symbolic roles, codes of hierarchy, the manufacturing of such pairs as the relevant and the irrelevant, fantasies of preservation, and chronomatics or time codings (for example, "later," "no longer," "not yet"). I am not trying to classify such discourse. I want to know how it works. In this latter objective, the critique of historiography from an anarchist cultural perspective is supplemented by the formalist claim of exposing the mechanisms of discourse, relations between signs and semantics which form the unstatability of narrative organization. This is the realm of acceptable cultural and intellectual unconsciousness, where the psychic and the cognitive overlap with discourse and implied practices.

To use Habermas's phrase, academic "historical culture" partially "steers" the apparatus of cultural containment, in that it fosters an intellectual channel of transmission which excludes loss of direction (cultural vertigo) or the decoding of value (loss of value). The historiographic form of such steering is that thought is geared to think of temporal processes as transcendent: irretrievable, collective, humane, total, nonnegatable, and so on, when, in fact, there are only temporal arrangements, combinations, inclusions-disjunctions, and so on, of uncommon cultural relations. In the sphere of culture there is no primary process and certainly no primary form of the signifier; only Western society privileges its culture by historicizing it. As I will argue, narrativization is a means/end structure reproducing discrimination and distinction; just because meanings are subjected to temporalization does not release them from hierarchy and power relations. Finding history as the cause of various impasses is the zenith of reactive thinking. Academic historiography falls under Lotman's formulation about "autocharacteristic" texts: a semantically extensive historical text written for nonacademics gives instructions, regulations, and directions about both the need for narrativity and historicity. The historical text presents itself as a model of intelligibility, of definition, where its effects are nonnarrative, even though such texts are read as transformations (Lotman 1975:83). In short, historical discourse will be shown to be isomorphic with academic discourse.

What I call academic historiography is, for now, this: a mode of writing in which historicity, historicality, or the historical is made a motivation, cause, factor, and reason for the existence of a phenomenon, and transmitted to a model reader as necessary for the reader's participation in some cultural series. I have in mind here condensed macro-beliefs like "tradition is constitutive of reality" or its opposite, "history is meaningless," which still conjures history as *that which must be thought about.* Instead, I consider historical thought to be part of a "shifter" function, included in what semioticians call the category of disengagement, wherein representations are split from coded acts of writing and made autonomous, manifesting an exteriority which one must think as providing one with temporal value (see Greimas and Courtes 1982:88). I argue that historical thought short-circuits present critical knowledge (for example, how capitalism works) by manifesting the present as incapable of being known or transformed without history. I treat historicity as an academic sign system, whose center is a narrative; but the latter is generated by obliterating its intellectual construction, so that the reader is in fact subject to an indirectly stated but systematic intellectual program in the consumption (reading) of a narrative presentation. I try, in this regard, to show the arguments put forth by narrative theorists such as White (1973) that historical thought is fundamentally characterized by literary narration are defensive protections of the historical discipline. Instead, I focus on the intellectuality of a model reader, arguing that the reader is designed to not think out all that is textually presented in the form of a narrative, and can only think reactively. I argue that there is a core of intellectuality closer to the metasemic (categorical) level than the literary, that historical texts have their most elementary functions, their history effects, not merely as forms of stories. Successful academic histories release narratability as a universal form of thought, an a priori container of all content. Thus, I argue that diachrony is secondary to semic investments, built-in meanings (predicates, definitions, attributes, and so on); before-after, now-then, not-now, or no-longer are secondary semantic blocks that refer to a culture's temporalization of its unstated but primary axiologies (see Greimas 1984:143). In narrating, academic historians promulgate the very presence of the discipline of history, yet because narrating is also based upon an acceptance of the myth of its ordinariness, the historical text is also an intellectual organization of a certain way of thinking. Minimal semantic distinctions like "good" and "evil" distribute "right" and "wrong" and "acceptable" and "unacceptable" (connotations) across many semantic systems; history texts redouble existing semanticized ideologies already built into a discourse. In this view, for example, Marxist narration can never, intellectually considered, be as semantically interesting as Marxist theory: narration is a way of evading semantics—refusing theorization—which, I argue, is intrinsic to certain command functions of Left history, especially the latter's projection of totality.

I do not analyze what Lévi-Strauss called anecdotal or biographical history, writings usually presented as exhaustive monographs, nor texts that are merely recirculated among historians (research summaries, hypothesis testing, and the like). I am not interested in what can be called "intra-mimetic" functions where historians send signs and codes to one another about internal problems. The kinds of narrative and narrative theory I have selected for analysis—Gay's "Short Political History of the Weimar Republic," Thompson's *Poverty of Theory,* and volume one of Braudel's *Capitalism and Material Life*—raise these domains, but they also engage the reader in the reproduction of thought, as the latter is recoded into historical thought. I focus on the spaces between such engagement, critical thinking, and history. Restated, I am interested in how the texts of historians use narration in order to deflect thinking, how they, as Jameson positivizes it, promote the idea that "history is meaningful, however absurd organic life may happen to be" (1981:261). I argue that such propositions from the Left (or otherwise) reproduce cultural overcoding: history is released from its full semantic workup and is empowered to serve as the category in the name of (common sense, desire, and so on), an activity that creates confirmation of passivity. In Braudel's *Capitalism and Material Life,* for example, the transcendence of history is accomplished, in part, by recoding demographic theory into a historical agent, then deployed as criterion in the very selection of historical significance. The unnumbered (for example, nomads, Indians) are thus made unnarratable and made to lack the very characteristic called history, this conjunction a trick on thought but which satisfies the present discriminations of middle-class readers who can thus directly analogize specific present-groups as "uncultured" (unemployed and so on). As I see it, analysis of such internal positionings generated by historians proceeds by extracting and isolating devices of disintellection; the aim here is not to compare historical texts to literary forms, logical models, theories of society, and the like, but to explore how, precisely, any phenomenon is rendered intelligible by means of historical narration. To pose the issue this way, of course, is to sever oneself from even the most critical of historiographers, who still grant transcendence to the historical text, sometimes by projecting cultural forms into such texts (White's position), sometimes by directly essentializing the historical as originating in a concern with death, a psychologism (see de Certeau 1975).

My third hypothesis is this: there is no primary object or complex that warrants calling forth the signifier "history"; in Hjelmslev's (1969) vocabulary, the "history" signifier does not coincide with any semblance or purport other than its articulated sign functions, such as "container," "referent," and "necessity." Released from both language and consciousness, perhaps history and all that is dragged along by it—unequal comparison, temporal compression, elongation of misery, and so on—might occupy a nowhere in cultural criticism. Is "what is living, what is dead?," regarded by many as the question of history, really a historical question?

Procedures

From the angle of procedure, two main points can be stressed. First, in using the term *code*, I am well aware that its critical value has been reduced by some of its practitioners to a false scientism and is thoroughly mysterious to others. I justify the term and its conjugations on account of its indexical value, which is to say its situational value. As I write this, the United States government has announced that it will "let" veterans have the "right to die"; another piece of the momentary social withers away. The nonapplication of lifesaving techniques has been officially called the "no code." This strikes me as bourgeois society notching another overcoding of legal discourse by finally combining those "about to die" and "no code"; discourse and bourgeois practice commingled in death and the absolute presence of absence (no code). Nonexistence equals noncode: this is what officials say without prompting. The conceptual value of code is simply that it always refers to the act of coupling signifiers to something else (the signified, meaning, concepts) in which grammatical, syntactical, semantic, ideological, and cognitive selections and implications are made pertinent. To focus on codings is to isolate the seams where criticism can read back to the valorization of the signifier and there think out how thought has been organized to commit itself to ideals, theories, hypotheses, associations, logics, predications, and the like. As will be made clear in the analyses, the code also includes the reader of historical thought, an unspoken but internal position of historical writings.

Second, my procedure of reading is rather straightforward. The texts analyzed are divided into lexias, tutor signifiers, which are dense connotations or points where partial meanings are momentarily collected, because I do not want to make statements about meaning and significance without presenting, as much as possible, the plurality of evidence and data analyzed. Obviously no one escapes interpretation, preinterpretation, commentary, substantiating an intuition, or simple projection. The lexias ensure that the reader can specify the object versus the analysis, and so, perhaps, by avoiding ornamental summary, the historical text as object can be seen in terms of its intellectual program, as it is successively manifested and narrated. Of the three texts, there is enormous variety in length and form: the lexias are the minimal intersection of predicates needed to establish their systematic organization and intellectual implications. I do not propose elegant models of these texts, along the lines of Lévi-Strauss or Barthes (see Lévi-Strauss 1964; Barthes 1970:28–29). Instead, I fully accept Todorov's proposal about reading, which is worth quoting at some length, because it designates so well critical contact with the "impurity of differences" of a text and does not stop with classifying what is read:

> A reading's object is the singular text; its goal, to dismantle the system of that text. A reading consists in relating each element of the text to all the others, these being inventoried not in their general signification but with a view to this unique usage. In theory of course such a reading verges on the impossible. It strives, with the help of language, to grasp the work as pure difference, whereas language itself is based on resemblance and names the generic, not the individual. The expression "system of the text" is an oxymoron. But it remains possible precisely to the degree that difference (specificity, singularity) is not pure. The task of a reading always consists . . . not in obliterating difference, but in taking it apart, in presenting it as an effect of difference, whose functioning can be known. Without ever "reaching" a text, a reading infinitely approaches it: it is an asymptotic activity (Todorov 1977:237).

Organization of the Chapters

This critique of contemporary bourgeois-academic and neo-Marxist historiography is organized in the following manner. Chapter one outlines some of the ways in which a language of transcendence, which involves appeals to cultural need, necessity, preservation, and so on, undergirds the repetition of cultural norms, and provides for the historian a specific cultural function that complies with academic purposes. In focusing on such transcendencies, whether as particular content or even language itself made transcendent, I stress the uncommon tie within academia, its semantic and intellectual self-formation, self-definition, self-perpetuation. This is the tautological function in which academia creates its beautiful images and forms, its reconciliations, combinations, syntheses. Chapter two isolates the theoretical plane of historiography, with its operations such as history shows, historical significance, or historical meaning. I argue that such macro-propositions connect historiography directly to the main operations of cultural integration. Here I ask questions like how is collective "unthought" (what the masses never think), or collective irrelevancy (what the masses do think) bound to historical thought? I try to specify how historiography presents forms of *nondisengagement* from history and how narrative theory is related to such thinking.

In chapter three I analyze Gay's extremely condensed version of a highly charged, compressed historical period, the Weimar "moment." The narrator's reduction of the fifteen years of Weimar (unless that is a mythic time) into seventeen pages of narration is a model of overcoding, a place where the historian's text becomes dictionary and the reader a psychologized Liberal interpretant, part of an acceptable and stable audience. Among other aspects, I focus here on how historical synthesis is accomplished when confronted with a "moment" of such extreme violence (the Nazi scene). How is Liberal social theory grafted to narrative transmission, to a collective audience? How has liberal historiography acted as the Sender of the Nazi context into cultural circulation? I stress the devices of narration in the liberal psychologization of thinking. In chapter four I critique Thompson's *Poverty of Theory*, whose positioning of history in contemporary culture reveals Marxism to be encrusted with bourgeois-academicism. Thompson's arguments about narrative are weak, but they voice many of the givens among the new social historians, especially that social history makes a critical difference in the present. Marxists, in my opinion, ought to

expose the real, including the normal capitalist functions of ex-
tortion (development deals), extraction of surplus value, unsafe
health practice, ad infinitum. But in Thompson's work, the macro-
theory of radical Marxism is decoded (Marxism is unhinged
from anticapitalism) and recoded (reassembled) into the self-
legitimation of narration, a remarkable act, there defended by
Thompson as a "business" (his term). Along with Said, Jameson,
and others, Thompson promotes the Marxist turn "to the subject" especially by reducing thought to psychological frames, yet
retaining the hegemony of narrative categories and themes by
which to model the "whole." There is no whole that can be
narrated: what collective form exists to tell the whole which is
not immediately ideological at this point? Thompson substitutes
narrative form for critical thinking and presents this as a research
program for the Left. Western Marxism here becomes an intellectual disaster. In chapter five I analyze Braudel's *Capitalism and
Material Life,* which I reduced to some four-hundred-odd lexias,
obviously analyzing what I took to be the minimal units of its
overall narrative program and trajectory. With *Capitalism,* one
passes into a text world not only where the historical profession
has found a high-modernist expression, in the shape of an acknowledged use of Structuralism, but also where it has validated
the internal design of the historical profession, the stampede to
social history. Social history means redescription, repetition (of
truisms), and recoding. The profession will not stay all that long
with Braudel, but it has already awarded his texts the status of
"masterpiece," so it seemed useful to probe how historians encode their self-definition through recoding how they "speak the
past."

In chapters two through five I focus on the subject of reading:
who is the model reader of historical discourse? In analyzing
these narrative texts chosen because they recode discourse (Liberal social theory, Marxism, Structuralism) and reroute it to a
nonprofessional audience, I inquire as to how these texts are
attached to that lingering imaginary thought of academic culture,
the "ordinary educated public." How do such texts allocate
forms of thought like "criticism" or the "spectacle effect" (macro-
perspective)? How are chrononyms or temporal segments like
"recent" or "no longer" fitted to logical modes, to social theories,

to grammar, to political norms? I try to make explicit the imaginary and symbolic worlds (possible and impossible desires, lives, thoughts) constructed by historians and what their pragmatic or existential implications are. To do this, I use the motif of capitalism to specify how these historical works both distance themselves from their enunciative context (academic norms) and educate this public mind as to what Capitalism is and is not (the "modern" within Capitalism). Instead of these texts' production of the ideation of *when* one is, *where* one is seems to me the minimal condition of social analysis: each of these historical works grants to capitalism the latter's own time, thus mistakenly conflating property and time, as well as promoting the transcendence of capitalism with the transcendence of history. All this categorical and intellectual confusion is performed by the displacements of narrating.

The primary strategy is to analyze in depth what Barthes called the metonymic skid, how the history text slides and moves to the limits of its own codings, recoding as it goes the very process of performing its enculturation. This is an essay, then, in the contemporary division of internal intellectual labor, the objective of which is to specify how successful presentations of the "history thing" achieve the status of cultural and intellectual stagings.

1

The Semantics of Transcendence As a General Academic Code

Preliminary Considerations

My aim in this chapter is to use examples, mainly from historians, of how transcendence serves as a generalized cultural code, which governs the academic performance of language.

Every historical text issues from word techniques, which consist of all the ways in which meanings are joined to expression vehicles, plus the complicit relations of readers to such texts (Barthes 1967:31). Word techniques can be listed under rhetoric, ideology, grammatical forms, poeticality, or any other organized metalanguage in which one takes a language object (for example, utterance) as something to be investigated as to its cultural and cognitive effects. In ideological propositions, for example, the intransitive

(1) The workers refused to compromise . . . ,

uttered by a company spokesman, is a technique that omits conditions, such as

(2) because of insufficient safety codes, the shop stewards began to . . . ;

whereas macro-symbolic propositions like

(3) inflation is a disaster

operate by combining "disaster" (=unprecedented negative change) with a subconnotation ("overexpanded") of "inflation." The proposition is ideological since "inflation" is very profitable for some capitalist sectors. Eco calls lexia 3 code-switching—in "inflation is a disaster," an assertion of a negative state is presented as a "universal," generating an interpretation that can "represent" the inflation context as autonomous (see Eco 1976:287–288). Our problem is how to pose whether or not there is an explicit form of the "language of transcendence" where its word techniques are displayable.

I can do no better to re-pose this than by presenting a textual sample of such transcendence and setting forth its reworking of codes:

(4) History is what hurts,
(5) it is what refuses desire and sets inexorable limits to individual as well as collective praxis,
(6) which its "ruses" turn into grisly and ironic reversals of their overt intention.
(7) But this History can be apprehended only through its effects
(8) . . . its alienating necessities will not forget us, however much we might prefer to ignore them (Jameson 1981:102).

Lexias 4 and 5 encode History as (a) a physical and sensuous living nonconceptual object; (b) no-saying ("refuses"); and (c) unalterable ("inexorable limits"), so a substitution for the Freudian "father". In lexia 6 History is Hegelianized, but in lexia 7 Hegel is hedged by recourse to invoking the dimension of events and relations; and lexia 8 subsumes the plane of events— immanence—to a kind of knowledge: history knows ("will not forget"), and in that omits nothing of essential value. Such subcodes, presented through signifiers of physical presence, negation (logic), inevitability (modal logic), Hegelianism (tradition), and a visual channel ("effects"), are thus means by which history acquires the status of a code: history is located in a place that one can do nothing about, but which affords history the power to enact its overall accumulative functions. Transcendence is shaped by making nonthought the occasion of thought: "history hurts" is the "ground" of reality, the obligatory must without which thought remains ungrounded. We could say that transcendence sets the imaginary to work in favor of some supposedly nonsubstitutable "must," which, in turn, is complemented by "positive" modals: to recognize history as necessity is also to participate in permission to act and to be certain, guaranteed by being overcoming desire. In this sample transcendence arises as the result of operations on semes: identity (the repetition of "is"), the sign form of which is assertion; irony, or making contradictory semantic fields imaginable; the disjunctive "but," which as a grammatical form protects the assertion from an excess (lexia 6 protects lexia 5 from the possible charge of reification); and closure, which through assertion stresses the impossibility that such assertions are only asserted! It is restrictive to regard all the operations of such codings, their purposes and effects, simply in the context of code-switching. It is preferable to suggest, following Barthes, that here transcendence presents thinking with a *structural* limit—the ideational effect of which is to preclude consciousness from regression. This renders a symbolic fullness—history is granted the role of Sender and Receiver of necessity, an autonymic (self-referential) function. In Barthes's terms, this left-wing "myth" is "clumsy" but on the way to saturating a reader in a "solicitation" to not think outside the confines of "reality" (see Barthes 1972:148, 154). It is really quite oppressive, both as written and thought. "Transcendence," in any case, is an act of signification, restricted neither to any set of signifiers nor to any substantialized signified (there is "catholic transcendence," "literary," and so on). And it is usually accompanied by a moral criterion; in Nietzsche's terms, transcendence is part of deception "in a useful way," where one overvalues what one has reduced "to a purposive and manageable schema" (1968:315). The transcendence code is on the side of the "need" for guarantees, performed by what Lévi-Strauss (1966:284) called the extraction of a scheme of interpretation which codifies and controls intellectual focus. In linguistic terms, I shall say that it supplies the signifier with support; it stops signifiers—meaning vehicles—from dissolution, from floating before subjects as chaos. At once signifying and social, transcendence is the force of intellectual inertia within potentially dynamic cultural thought, an "it must be" presented as addressed to no one, a postulate of reactive thought (see Clastres 1974:33; Blanchot 1981:159). For our purposes, to which I will return, it is also the myth of "contact" between thinking and the nonthought, out of which thought itself is putatively generated.

Functions within Immanence

Bourgeois-academic discourse claims for itself the role of arbitrating the meaning of contradictions, starting with its function as a corrective to the deficiencies of categorical definitions. Here is a passage from Marcuse in which diagnostic thinking culminates in a positive transcendence that both flattens the impact of immanent contradictions and forestalls psychoanalysis from being considered merely discursive, which is to say, from being considered a codifying discourse. Marcuse writes:

(9) It is not the conflict between instinct and reason that provides the strongest argument against the idea of a free civilization,

(10) but rather the conflict which instinct creates in itself.

(11) . . . instinct itself is beyond good and evil.

(12) and no free civilization can dispense with this distinction.

(13) . . . the sex instinct is not guided by reciprocity

(14) . . . but is there perhaps in the instinct itself an inner barrier which "contains" its driving force [self-knowledge of this instinct]

(15) Is there perhaps a "natural" self-restraint in Eros so that its genuine gratification would call for delay, detour, and arrest?

(16) Then there would be obstructions and limitations . . . set and accepted by the instinct itself because they have inherent libidinal value (1955:206–207).

Marcuse's language takes a neo-Marxist cultural analysis straight to hysteria; the signifiers organize this. It is not difficult to discern, through the overall *exergasia* or repetition of the figure "not," that (1) the "strongest" argument against "liberation" is on account of the transcendence of instinct itself, its being beyond good and evil; (2) once this barrier to liberation is presented as the case, what lexia 13 calls the absence of "reciprocity" within the instincts is quickly opened to cancellation, performed by the hypothesis of lexia 14's "perhaps"; (3) the short-term negative transcendence of the instincts—what civilization calls repression in order to protect the gains of Eros—or the "bad" transcendence of Freud's pessimism, is not the correct "inside" of the instincts according to Marcuse; (4) the "real inside" of instinctual transcendence is set forth in lexia 16 as an "instinct" encoded as recognizing long-term identities and desires, so that it sets its own limits in order to protect "libidinal value." The instincts are to be thought of as capable of "good transcendence," this one attached to the "integral identification" achieved in the more original and primary "narcissistic maternal" phase of the ego (Marcuse 1955:210). Nonrepressive civilization can thus proceed once the appropriate, but unspecified audience, reexperiences such good transcendence or, what amounts to the same thing, undergoes experience of these signifiers, a correction to the malaise of existing negative transcendence (the rule of the performance principle over the subject). "Mommy" is at the basis of transcendence, the latter linked to the resolution of immanent neurosis. Those who know this positive transcendence are thus empowered as agents of immanence. Everything of value, in fact, is restored by the only kind of language which can convey such restoration, a language constantly gesturing toward a return to the presemiotic, the precultural. In an attempt to undo the neurotic creations of "tragic" psychoanalysis, such new-Left writings perpetuate an excessively neurotic relationship with language. The "true subject" is discernible through the transcendence of a "good instinct" grasped by the immanent transcendence of a discourse. Immanence is the scene of access to transcendence, a cultural formation to which we shall return later.

Radical semioticians have forcefully argued that signifiers such as "rationality," "explanation," "understanding," and "intelligibility" are not detachable from symbolicity, in which the latter can be considered a surplus of indefinite figurations and implications (see Eco 1984:158–163). The display of "truth," or answering of questions, or concretizing of concepts is insepa-rable from semio-cognitive acts of hierarchy, pertinence, stability of signifiers, multiforms of comparison, and taxonomizing, ac-tivities of an institutional order (see Greimas 1976:9–43). The humanities, treated as a bureaucratic writing, have no systematic interest in a critical theory of signification insofar as one believes language some sort of universal equivalent, a money of all pos-sible meaning, an overcoming of distance and gaps (see Deleuze and Guattari 1977:240). Why should language, a "product of human ingenuity be allowed to put an end to the very same questions to which it owes its existence"? asks Feyerabend (1970:209) about the hegemony of "normal" scientific discourse, on account of the latter's disposition to narrow the range of its interpretants. We can note that the presence of sign functions— of guarantee, restoration, correction, and so on—provides im-manent acts of judging or condoning or lying or negating— metalinguistic actions—with an aura of transcendence, so they are modes that ensure a containment of the full implications of meaning utterances.

There is a continuous institutionalizing of positive or negative need in bourgeois-academic writing, where thinking defuses critical force by focusing on *absence and presence* as transcendent structures. Following are two samples of such discourse in which attempts to stabilize signification by attaching it to transcendence manifests first the positive, then the negative form of absence/presence. The prominent new-Left critic Lasch writes:

    (17) History is part of a political and psychological treasury
    (18) from which we draw the reserves that we need to cope
         with the future (1979:25).

Following some suggestions by Eco (1979:18–23), there are, first, some virtual properties to these signifiers: "treasury" can be decoded by a reader as part of a narrative if the reader favors its metonymic "history," in which case emphasis is thrown onto the realization of a "future." Transcendence is inserted in narrated means, with an implicit narrative goal, in which the paradigmatic sense of treasury is suppressed. "Treasury" is not inherently shorn of its cultural-semantic roles by reducing its implications to a narration function. But at the same time, if "treasury" and its qualifiers—"history," "political," and "psychological"—are accepted in accordance with the sense of a means to resolve a lack, the narrative aspect falls under the category of a stereotypical plea: a case of persuasion linked to competing "cultural" claims, in which it is suggested that only history cannot be replaced or substituted (and which frees history from signification, from the materiality of culture). But we can postulate that a reader is also built into such "seriousness": insofar as "treasury" is connected to "reserves," a state, the former the condition of the latter, the "future" is made ideational (imaginable) with an underside—"there is no future without such a treasury." In other words, a greater, larger, absence would occur in the absence of the acceptance of this proposition. There is more. Which sense of "treasury" is a reader to abduce: the "treasury" itself or "drawing" from it? If the latter, "to draw reserves" implies a kind of central bank. Are the "assets" of this "reserve" distributed according to standards of "demonstrable coping"? This minor, almost tiny, "cultureme" is interesting insofar as it is congruent with the "serious" *made* part of a dreaded absence, "treasury" a guarantee of the "profit" in a "history-to-be." The centralization of such a need for history presented by this discourse would seem to be an implicit pragmatic implication, perhaps to be realized in a Ministry of History.

Within mainstream bourgeois-academic culture, one often can locate darker and more tortuous twists to such transcendencies. Whereas cultural critics such as Lasch idealize and overvalue these imaginary constructs and make their nonexistence unimaginable, an affirmation of nonnegation, more realistic writers such as Shklar invoke transcendence located at the very intersection of immanence and "necessity." In the summer of 1979, *Daedalus,* a journal that often presents liberal intellectual programs, published an issue on "Hypocrisy, Illusion, and Evasion," where scholars presented interpretations of "public life" in connection with this topic. Shklar's piece contains an interesting passage:

(19) The only voice that damns hypocrisy to some purpose is one that laments that the society in which we live does not live up to its own principles, promises, and possibilities.

(20) This outraged jeremiad is the mark of a moralistic rather than a moral society perhaps,

(21) but it is not without effect,

(22) because this type of anti-hypocrite does at least have a sense of what is wrong,

(23) rather than only an urge to blame.

(24) He may well frighten politicians enough to inhibit them to a significant degree.

(25) Even the participants in the system of hypocrisy perform unintended services to liberal society.

(26) Each fears the other enough to restrain himself.

(27) Their discourse conveys little moral urgency, but it does discourage fanaticism.

(28) The politics of unreconciled political neighbors are not as liberating as earlier liberals had hoped, not as edifying as had been expected, and certainly far less democratic,

(29) but they make for a society superior to its known alternatives.

(30) It could hardly survive without hypocrisy (1979:24).

Restated: all of the "damns" uttered against hypocrisy are canceled by the narrative result of lexia 30. Only one form of "grief," the "lamenting jeremiad," emerges with "voice" or the empowered right to demand coherence pertaining to society's disjunction of "value" and reality. This jeremiad, unfortunately, never occupies the existential territory of the moral—the "moralistic" is as close to the moral as can be achieved; the "at least" of lexia 22 grants this figure of morality event status, restricted to acts that devalue the grammatical subject of lexia 23 ("urge to blame"); with lexia 24 the lamenting jeremiad goes into action— the jeremiad's grief issues in the result of "fright," which presumes that politicians are already encoded in the role of self-limiting their actions in the face of a psychological "power"; at lexia 27, the jeremiad and "frightened" politician meet in what both succeed in expelling—the "fanatic"; lexia 28 suggests just how distant all this is by comparison to standards and norms of an ideal order, but it too is annulled in lexia 29 as soon as the comparatizer is mobilized—"known alternatives" or what actually exists as phenomenal social systems. Reality, which now occupies the slot of transcendence (lexia 30), is thus written as a need—without hypocrisy, no "survival." Each lexia progressively opens enough space to release successively the conjunction of hypocritical survival located within immanence as the latter's needed semantic structuring of public life. This negative truth is implicitly encoded as (1) the exclusion of nonjeremiads from political existence, the exiling of those who transgress the line between moralistic and moral; (2) the reduction of political existence to the psychologically based "outrage" and "frighten" and "worry," at which point there is rendered an acceptable form of Liberal morality (and attached, somehow, to obsessions with appearance); (3) a trace of Hegelianism, stated as "unintended service," which, of course, is today a form of the long-term self-preservation of Liberalism; and (4) the trace of a "failed" history ("had hoped," "far less") or the continuously untranscended past presented as not-possible to transcend. That 'horror' is super-annulled by appeal to an immanently based transcendence—the lack of present-now alternatives (none of which is considered), so that the final enthymatic conclusion "could hardly survive" makes "hypocrisy" a classification of that which "no one can do anything about." The effect: one should not try to cognize hypocrisy as a social relation but rather as transcendent to a society where what is, is connected to "must be." The receiver of the full message can only be intellectually deflated by this presentation of the necessarily absent morality.

The texts from Lasch and Shklar are specimens of what Barthes categorized as the language of "essences and scales," the aim of which is the immobility of political-intellectual criticism achieved by a "weighing" of alternatives so selected and combined (presented) as to freeze criticism or set it within limits that in no manner threaten any institutional practices (1972:155). Better yet, such codes and subcodes pertain to "half-thought": if all the codings were fully stated, such discourses would lose their trajectory; but such texts can only achieve their effects if their codes are unstated. In addition, these utterances are oriented toward the mode of commands, and invest the transcendent with a surplus of *semia*, the very expression of which is aimed at an audience not of readers, but of conciliators; the latter's speech duplicates by imitation an Academic Ideal Encyclopedia, where meaning is coded by continuous reactive significations. "Treasury" or "hypocrisy/survival" actually refer to meaning conditions where speakers are riveted to legitimations presented to thought as if "treasury" and so on were found at the basis of moral thought. This use of sign forms is usually found in contexts where both "need" and "abandonment" co-occur: one is to think in the signs of a code that confirm a need, a code which is then used for the abandonment of tactics and means that might transgress such transcendence. One is released from excessive thought/signification (from having to think) and yet contained by it at the same time. And since such signifiers are so heavily narrativized on the side of a pedagogic effect (for example, Lasch's "cope" is far more a latent psychological story of learning than, say, "eliminate surplus labor in the future," a proposition with definite implications), one can only "abandon" oneself to a scene of instruction: "cope" is tied to a direct academic practice, that of adjusting, just as "correction" with Marcuse is tied to offering a Utopic resolution.

Let me stress that some semioticians argue that every sign manifests, beyond its relational value(s), a function of itself: this is clearly revealed by lexias 17 and 18; such propositions self-promote their own performances (for example, the infinitive form "to cope," which produces surplus time). Neither Lasch nor Shklar remotely considers that a full and complete exposure of their significations could result in their being seen as part of a prosthetics of academia, devices to restore bodies to circulation and function (see Eco 1984:208). It is not anywhere acknowledged by them that such sign forms might represent what the Tartu group has called deritualized but hierarchical texts used for magical purposes (intellectual bewitchment) (see Lotman and Pjatigorsky 1977:134). At any rate, because such significations support capitalist culture by perpetuating its elementary cultural categories—exchange, loss, acquisition, pseudo-communion, and so on—transcendent discourse deflects criticism precisely by confirming means and tactics that are discontinuous with the contradictions and issues it so fervently writes about. One sees here academia stretched to the limits of representation.

Another type of sign use and coding should be mentioned here, since it is so much a part of academic culture, and particularly favored by historians. This is the invention of *concerns* that enforce a sense of *loss,* somewhat stronger than current usages of "lack" and "absence," the latter usually operationalized according to an overcoming/resolution schema (as Lacan uses the term "lack," for example, it is completed or fulfilled in the subject's assumption of symbolic roles that "absorb" excess ideation). "Loss" is more radically reactionary because here one is involved with the signified of "permanently separated from," a temporal and physical exclusion that combines a positive transcendence of the past with immanent instructions on how to read the present. For example, a recent historian of the changes in media, adopting Foucault's schema in the *Order of Things,* obeys the "historicist" rule to understand each era "on its own terms," "in context," "without anachronism" and stresses that in the switch from typography to film, "there is no continuity from one period to another" (Lowe 1982:161); once this culturally discontinuous "space" is affirmed, one encounters this astonishing narrative enthymeme: in passing from books to images as forms of public exchange, there really is continuity, for

(31) the human being now possesses less of an interior than formerly (Lowe 1982:161).

One would like to know how the quantifier "less" can be pulled from "interiority" (it implies books are worthy for interiorization) but, as always with such assertions, one is dealing here with highly overcoded signifiers rattling around within myth which, for its part, is ready to be transformed into a factual system (Barthes 1972:134). The conclusion that one is supposed to draw is guided by the verb of ownership ("possesses"). The implicit presupposed is "no longer," the contrary of "now possesses," which enables the propositional content to achieve an effect: "no longer" is made a plus-value on the assumption that the reader shares the assertion of the negativity of "now," the book "rising" as the transcendent object. "No longer"—a temporal absolute—carried by such "loss," is heavily coded: (1) the first coding, what might be called the second articulation of historians, is the application of "before and after," *after* a change, however abstract ("Book to image") has been made pertinent in the first articulation (the selection of an event); (2) a psychological encoding, signaled by "possesses" insofar as this signifier opens onto a sense of "alienation of mind" in the "now" (one supposes) and transmits (3) an entirely gnostic encoding, conjured by the signifier of "interiority," some special place or zone found "deep within" the subject; (4) a grammatical encoding, ellipsis, or the dropping of the middle terms of comparativization (what is removed from the consciousness of the reader here is the comparison which, in Genette's terms, "impregnates" "now and formerly"; see Genette 1982:111–113). One sees that "loss" is an entirely stabilizing function, in that the "concern over loss" encodes, in advance, an aim for academia which is embedded in structures of retrieval or restoration, mourning and pseudofact, announcing collective loss for an audience alienated by excessive images, the latter written out from one's thoughts. The Positivity of the Book is yet another achronic positivity, that of maintaining academia's own practice.

One knows that historians dread the category of the anachronistic, setting it against chronology, the latter reduced to a semantic fusion of time and space (the identity of that and then). I want to suggest that anachronism is a military tactic within the historical discipline, leveled at those who bypass the historian's modes of access to the past; it is also used by historians to present the claim that there is a transcendence of place belonging to reality, a claim often joined to the maintenance of accessing a past. For example, in a review of Fitzgerald's *America Revised,* which (timidly) criticized the writing of American history for grade school students, Woodward acknowledges the "insights" of the work and then goes on to state what is "really" of significance concerning the putative dearth of "genuine historical thinking" in America:

(32) one would have had to take account of more *basic traits* and *quirks*

(33) of the *American mind* that are *far older* and *more deeply* rooted

(34) than the texts and school-texts and pedagogical fads that pre-empt attention in this book. They go back beyond Jeffersonians (1979:16; italics added).

The italicized items are all overworked signifieds of academic culture: (1) "basic traits" opens onto the territory of the *primary,* which enables this historian to claim the status of a (nineteenth-century) scientist in his grasp of a "problem"; (2) "quirks" are long-term *character* relations, what is unique or specific to (3) the "American mind," which is surely the result of historicist colligation (over condensation) and invoked to displace the reading it rejects as too surface/superficial; (4) "far older" aims at establishing an *unanachronistic* history, or the treatment of time according to a longer chronology (= "more real"), and the (5) "deeply rooted" plays off the fantasy of achieving unity located in time now—what Deleuze and Guattari call "autonomous centers of organized memory" which allow the subject to at last realize meaning and value (1983:35–36). The demand here is not for a true story but *the* story, the grammatical mark of the definite article transferred to teller and reader as a negation of the partial story, an unforgivable intellectual space between "the" and "true" which this historian wants to close. Woodward's review is the presentation of a desirable model of inquiry and research whose object is the maintenance of academic culture as the systematic closure of story, with the stress on closure. Here academia is the implicit subject of transcendence, because it assigns and gives value by preserving for itself what Kristeva calls politics *simpliciter,* the "one and the only meaning" (1982:84), where "the" and "true" meet.

Nonacademic readers are built in to occupy the social positions of such discourse, positions analyzed in detail in chapters three to five, roles accompanying academic discourse which are co-coded with the self-promoting, self-sustaining, and self-valorizing stabilization of the linguistic apparatus. One's assent to contradiction as necessary (Shklar) or regression to noncontradiction (Marcuse) are not just pure oxymorons but also the ideations that reproduce reaction. For now I want to stress that the academic functions pointed out can be suggestively compared with contemporary monetary relations, and in a way that leaves the liberal-Marxist sense of history devoid of conceptual value (see chapter four). Mandel (1980) argues that the collapse, since Bretton Woods, of any international monetary system (no unqualified form of storing value) is a "sign" of increasing destabilization due to unavoidable competition among the many sectors of capitalism. Capital can only be expanded in one department of production while pulverized in another; only multinationals, (some) States, and a few select individuals and institutions can reproduce their existing social relations, let alone expand, from self-financing, the latter today the idealized post to keep the accumulation form intact, to play the game of competition. Self-financing is really the contemporary form of access to the status of an economic "gainer," where accumulation is no longer a narrative telos but itself direct social reproduction. Self-financing has been redesignated for radical cultural analysis by Baudrillard, who has stressed that the category of *self-referentiality* in all advanced cultural systems is structurally equivalent to self-financing and allows one to postulate connections between the functions of these different forms, functions that return us to the real transcendence of pure context, the status quo in perpetual motion:

> The sign, in which a signifier referred back to a signified, in which a formal difference still referred to what one could call the use-value of a sign has disappeared in favor of the form-sign [which] describes an entirely different organization: the signified and the referent are now abolished to the sole profit of the play of signifiers, or a generalized formalization in which the code no longer refers back to any subjective or objective "reality" but to its own logic. The signifier becomes its own referent and the use-value disappears to the benefit

of its commutation and exchange-value alone. . . . It approaches its structural limit which is to refer back only to other signs. All reality then becomes the place of a semiurgical manipulation (Baudrillard 1975:127–128).

On this view the shift to self-financing and the sign functions of stability are conjoined in any number of current social binds highlighted by noting the appearance of reactive social-linguistic formations: women and children are transformed into signifiers of poverty when surplus is rerouted to the military (class division within gender, and synchronous with affirmative action's minimal integration of women into the professions); the revival of "value" is stabilized by those still working whose higher real wages benefit from Reaganomics; while, to head off the negative consequences of this reaccumulation of value, some insist upon a new intellectual accumulation, achieved by intensifying syntheses of knowledge (for example, periodization as base for strategy) not the speeding up of deconstruction (see Jameson 1984:65). More basic is the flat equivalence between the "economically unintegrables" and the functionally illiterate, whose discourse, in advance, is unexchangeable, because their signifiers are inarticulate; they appear uncoded, the cardinal defect of the uncultured. This is a social world, in all its forms, where context alone constitutes which differences make a difference, but a context now understood not as a scene, a place, but sites and operations of reactive but nonuniversal differences, conjoined to the self-referentiality of a particular hegemonic context. Incommensurable contexts, whether economic or cultural, are pluralized to the point where overproduction in each sphere is dominated by managerial functions, in order to rank differences (see Baudrillard 1983c:127).

Transcendence of thinking hierarchizes and restricts this expanded self-referentiality. Depending upon how fast the division of labor affects practices, the mind seems to be hurled through a process of recoding: innovations of exchange, but without change, which might be a motto for the so-called Age of Information, since information is really only Capital. Transcendence becomes, for each individual, his or her *mot d'ordre*, the self choosing to privilege empty forms, as Deleuze and Guattari (1980) point out, which is another way of saying that academic discourse fixates on simulacra of wholes. One can supplement Baudrillard's position by pointing out that "bourgeois culture" has no center but is not decentered either: it is only about positivizing signifiers in one system (for example, subjectivity) which can effect a change in another (for example, Capital). One does not need to know anything apart from what such knowing does: thinking is obligated toward transcendence within the academy because "universals" (as stereotypes, models, paradigms) are still required for this particular context, but even here, the segmentation of discourse (fields, disciplines, and so on) requires less and less of any intellectual justification by comparison to performative criteria (reproduction).

As Western society withdraws from its prior narrative stabilizations, signaled in current historiography as the proliferation of "histories" of welfare, social policy, and managerial roles, transcendence also appears in grotesque expressions of *refuge*, grafted to the idealization-fetishism of special cultural objects, the latter called upon to provide thought with an anti-interventionist project. The following lexias are a case in point, where the attempt to transcend the whole of contemporary double-binds satisfies the demand for academia to limit access to criticism by withdrawing into the imaginary:

(35) Literature . . . is the most revealing mode of experiential access to ideology that we possess.

(36) It is in literature, above all, that we observe in a peculiarly complex, coherent, intensive, and immediate fashion the workings of ideology

(37) in the textures of lived experience of class societies.

(38) It is a mode of access more immediate than that of science, and more coherent

(39) than that normally available in daily living itself (Eagleton 1976:101).

First of all, note that "literature" is defined by its location: it is even better than studying people because, as an object, literature already "contains" the superlatives of all "good objects"—"most revealing" and "more immediate" situate literature as *open* and *accessible*, displaying itself in ways that are *closed* and *inaccessible* in both "science" (lexia 38) and "daily living" (lexia 39). One can ask: what about literature that refuses all these functions attributed to it? And is it no longer slightly strange, after all, that the signifier "peculiarly," which conveys the "special" status of ideology here, is realized in lexia 37 as "textures"? Literature is recoded as the best of all *sensoriums*, with the implication that of absence of the "complex, coherent, intensive, and immediate" from "daily living." How could this be so? Put another way, the mechanisms that enable literature to be considered as simultaneously a knowing and doing, like condensation or narrative voice or prolepsis, are not themselves "literary." Why not analyze prolepsis within the bank system? The not-knowable of the not-literary is thus consigned to critical oblivion by this Marxism of literary transcendence, a Marxism very recent, very popular, which pulls out of "reality" by means of its very definition of literature (definition is an action, which confirms the Stoic teaching that every sign use is an action).

Cultural transcendence can be explicitly a mirror function, a mélange of motivation and justification. *Academe*, a bulletin of the American Association of University Professors, publishes articles where professors circulate, for themselves, a recoding of issues and problems. (Like the polyphonic novel, *pace* Bakhtin, *Academe* has more than one plot line: it provides a list of universities that have violated hiring practices, it addresses academic renovation, investment strategies, and so on.) In the May-June 1982 issue, a philosopher raised again the question as to the status of the "humanities," and engaged the topic by referring to Karl Popper's epistemic condemnation of systematically misleading questions: the humanities are not the kind of activity subject to the question form "of what use are the humanities," since "use" is presupposed to rest upon "objectivity" and/or "practical activity." The rejection of this question form's application to the humanities aims at a kind of "de-supposing," whereby the humanities can be disengaged from comparison to "natural science" and utility, and here is the shape of this disengagement from the "wrong" question form:

(40) The business of the humanities is not to map the empire of nature nor to outline the contour of institutional man
(41) but to chart the soul:
(42) to exhibit and to expound a world of concrete immediacy
(43) of dramatic, rather than utilitarian, relationships.
(44) In the humanities we see *ourselves,* though not always happily and often not even forbearingly (Hoffman 1982:27, italics added).

One sees here a very strong symmetry between the code and the message: the codes (or subcodes) are based upon an attempt at communion—"immediacy" and "dramatic" and "self-seeing" promise maximum participation and saturation governed by a psychologically based desire for knowledge as gratification; the conative function is dominant and so is redundancy (the information of "immediacy" and "drama" and "self-sight" is insignificant). Only the lexemes "business" and "chart" and "soul" do not quite fit the encodings, so that their splicing stands out: "business" is antithetical to "soul" unless one assumes the operations of another subcode. It can only be one that attempts some sort of collaboration or maintenance of a practical link between sender and receiver, here that academia has a "job" or a "mission." Maximum idealization (soul) meets labor (business), a conjunction that presupposes the fantasy of unlimited temporal growth, guaranteed by the ever receding soul. This is a revival of the static Quest routine, belief in an endless accumulation that can never be exhanged, because exchange itself closes the game of the soul (see Guirard 1971:13–14).

Compared to such ritualistic acts which try to ensure that academia fulfills the objective of a camera lucida—an opening to transcendence—following is a sample of the popularization of transcendence, included here because it illustrates how language can be unhinged from a past academic discursive practice and placed in a consumption circuit, a pure myth in the everyday, which conforms to the cultural divisions of the present. (A frightening idea: the present of society is the past thought forms of academia.) The Ohio Match Company prints on its matchboxes (in 1982) the title "origin of words" and one reads:

(45) Etymology . . . can be an interesting and romantic adventure.
(46) It traces words back to their real life beginnings.
(47) It leads us into the studies of mythology and history and of great names and events.
(48) Even today new words are forming from the colorful language of sports, show business, the space program, and other professional fields.

The academic will, of course, get a little testy: the pursuit of scholarship and knowledge is antithetical to lexias 45 through 48, or so it seems. But the axiological component, the attempt to reproduce values immersed in a *creation/reproduction* dyad, where fundamental hierarchies are just given, involves the whole of bourgeois-academic culture. These lexias serve to conjoin value and name, a pathological act of signification shot directly into the social (of one's mind). Thus: (1) the switching on of "etymology" by the verbs "traces and leads" fuses language with "great names and events" (lexia 47); (2) such "names" are, "historically and linguistically," marked by the *infrequent* so they embody, already, an act of "creation" ("real life beginnings"); (3) there is a connection between "meaningful" ("great names") and "color" which pertains to the iteration ("even today") and repetition of language: the present-now "new words are forming" embeds "sports, show business, and the space program" in "professional fields" (lexia 48). Now here, in a mass society, where language tends to be avoided in its figural and machinac aspects (the first leads to the charge of opacity, the latter to the exposure of metalingual positions), language is made transcendent to the extent that linguistic creation is defined as part of a "colorful" *and* a "professional" activity, a case of hierarchy presented and realized through equivalence (see Group μ 1981: 19–21). The "professions" are empowered to write with a "language" that is a priori on the side of "life" (that is, it is "colorful"), whereas its "addressees" (consumers) are subject to "etymology" (the axiom that the origin of a word equals its "real life," lexia 48), thereby satisfying an exclusively reproductive function: one consumes a sociolect where value and name are identical, which makes speaking a crystallization of hierarchy and status (see Barthes 1977:168; Kristeva 1975:52). When matchboxes confirm the transcendence of culture, "mass society" is not to be conjured as the villain: what is written on the box shows that there is no space remaining as a residue from sign-distortion.

Primary Intellectual Effects of Transcendence

If transcendence is a permanent possibility of semiotic-intellectual destruction, because its minimal function is to make unthinkable the negation of that "which ties one to reality" and holds one in place, this superfunction today is perfected in contexts where language is hypervalorized as the "indispensable," "needed," "necessary," "required," and so on, basis of enculturation. Socio-cognitively, language is projected as released from contradictions. Thus, when the Genoveses call for the "politics of mediation" built around the adjectival "irreconcilable," or Shklar writes about the "could hardly survive" and its implied performative threat ("would not survive"), or Woodward invokes the "more deeply," there is released a double coding of *exorcism* (one expels some imaginary other) and *integration* (through negation, limit, dilemma, contradiction, etc.), a reactive binary coding that oversees immanence (see Joos 1968:152–153 on the social matrix of modals). The implied fear of the absence of hypocrisy is hardly only a form of our reactionary cultural deep freeze; like the Genoveses' scheme, for example, it requires the *accession* of subjectivity to the demands of being-able-to speak, authorized by the full weight of a discourse (psychoanalysis, Marxism, etc.). When such discourse fills the slot of transcendence, of passing on the right to occupy the right to speak, it would seem that even "extracultural" spaces (for example, those activities seemingly uncoded by the division of labor/signs) become subject to what Lotman has called "closed, inaccessible, or completely unintelligible texts," linguistic performances used to *segment and isolate* subjects by reference to their capacity to make or use a language (see Lotman 1975:62). In our society, the tax codes, literary theory, rules for the production of various curricula, and the like, are part of what one can call an ideology of the form of language, which concerns, above all, connections between the transcendence of language and access to culture. To return to Baudrillard's terms:

> ideology is the process of reducing and abstracting symbolic material into a form. But this reductive abstraction is given immediately as value (autonomous), as content (transcendent), and as a representation of consciousness (signified). It is the same process that lends the commodity an appearance of autonomous value and transcendent reality—a process that involves the misunderstanding of the form of the commodity and of the abstraction of social labor that it operates. In bourgeois (or, alas, Marxist) thought, culture is defined as a *transcendence of contents* correlated with consciousness by means of a "representation" that circulates among them like positive values, just as the fetishized commodity appears as a real and immediate value, correlated with individual subjects through "need" and use value, and circulating according to the rules of exchange value (1981:145, Baudrillard's italics).

Formalized, the transcendence of contents presupposes the immanent stability of some category of content as its semantic classeme, that is, a category of the *nonfigurative* permanence of content. For the Genoveses, the nonfigurative = "irreconcilable contradictions" *located* at the psychic and "historical" levels but *accessed* only through psychoanalysis: one is blocked from "reality" (content) if one rejects the discourse (psychoanalysis). What energizes the attempt to realize value, the form of which is positive signifiers, is the very axis of need-transcendence which sustains the entire structure. Recall the Genoveses' minidiscourse: "irreconcilable antagonisms" transcends, it sets going, both tragedy (negative and positive value) and representation (for example, images); it should be obvious that unless one is willing to speak the code immanently (psychoanalysis), one is cut off from transcendence (knowledge) and from the right to represent values (immanent talk). The couple transcendence/need determines the way in which immanence is made accessible; it is, I think, the academic opening, where contact and code with institutional ideation occur at once. I am going to conclude this chapter with an analysis of what I think is a model case of such academic transcendence, the making of language into the content of cultural transcendence, there defining what informs the immanence of academia, its setting up of acceptable modes of access to culture in the first place. The analysis of transcendence becomes a reconstruction of how access to culture is made possible yet controlled by academic functions.

Academic Transcendence of Culture

I would like to pursue here a systematic analysis of Vico's notion of the transcendence of language as a defining instance of immanent cultural positivity and connect it to an example from current historiography. I trust that it is clear that by language transcendence I mean isolating how language is overvalued, made accessible (or not), coded according to class and cultural functions—how, in short, language can be stabilized so as to mediate between immanence and need, as contact and code, so that immanence or the plateaus of perception and thought are accompanied by their "right" forms of linguistic mediation.

Vico so blended notions of metaphor, psychology, etymology, philology, and so on, that late "Vichians" have awarded *The New Science* the title of "master text," just as, later, we will see Braudel's work receiving the same hyperestimation. According to White:

> one can find a pervading ambivalence in [Vico's] thought on all the important questions underlying the quest for a science of man, culture, society, and history. . . . Instead of being a champion of either the masses or the aristocracy in society, Vico found virtues in both. Vico's genius . . . must lie in the totality of his vision, its amplitude, his affirmation of both the negative and the positive sides of the dialectical process (1976:202).

Note that Vico is credited with transcending the logic of either-or: his texts achieved the threshold of both-and. But at the same time notice this: the "dialectical process" is made up of "positive" and "negative" wherein *both* are affirmed (as necessary) and so, really, the negative side is rejected: in advance, the dialectical process culminates in "affirmation," which is really then a suppression of either-or. At any rate, it is on account of his strategic cultural placement of metaphor that Vico is granted the status of a key ancestor of academe.

The presence of metaphor in any discursive system is potentially innovative; every metaphor can be used to assault a preexisting codification (for example, "tricky Dick," which plays off phonetic signifiers, enabled commentators to create cultural "resemblances" between Nixon's psyche and actions, but "tricky dick" also can refer to a specific erotic arrangement, as well as to codified unsavory social attributes of anyone named "Dick"), so metaphor can always be associated with semantic pleasure, fun, and the expansion of the semiotic elements of a given cultural system (see Eco 1979:73–76). Metaphor appears as a force, at once presignifying (collective), polemical (countersense), an interpretant (of another sign, another register), a postsignifying multiplier of sense (see Deleuze and Guattari 1980:183). But we stress that academia also has a bureaucratic-linguistic role for metaphor, which turns on the omission of preexisting senses, or usages, these disappearing as the metaphor is presented. Metaphor can appear to embody one of the "essences" of language, because it is a linguistic act that can be used to escape from subjection to language: metaphor as the embodiment of "imagination," because metaphor can institute thinking about proportions between cultural units (see Eco 1984:101–103). Genette (1982:111–113) provides a quick sketch of the modern hypervalorization of metaphor and analogy in which the privilege granted to metaphor has paralleled deintellectuality, insofar as the reliance upon accepting metaphor and analogy as "root figures" has made it more difficult to sort out operations involving comparison, whenever nonpoetic ideation is involved. An unmotivated comparison ("Society is like an unsatiated Mammon") or a motivated one ("Society pursues innovation like an unsatiated Mammon"), the presence or absence of modalizers ("Society is like an unsatiated Mammon" has a modalizer, but the construction "Society needs to . . . " is a mere identification, since it omits the compared and modal forms), implies that metaphor is not necessarily a cognitively beneficial instrument, always able to formulate "a notable illumination of the obscure and inchoate" (Fernandez 1977:104). With Eco (1984:102), we can ask how metaphor can be thought of as a "network of proportions between cultural units," that is, how it codes immanent differences with continuous meaning. With this in mind I want to analyze Vico's systematic embedding of metaphor in a theory of language and show how, once made transcendent, language thought of as metaphor acquires a social power, an academic one, a sort of omni-present use value built into language with a very restricted exchange value.

Vico's consideration of the role of language in the history of social institutions acknowledged the principle of uniformity or the inertia of culture. Indeed, he assumed that, as a principle of social philosophy, "the human mind is naturally impelled to take a delight in uniformity" (*The New Science*, par. 204; hereafter, just paragraph number). The mind is both known and displaced by metaphor, for at the time of utterance, residues of affectivity, desire, and so on, are caught in expressivity. Vico argued that, in the third phase of "history," after the collapse of the hieroglyphic and poetic systems, language appears more and more abstract ("unmotivated" in semiotic terms, referring only to conventional links between sound, thought, object, interpretant) and restricted to social requirements such as rules of law and contract. If, as Barthes believed, modern society signifies the direct "rule" of language over the selection-combinations of "parole," it is quite clear that Vico also saw this distinction; for Vico the history of language and society is a movement from "speech" founded on a "common mental dictionary" (what today would be called a fund of invariant semes) to language "proper" where signs are fused with logic and grammar or stripped of their participation and saturation with the affective (pars. 447–455). The story of language in this third phase is one of decline in subjectivity, marked by upheavals like rhetorical debates, "events" within the academy. The three languages—the first mute or speech by hieroglyphic marks, the second poetic, the third "articulate"—began simultaneously but their history is one of progressive exclusion of the hieroglyphic and poetic modes.

The first language, mute and hieroglyphic, was organized around the channel of families and individuals where monosyllables and certain imperative forms dominated. Vico is obscure about all this, but it seems that in this early society's hieroglyphic expressions, objects were used as natural signs and transformed into iconographical *pleromata* painted, carved, and the like, but not reduced to schemata where, for instance, a single brush stroke prefigures a suggested whole or gestalt (image figures that transgress perception; see Lyotard 1984:62–63). As spoken, this first language is not linguistic: it lacked double articulation of its materials, and there was a tendency for it to have such complete determination by "speakers" that it was unstable to the uninitiated, a code overtaken from the inside by the messages of speakers; hence Vico cites gesture, physical objects, idolatry, divination, sacrifice, and use of auspices as modes of this first language (par. 938), all requiring very strong visual cotexts. Those who "spoke" this first language were incapable of identifying themselves as the "subjects" of their own experience of language; and they lived what Vico identifies as an iconic existence: the grinding involved in acts of chewing *was* eating and eating was not an analogue of existence, it was being (par. 693). The specific achievement of this first language was singing (par. 230), based on the spondaic, emitted as a natural sound because its vocalic shape was determined by a material constraint, what Vico calls the "slowness of mind and a stiffness of tongue." Arising out of psychic distress and fear because of all that they did not comprehend, this initial cultural state is characterized by Vico as the virtual identity between language and psychology.

The second language, that of tropes, was generated out of a contradiction within the first language since the hieroglyphic could not mirror-reflect itself; the tropes stylized idolatry, auspices, sacrifice, and divination, manifesting a sort of secondary revision of the excitement of "primary" existence. This second language is a stage of failure, a desperation for signs, a lack, of primitive (European) culture to render complete and whole (continuous) the primary truths of their existential matrix. Sacrifice was not made *for* poetry; poetic effects were not just congelations of language in an aesthetic mode, the implications of which Vico is quick to suppress (as are his commentators). Vico does say that the earliest collections of fables were *true* narratives (pars. 401, 408), for in them the savagery of the first "fathers" acquired the force of representation:

> A fair trace of it has remained in the ancient Latin words *pipulum* and *pipare,* in the sense of "complaint" and "to complain," which must be derived from the interjection of lament, "pi, pi." *Pipulum* in this sense in Plautus is generally interpreted as synonymous with *obvagulatio* in the Twelve Tables, which must come from *vagire,* which is properly the crying of children. . . . Song arose naturally, in the measure of heroic verse, under the impulse of most violent passions (par. 449).

Poetry is manifestly *not* at the origin of language; interjection is, for example, not a poetic mode. Vico then goes on to narrativize metaphor instead of analyzing it, and this is its story: (1) the giants, frightened by thunder and lightning, (2) stopped their grumbling and shouting and ignorantly thought that the sounds of thunder and the "hissing of the earth" were "sent to tell them something," (3) out of which divination and sacrifice were practiced to interpret such sounds and events (pars. 378–379); metaphoric effects were lived (par. 376), and (4) the fables preserve this *physical* history. In other words, the fables or metaphorical language as we understand it, were true explanations: "Thus the many Joves the philologists wonder at are so many physical histories preserved for us by the fables . . . they were called theological poets, or sages who understood the language of the gods expressed in the auspices of Jove" (pars. 380–381). And although Vico often repeats that the three languages began at the same time (which is opaque), it is also clear that poetic language (metaphor) overcame a poverty of language: "The fathers alone must have spoken and given commands to their children . . . who, under the terrors of patriarchical rule . . . must have executed the commands in silence" (pars. 453–454). Poetry added—supplied—pleasure as difference, the difference of pleasure serving as a distancing device in a culture lost within immediacy. Poetic language is sublime because through it the "deficiency of human reasoning power" is overcome.

What does metaphor share with the first language, initially mute and hieroglyphic, yet attached to divination and especially the sacrifice of auspices? What is continuous between metaphor/poetry/fable and a first, prepoetic, society? Vico nowhere directly states their connection; but indirectly, that is to say in a passage where he does not explicitly reflect upon culture and metaphor, an identity is posited between metaphor and sacrifice in the sense that both participate in or bring about the enlargement of what is not understood: both simultaneously over and under value (see pars. 816 and 401). Metaphor is not simply a *genere fantastico* through which a society invests or entitles amalgamations and relations which are then used as a grid for identities and distinctions. The act of sacrifice makes "the god bigger, to exalt him, and at the same time to increase his strength by offering," as Benveniste (1973:481 ff.) notes; Vico characterizes metaphor as "true and severe narrations . . . gross . . . then altered, subsequently became improbable, after that obscure, then scandalous, and finally incredible" (par. 814), "which could not feign anything false" (par. 408), so that metaphor is initially an *enlargement (expansion) of ignorance*. Metaphor is doubly related: first, as sacrifice and ignorance (the belief that "blood reveals"), metaphor embodies real practice; and metaphor represents, later (by sympathy), a "credible impossibility" for those heroes who no longer "spoke" the language of sacrifice and the other "arts" of the first humans. In sacrifice, a nonnarrative act, men diminish themselves (as subjects, as consciousness, by enlarging nature and the gods); *in metaphor one enlarges language* (as fable and narrative). It can be argued that the novelty in Vico is that he does not negate the noncognitive basis of poetry and metaphor, ignorance and fear, which for him is the transcendent human situation. Vico tells us that poetry emerged out of a lack, a need, resulting from a

> deficiency of human reasoning power that gave rise to poetry so sublime that the philosophies which came afterward, the arts of poetry and criticism, have produced none better, and have even prevented its production (par. 383).

The sacrificial misunderstanding in the Age of the Gods, the self-positing of being-for-the-gods, is congruent with the metaphorical answer to that misunderstanding: first fear, then the power of sacrifice, then fables that were continuous with these "violent passions of fear and joy" (par. 463). Poetic language was founded by heroes (par. 443).

What is radical here is the simultaneous transcendence and narrativization of metaphor, after the close of the Age of Heroes. "Linguistic" or poetic language was an aristocratic invention, their link to a constant of human nature, the demand for immediacy, however presentable. Poetic discourse, reiterated by Vico as sublime, connects us to what Bakhtin calls the Epic past; it is a way of "speaking about the *inaccessible*," before which one is "reverent" as with one's descendents (Bakhtin 1982:13, italics added; see the Ohio Matchbox example cited earlier). As Todorov (1982:234) puts it, metaphor is thus natural and acquired. Metaphor is an opening, it seems, to the inaccessible past, even when this past is contained within the present.

Thus Vico is one of the authors of the belief that metaphor equals something like the "life force" of discourse, the mingling of all the "passions" and "mind" in combinations whose presentation connects with the underlying world of the presocial. Metaphor is at once strength, power, force, difference, and sign. It is superiority in the Age of Signs. Of course, this is a complete overvaluation of metaphor in which metaphor is invested with the role of manifesting the transcendent human power to create linguistic culture (story, fable); this language, in a society that is no longer heroic (one dominated by contracts, by the risk of the Other as liar) enables those who possess the metaphorical "force" to gain for themselves an enormous advantage: they project *nondistance*, linguistico-cultural existence closer to the "origin" of the human race, to its strongest transgressions, aspirations, expressions, confusions, and, above all, sense of learning, because metaphor invents new connections between stable but boring (conventional) cultural semes. With the close of the ages of the theological poets and the heroic fables, the end of a language "naturally open, truthful, faithful, generous, and magnanimous" (par. 817, which could be compared to Nietzsche's description of the aristocratic mentality with its lack of cunning and guile), enlargement by means of metaphor faded into mere fables, the overtaking by metonymy, shown by contraction: "Jove became so small and light that he is flown about by an eagle, Neptune rides the waves in a fragile chariot. And Cybele rides seated on a lion" (par. 402). Fables here become only signs of the past, not "natural significations." This is the world of the contract (hence the contraction of metonymy), the vulgar languages. Under the reign of law and prose, words became smaller than things. Here Society empowers universal concepts to achieve "agreement upon an idea of common rational utility" (par. 1038), and the cultural indices of this are the triumph of philosophy and metaphysics, where metaphor is tamed in favor of squaring (or flattening) ideas so as not to violate socially adopted ideation. Under the reign of culture, reason, thought, law, and universal concepts, metaphor gives way to a "malicious wit" and "dint of reflection," and so becomes stripped to semiotic status, the elimination of semantic force, a mere sign of the heroic past, a lapse into an accursed delirium when uncontrolled (out of context). Vico does not hide his disdain for a culture based upon significations in which metaphor "lives on" only as the secret transcendent power to animate and is everywhere confronted by the "people's" speech utilizing "vulgar genera" (see par. 460):

> languages are more beautiful in proportion as they are richer in these condensed heroic expressions; that they are more beautiful because they are more expressive they are truer and more faithful (par. 445).

Poetic invention, then, is devalued and overvalued in the third age, which lives an endless Socratic test in which every idea is subject to equation, instrumentality, truth. Poetic invention preserves the ideal of a subject separate from contractual ideation, for metaphor continues, in advance, to outline and trace the territory of a subject who recognizes the existing deficiencies of a mere sign system. By comparison to the great past of "poetic wisdom," Vico devalues the present autonomy of law and philosophy, which is to say that his history of languge has a real immanent function.

Within his own Christian society Vico reverses and overvalues the academy and its elementary function. The "once upon a time" (almost itself a pure time-coding of metaphor) excessive combinations of fantastic poetic comminglings is subsumed within the academy's formulation of analogical axioms where metaphor is placed in the service of institutional life. In his "Practice of the New Science," Vico loosens metaphor from history by recoding it as both a principle of historical continuity and social control, with the emphasis on the latter. The "Practice" codifies how language has "need" of the academy. This 'need' is based upon a philosophy of matter. On the one hand, matter is defined as formless, semically marked by the "defective, dark, sluggish, divisible, and mobile," and where the vulgar desire, on account of their refusal to stay in place, a disordered world (the discontent); on the other hand, in the face of this disorder, only form is to perfection as order is to constancy, in which form is the "quality of counsel" realized by the wise and strong, who desire fulfillment of their craft (perfection), beauty (order), and harmony (constancy) (Vico 1976:453–454). As this vast academic system of positivity is made operational (given a narrative purpose), its function is *to prevent an outbreak of excessive metaphor within culture;* culture is to be spared regression to the stages of the theological and heroic, while academics are to oversee the preservation of human society. Put another way, the academic is to ensure that metaphors on the side of form and its attributes are those of, at best, a "robust and prudent eloquence," where the aim is to ensure a sense of "shame and duty" among the unknowing. (par. 1101). In an "unheroic" age (contracts), the academic should encourage a discourse where its performance maintains respect for the imaginary "common sense of mankind": academics should stress metaphors that enjoin "counsel," engaged with "propriety" ("serious and grave men"), "respect of being, order, beauty, and harmony," so as to "preserve their states."

The academic is responsible, then, for judging and preserving how one can present a restrained *sublime element* in culture, which is the only poetry available in a society of significations or for the mind that is in control of society, the latter no longer an intensive expressivity. Vico, of course, urged that, within the society of signs, knowledge of jurisprudence was essential (see Kelley 1976:21–26). The masses are left with academics overvaluing their common sense, their intuition, their topics, their proverbs, maxims, and cliches, precisely forms of language that preclude knowledge of law—what dominates their actual present. Academics thus take charge of the rules combining different semantic networks. The sublime—what Genette (1982:48) subtly calls "obligatory and reserved"—appears in utterances with maximum contact ("robust") accomplished through minimal means ("prudent eloquence"), and is an intellectual transcendence (which blocks ideation from joining with formlessness) now overseen by academic discourse. One is thus in the realm of an academia understood as intellectual repression ("Human passions must be moderated since they can be") performed in the name of preserving the masses' "instincts" from dissolution (see par. 1410).

The mixture of myth, logic, gnomicism, and historical theory found in Vico is not present in contemporary academic historiography in as interesting or reactive a manner. Today language and metaphor are liberated to serve as pure forms which promote the collapse of critical thought into aesthetics. Late "Vichians" continue to search for the appropriate sublime code to shape cultural and linguistic transcendence: the sublime "poetic" is an essential component of bourgeois-academic culture, insofar as it is found over and over again as an axiom of distance from mere signs, from the Law, a contact with affective experience. A recent essay by a historian restates all of the cultural and political issues in which, today, language is promoted as a need in order to support the effectiveness of recoding historiography. It seems one wants a signifying practice in order to salvage subliminality, the "academic drama" of mixing the right signifiers of metaphorical contact (poetry) and un-metaphor (code, law).

LaCapra (1980:247) starts out by trying to synthesize Heideggerian and Derridean notions about thought and textuality. He argues that the historian's relations to the past can be placed under a "dialogic" model. A past text, its social milieu, and the present historian share the figure of *inscription,* which is inclusive of how past-present experience is registered, marked, signified. Inscription establishes that the historian is to treat past texts as successive acts of writing, the latter made the self-production of information, meanings, conclusions, judgments, hypotheses, guesses, ruminations, isotopies, and so on; a past text is also inclusive of the ways in which a text rewrote its own formation, releasing its sense of history and contextual linkages, so that finding the images and senses of history in the text is part of the endeavor. Every "great" text is always about History in some manner. This aspect of a dialogic model is drawn from Derrida's reading of Freud's "mystic writing pad," in which a text, like a subject, simultaneously annuls and preserves self-formation. The role of the present historian is analogous to the psychoanalyst, after the "bad" (reductive) traits have been expelled from that profession: the historian translates, effecting the emergence of coherence so that past texts, like patients, exhibit their topographies, dynamics, exclusions, and economies of signification (the Deconstruction model). The historian, then, shifts back and forth between tradition (language, canon, what must be read) and texts that modify, transform, extend, and contest that tradition. But in this grafting of psychoanalysis and deconstruction, more emerges than such reappropriations. Here, the purpose of this inscription model is to enable the historian to "think the unthought" of every text and rehabilitate these subliminal ideations, these "strong" displacements performed by past writings: the historian is to find within tradition

(49) what is submerged or repressed in it
(50) and entering the submerged elements into a more even-
handed contest with tendencies that are damaging in
their dominant forms (LaCapra 1980:249).

Lexia 49 presents the historian who, as psychoanalyst, is to focus
on the surplus of banished signifieds, signs that undercut the
domination of tradition; lexia 50 states that, once restored, such
meanings can be used to restrain the misapplication of the master
texts of Western culture in the present (see Culler 1982:89–110
for a full discussion), an acknowledgement at first of the false
monumentalism of past texts. By showing what it is that Hegel
could not think within the context of what his text says, one
loosens tradition and rereads it through its necessary positivity
(perpetuation of some "must") and fundamental lack (of knowing what it was doing, of what it was saying).

This model of inscription is intrinsic, however, to the new
academic strategy of using versions of "reading and writing" as
basic metaphors of all possible social and cognitive relationships.
But the inscription model is also supplanted; its function fulfilled
by imaginary contact with tradition, the full dialogic model
henceforth emerges as the basis of "speech" insofar as "dialogue" is to result in *exchange* with the Other, an exchange "sensitive" to the others displacements and one's capacity to be open
to other voices (see LaCapra 1984:297):

(51) Insofar as it is itself "work-like," a dialogue involves the
interpreter's attempt to think further what is at issue in
a text or a past reality,
(52) and in the process the questioner is himself questioned
by the "other."
(53) His own horizon is transformed as he confronts still living . . . possibilities solicited by an inquiry into the past
(LaCapra 1980:251).

This model is supposed to preclude both antiquarianism (knowledge of the past for its own sake) and presentism (nonacceptance

of tradition) (LaCapra 1980:255, 272). But it generates this through the privileging of identity, continuity, necessity, and an unbreakable link between current discourse and the world of past texts, precisely attributes that have to be demonstrated in the first place as something other than the academic projection of the sublime (the past as an obligatory "must know"). "Dialogue" cannot transcend the distance between past and present unless it is first shown that present is in fact the "same" as past (their difference residing in their being only versions of the other), but if this could be established, it would actually only devalue a "history of texts," since all dealings with them would pertain to nonhistorical repetitions of cultural issues, problematics, themes, and the like. The sublimity of dialogue (as model, as transcendence) is a relation within the orbit of continuity. Note some codings: (1) to call dialogue "work-like" is to graft an economic code onto academic writing—one sees here the frequently used figure of labor in order to create the aura of value; (2) the supersign—"solicited"—belongs to a code of pseudopragmatics, Vico's "good analogy" evoking an unspecified sense of the means of contact with the "poetic" plane of past texts.

In fact "communication" is the substance of this "code of transcendence" (here the transcendence of the surplus power of tradition *and* the implied need for present-now discourse), of this "dialogic" hypostasis. Communication, in the precise sense of a dialogue where a "contest" can co-occur, must have direct address between an I and a you who shift in relation to each other, where intonation, the use of imperative forms, or the capability of "breaking off" from each other are at least realizable conditions (see Banfield 1978: 415–454). Writing can simulate communication, as in letters. But the "great texts" of the past are always an "it," and dialogue is more readily a discussion where opposing interests are at stake, where one might confront the utter groundlessness of one's beliefs (see Perelman and Olbrechts-Tyteca 1969:35–36). Nothing of this sort can happen in relation to past texts, except, of course, through a discourse that treats language that way. The epiphany of this New Hermeneutic is the use of "dialogue" and "contestation" so as to "talk between" the tradition and dismemberment, so that norms and conventions can be reconstructed

(54) that may be more durable precisely because they enable us to better contend with criticism and contestation (LaCapra 1980:272).

Dialogue with such a past merely refigures Vico's promotion of to "counsel and preserve." The academic must not relinquish or abandon transcendence, accessed through the right to immanent discourse (dialogue). One is, at all costs, to reject sign practices and signification acts that break out of the subliminality of "contact."

Conclusion

Transcendence encodes intellectual criticism to restraint before that which makes it possible, accessible, exchangeable, and so on. This occurs because: one is socialized/intellectualized (there is no difference) to focus on the missing, the absent, the not, the not-yet and no longer, the completion, the answer and question, the correction, and the like; thereby one is to practice a general elision of what is here-now, unless it is already transcendentalized. What *is* here-now is not, then, now. As these issues concern historians, one function predominates: their insistence that an engagement with history and what is left of the present is set up as the transcendence of the past, where present-now form, desire, and thinking is already engaged in the past and one has an imaginary obligation to history which cannot be broken without losing access to the present and the future.

Now I will turn to the historical, insofar as it can be shown to be functionally congruent with the subliminality of metaphorical exchange; where "to be historical" at once repeats contact with that which transcends the subject and distances one from the nonsubliminal present, and is a mode of access to the future. The historian's presentation of all this occurs in both historiographical statements and concrete narratives. In the former, propositions about "history" and "historicity" are not yet themselves entirely immanent (storified) but are embedded in theories of narrativity and story. Borrowing Greimas's idea of disengagement, involving notions of how a discourse can semanticize contact, access, and distance to various realities, while shearing off attention to its own acts of semanticization, I will try to show that historical theory can be rethought as a case of nondisengagement from history (for example, Jameson's "history hurts"). I will examine next how history is hinged to sublimity on a conceptual plane, whereby the plane of immanence (Deleuze) is closed and inaccessible to those who are culturally without history. In other words, I am going to argue that the narrative theory of history is best considered to be itself a device that tries to codify history as a necessity, certainty, obligation, and belief for cultural-intellectual existence. I shall examine the construction of historiography as it elaborates the legitimation of narrativization, the latter treated as the recoding of reactive subjectivity. And insofar as the "philosophy of history" has in fact become the academization of history, I shall focus on historiography as the modeling of a simulacrum of nondisengagement from history.

2

Historiographical Rejection of Cultural Disengagement

Preliminary Considerations

There is no "lack of reality" to "reality," as Lyotard (1984:77) puts it in referring to the accent and meter of experience, the depths and speeds of history in culture. But to achieve a cultural effect, like the belief that one is "near" an end or "far" from a contradiction, historical thought has always had to turn itself over to an adjacent discourse that could empower historians to narrate. Direct models of history as with Marx are rare; it is usual that historians eschew a discourse on and of history in favor of the more limited task of making a discourse suitable for narration. Butterfield (1981:101) reports that the kind of story told by the Yahwists in their support of Solomon's wars was precoded by Mesopotamian "Wisdom" literature: the Yahwists transformed Proverbs, a discursive form, into acceptable stories; through such stories, Solomon's aggressions were attached to a "jealous God," which Solomon could immanently exploit. The historiographical ideal of the "story for its own sake" is, as numerous commentators have shown, a form of writing that not only denies that it is, in fact, a writing—that is, a transcription—but also aims at the equivalence between discourse and narrating, their identity. In our period, psychoanalysis, Marxism, and neo-Behaviorism are a few of the discursive modes of access in the recoding of historical thought. The status of these discourses throttles a "critique of historical reason," for how could the singularity of historical reason be established given the multiplicity of these differentiating discourses? The categories of a possible critique of historical reason are inherently unstable semiotic entities (for example, neither economic nor social nor political nor psychological categories can be elevated to the status of necessary forms/relations without bringing along their own definitions and semanticity). Here one can cite the failure of Sartre to write such a "critique" as an implicit recognition that "historical reason" has evaporated as a conceptual representation. Certeau (1975:57), in accordance with the accepted contemporary tendency to downgear explicit problems of historical reason, in favor of a discourse that results in "historical products," acknowledges that history does not yield transcendence—as written, history is not about the emancipation of Humanity, and the latter is not, therefore, the transcendent content of the plane of immanence. Instead, Certeau has tried to recuscitate historical thought along the lines of "modernism" to render historical thought conformable to the Age of Information and "models." Recognizing that the "totalizing" capacity is sheer illusion (we are no longer participants in the nineteenth-century's formal faith in history), Certeau states that today historical thought

> intervenes by means of a critical experimentation of sociological, economic, psychological, or cultural models. One can say that it employs a "borrowed tool" (Pierre Vilar), which is true. But more precisely, history, by a transfer of these tools to areas outside their elaboration, puts them to the proof in the same way that an automobile used for tourism and which is made to operate on the trace of a course, moves at speeds and under conditions which *exceed* its norms. History becomes a place of "control." There it exercises a function of falsification. There one can place into evidence limits on significability relative to "models" which are "tried" by turn in a history of areas foreign to their elaboration (1975:93).

On this view, the thinking of "historical knowledge" should be determined by the "profession": the latter successively whittles away the inappropriate or malfeasant models of knowledge, so that each successive wave of historians starts off knowing what the profession has negated, what not to do to the past, so that an endless experimentation is at last autonomized. History as a scientifically modeled discipline emerges as the transcendence of its own cultural contradictions, an ingenious and typically historical solution (nothing is answered, but recoding is projected as a liberation).

The problem with this view, offered against the trivialization brought about by traditional political history, is that it presumes that the political and intellectual operations of bourgeois-academic writing can be neutralized by a kind of generalized accumulation of exceptional knowledge (Certeau 1975:100). The past can then appear in its utter specificity insofar as historians have a clear sense of what not to say. In trying to open the past to modern discourse, Certeau does not realize that most historical texts are flatly anti-experimental, that he is describing an idealized immanent-transcendence to be carried out by an avant-garde of the profession. Certeau flees from the generalized academic myth—that their texts are only secondary elaborations, yet "necessary" on account of their proximity to *and* distance from more "primary" texts and social relations.

The place of the "secondary text" is by no means settled or clear in modern culture. The writings associated with Mill or Aquinas or Marx or Freud are "primary" since they provide public life with models of existence, contradiction, logic, and philosophy, and are believed to be continuous with information and data. Whatever exists or has existed can be considered primary data; and as this primacy is redesignated, coded, named, narrated, and so on, academia undergoes further subdivisions: what was once a secondary source is shifted to the primary (the dissertation process is paradigmatic here). No doubt certain texts, like those of Marx, invent particular thematic domains and recode the activity of argumentation and theorization. But this process is mythified: its temporal logic is that Western culture has only to produce from time to time other primary texts or a repertoire of texts to replenish the sense of intellection and cognitive progression. This is a historicist program spun by the self-referentiality of the professions. The putative "secondary" texts of bourgeois-academic writing are just close enough to these primary texts to test and reevaluate them so as to preserve them for a public, or conversely, to announce that in some areas, certain texts are no longer necessary. The permanence of bourgeois-academic discourse is established when such secondary elaborations are said to be only based upon the primary and yet are also far enough from the nonspeaking masses so that a *tutelary* coding is required as its fundamental "mediation." Gellner (1974:207) has argued that academic writing has the immanent function of bureaucratizing "effective knowledge" because bureaucratization is itself an "effect of history"; because "we" have a Faustian past, our secondary sources are essential to preclude "individuality" and "idiosyncrasy" in the production of knowledge. The historian's secondary text in this post-Faustian world is a crucial means by which our culture accesses its past and its future all at once:

> if powerful, communicative, cumulative, manipulative knowledge is available at all, then it must be of this "regular" or bureaucratic kind. The growth of knowledge presupposes its communicability, storage, public and independent testing, independence of anyone's status, identity, moral or ritual condition, and so forth. This is what makes such knowledge powerful, and it is also what makes it "cold," "disenchanting," "mechanical." This is the only "proof" which, in the end, is available. We choose a style of knowing and a kind of society jointly. All in all, mankind has already made its choice, or been propelled into it in truly Faustian manner, by a greed for wealth, power, and by mutual rivalry. We can only try to understand what has happened (Gellner 1974:127).

"Communicability," "storage," "public," and so on, are here functions of the "story of knowledge," linked to the fatalistic acceptance of what Habermas has called the coupling of a cultural system, treated as a motivational domain (the Faustian past), to the management of intellect; the latter is to administer contradictions between temporal rationality and present irrationality. Note the historical components: "bureaucratic" knowledge has two stories—the first is willed ("choice") insofar as it is continuously "propelled" so that positive and present-now discursivity has no other basis than to work through past, the latter encoded, implicitly as a force of the present. Second, bureaucratic knowledge is transcendent (surpasses the subject, determines the social) and a historically necessary form of the real (see Habermas 1975:87–88). One passes from the alignment of the categories positivity/bureaucratic/past/chosen directly to the necessity of the present-now context of "only try to understand," a passive knowing and reactive mode of thinking.

What Gellner's text manifests is the release of historiographic transcendence, a metalanguage on history, which recodes an axiom of predestination: there are primary cultural truths (Faust) which are made in the past and effective now, a conjunction and determination accomplished by a (collective) subject ("mankind"). Implicitly, the historian's narrative texts function as so many scenes of necessary instruction insofar as they connect what happened to why it must happen again and again, now. Among historians, their collective willingness to identify with such bureaucratic self-institutionalization as both content and as an immanent justification often leads them to project that in ascertaining "what happened," they are only like engineers or architects, reconstructors of a past, gardeners of history (see Hexter 1961:210; Gardiner 1961:45). Their activity is self-reduced and idealized at once because historical knowledge is reduced to a secondary elaboration yet is culturally primary, since it embeds the present in versions of "must." The cultural hermeneutics of historical discourse is thus generated by the separation between secondary and primary, a separation that allows historians to recode the idea that they are transmitters of the past (the primary) and present textual solidification of the past in accordance with evidence and documentation. We shall see later that this is sheer fantasy, especially the idea that a historical narrative has any necessarily continuous relationship to what it cites as its own basis (the footnote). For now it is enough to point out that one has to reject altogether the notion of that separation of the secondary and the primary which is called forth to provide legitimation: it is only through the constant machinery of the so-called secondary elaborations that the primary sources are allowed to reach various audiences. At the outset, such self-referencing by historians, which allows for their labor to be thought of as a double transcendence, of the past in the present and of some need in the present, should be rejected in favor of refocusing upon these secondary texts insofar as their imaginary and symbolic operations organize appropriate forms of *doxa*. The culture of the historical text is primary only within frames of learning because these texts code and recode social and intellectual roles. Their ideation (the processes of similarity and contiguity) refurbishes the symbolic (what Peirce called "thirdness," which is inclusive of law, code, must), so that appropriate predicates always "inhere" in their subjects. In the terms proposed by Moles, the "historical text" might manifest an "experience of necessity" (Jameson's "history hurts"), hence of a "super-realism" (the "real" determines "culture"), but only if it orders itself first as

> an elementary form . . . to assure . . . at least . . . foreseeability. In other words, to foresee means to see beforehand. Foreseeability is the receptor's capacity to know, as the message unfolds in time or space what will follow on the basis of what has been transmitted; it is the capacity to extrapolate . . . to imagine the future of a phenomenon on the basis of its past (1968:55).

We shall say that instead of the primary-secondary axis, historical texts are part of what Sollers (1968:325) has called "matrices of transformation," placed in the service of a process of integration. That is, narrative thinking does not pertain only to narrative effects but to social systematics as well, to how one thinks, what one thinks, where one thinks, and so on. Neither Certeau's "intervention" nor Gellner's bureaucratic celebration—both defensive significations—raises the appropriate cultural starting point for a critique of historiography.

We start then with the cultural fact that there is no zero degree of historical writing—such texts are only determined by their cultural/intellectual functions and, in that, they do perpetuate Peirce's sense of thirdness, the promulgation of symbolic laws (for example, Gellner's cold knowledge equals passive subjects of knowing), identities, rules, maxims, instructions, templates, analogies of continuity or discontinuity. And without a narrated story there is no history text at all. In what follows, I shall assume the correctness of this epistemological frame—that historical thought is located, intellectually considered, near its suppression of the nonnarrated—because the kinds of historical narratives fully analyzed later do not allow the nonnarrated (theory, definitions, forms of voice and mood, argument) an independent status. This starting point recalls the principle of the arbitrariness of culture: "superstructures are faulty acts that have made it" (Lévi-Strauss 1966:254), so that one is really analyzing the presumption of claims to conceptualize history, to release it as a non-arbitrary meaning.

Denarrativizing the Model of Story

With this in mind, much of the philosophy of history can be rethought as an institutional discourse about why it is impossible for the subjects of modern society (individuals and groups) to disengage themselves from history, the latter equated with the sense of thirdness or thought of as symbolic ("history hurts," "irreconcilable antagonisms," "loss"). Everyone knows cultural syntagms such as "in history," which symbolizes history as a container or "because of history," where the category of result and its interpretant, a sense of consequence, encodes Fate as "historical life," or the symbolic based upon a sort of "historical zoology" wherein figures are marked "by history" (Berlin's *Hedgehog and Fox*) or "historical significance," which measures distances between value. Such syntagms are derivatives of what Faye has called overtelling and Lyotard a *meta-récit:* the predominance of some master story that absorbs its peripheral versions (little stories) and closes gaps between past and present (see Faye 1973:102). The recoding of the signifier "history" as a container or limit or base testifies to the ideological function that is accomplished by the dissemination of the signifier "history": the history signification can be made to float, because in every one of its usages *it could be replaced* for a gain in sense. For "history hurts" one can say that "society is intractable" or for "because of history" one could specify any predicate that opens to an action. That it cannot be replaced is the business of historiography.

In a famous essay, Charles Beard (1946:4–14) noted that historicist syntagms ranged from logical codes ("history" as a form of proof) to iconographical illusions ("history shows"), from serving as an answer to an ancient epistemic riddle ("History repeats itself," which would validate Parmenides) to legalisms ("the verdict of history"). Beard went on to state that "historical knowledge" often hovered between an almanac and the law (practical information and total determination) and called for ending the extreme vagueness of the term "history" so as to salvage historical knowledge from the plurality of excessive signification (that is, from its overaccumulated usages). This is how Beard resolved the contradictions of the signifier "history":

(1) History-as-actuality . . . includes all the humanistic sciences and all the data upon which they draw for formulas, axioms, proofs, demonstration and illustrations;

(2) and it is against knowledge of this comprehensive history that the abstractions of the humanistic sciences are to be checked for validity . . .

(3) History-as-actuality is one thing;

(4) written-history purporting to describe all or part of history-as-actuality is still another (1946:12).

What is interesting in Beard's statements is the combination of affirmation and refusal: (1) the continuity between event and representation, the absoluteness of lexia 1, affirms the substance of the nonsignified—as "actuality," history does not come coded in any particular shape or form ("includes," "all"); (2) this actuality is here concrete and total and operates to modify, qualify, de-reify, and so on, the "abstractions" of other knowledges; (3) since Beard recognized that "history-as-actuality" and "written history" never coincide, an Ideal Narrator is presupposed who can blend sign and thing, event and *diegesis*, so lexias 3 and 4 also refuse to consider why these levels are so disparate in the first place. History-as-actuality is always, at x moment, as complete as it could be. The very gap between actuality and writing relies on the dramatization of actuality: an imaginary relation is posited as the transcendence to-be-known, but which cannot be known if it is rendered abstract. Only by assuming historical knowledge to be continuous with historical actuality does Beard's formulation make any sense. Story telling is this continuity, hence the real question about abstract versus concrete knowledge should be posed as: how is comprehensive history tellable? Recent historians like Kuzminski hold that history-as-actuality is made up of "an objective, pre-interpretative, pre-explanatory reality immediately accessible to anyone who confronted it" (1979:337), which closes the gap perceived by Beard by making narrative history one with what is told.

The presupposed irreplaceability of history allows such authors to bypass contradictions located at the level of story, the latter made into an unconscious presentation form of certain effects of meaning which are insinuated in stories: I have in mind here designations like Aron's (1961:43–45) conjunction of "dramatic change" with "historical life"; Gallie's (1964:45) "sense" of "historical life" and "compelling thoughts and feelings"; Chesneaux's (1978:143) horror of the loss of future through the nonappearance of Past-in-Present; or Marcuse's (1969:98) equation between "historical knowledge" and "dangerous insights" which belong to "subversive contents of memory." These nonnarrative effects can only be presented narratively, as we shall see. We would like to ask: if to "historical" belong "drama," "empathy," "struggle," "loss," and "subversion," then are the "undramatic," "unempathetic," "nonstruggle," "presence," and "nonmemory" part of the "unhistorical"? Do such modalities vanish if history is not actual—that is, are "compelling thoughts and feelings" specific to the impact of a story or not? When is "subversion" historical or nonhistorical—that is, part of a story or not? If the signifier "historical" is always translatable (decodable) into lists such as the one given, then one can suppose that narrativists like Gallie and Hayden White are correct in their assumption that story and history are co-coded significations.

But when Moore (1966:508) says that the nonhistorical has to be overcome so that "subjects" can be created in the first place, or when Foucault (1970:367–370) suggests that the nonhistorical is part of a refusal to accept the "inevitable" oscillation between limit and totality, or Jameson (1971:390) expresses the historical as a multiplication of "the horizons in which the object is maintained, to multiply the perspectives from which it is seen," is one to believe that the nonhistorical amounts to "nonsubject," "nonoscillation," and "nonmultiplicity"? Such negatives appear over and over in historiography as the equivalence between nonstory = nonhistory, and what is distinctive about them is their utter reversibility (positive and negative), suggesting a rather fluid semantic network. What Said (1978:311) has called the reduction of history to "legislated accidents" is prevented by positive syntagms like "compelling thoughts" = sense of history, incantations against fissures in the signifier "history."

At any rate, if the "history" signifier always appears through another discourse, a semantic system, then we must also say that such semantic meanings are invariably narrativized—that is, it is the form of story which shows the initial organization of the signifier "historical."

Borrowing from the formalist Tomashevsky, we can say that whenever the type "Because of . . . , then B" appears in written form, then story is already minimally present as a cognitive form insofar as the causal and temporal are supposed to be coincidental (1965:67–68). Tomashevsky thought that there was a close connection between story themes and causality, that the latter organized the former and was at once a fusion of "logical and causal-chronological order" (1965:66 ff.). As reformulated by Bremond (1973:46 ff.), the "because-then" relation comprises the nucleus of story logic, and allows story to be analyzed along two lines: narration consists of the series of transformations in which story material (theme, motif, actions, kernels, catalysts, etc.) results in either a story of improvement or deterioration, these transcensions becoming not plot in the sense of tragedy or the like, but rather components of a model of open and closed processes. Opposed to "local causes," which can be added line by line (inclusion of informants, de-submerging a story motif), an overall narrative transformation can employ only these two forms of "complete causality." For Bremond, the structure of a story is "independent of the techniques that take charge of it," which is metaphysical in the extreme because it projects positive and negative as constitutive of thought. In Chatman's (1978:19–27) synthesis of story and narrative, building upon such logical scaffolding, to story belongs events (actions and happenings) and existents (character and settings), so that to story there is always a specific referential core (its "aboutness") and its encodation, its how or the organization of the telling. The instance of narrating has to be sharply distinguished from narrative media (for example, words, photographs, musical chords), narrative content ("ideation"), and story proper (events, or what Barthes called existents and occurrences, the former a list of substantives and the latter irreducible acts/verbs). Narrative criticism then is supposed to focus on separating narrating and narrative enunciation from story so as to expose how a story is told, the how usually displaced and hidden from the normal speed of reading. The interrogative "how" leads from story to telling, its organization, composition, and so on. "How" leads to structures, rules, codes, and forms, what we can call the vast territory of the Machining of the Said, apparently autonomous pluri-potent mechanisms of transmission to members of culture. Genette, for example, has shown that in past-referring sentences with a preterit, such as "Napoleon died at Saint Helena," generally accepted as the antithesis of statements of dispersion and multiplicity, there is nevertheless a trace of the narrating voice because the event has occurred before the narrating. There is an anteriority grasped by a posterior voice, which presupposes hierarchies of speaking at the level of telling (see Genette 1978:212–215).

For our purposes, we want to show that relationships of semantic investment are presupposed by narrative operations, that narrating presupposes prior acts of intellectual stabilization which are not temporalizing activities. I am not suggesting that logical or aspectual modes underlie narrating and make it possible; I am saying that it will be useful to stress that a typical academic narrativization is only successful if one shuts one's mind to the overall organization of narrating (the reader should note here that literary works, like Borges's stories, which are often about narrating, are very remote from historians' narrations). For example:

(5) After Watergate, Nixon was depressed.
(6) As a way out of his predicament, he accepted a publisher's offer to write a book.
(7) The act of writing so relieved him of his immediate misery
(8) that he felt able to speak out on what he regarded as important policy decisions facing the presidency of Carter.

Lexia 5 is the informational core or the stative; lexia 6 is an argument required by the predicate "was depressed"; and lexias 7 and 8 stand for arguments that transform *and stop* proposition 5 (see the superb article by Ryan 1979:138). Stories like this one appear only within narratives: lexia 8 could be added to (for example, another then-clause could be offered), its informational function subsumed by each successive story (sometimes understood as three propositions, linked by a stative like "was depressed," its reversal, and an action responsible for the reversal) and embedded between, conjoined to, disrupted from, overlapped with, and braided to other stories. The story is not exposed as a cognitive form, because predicates like "was depressed" are already interpretations and so result from the choice of and exclusion of other predicates, whatever sense they emit; to say "was depressed" is synonymous with a rejection of other predicates ("was bored," for example), but whatever predicate *could* fill the place allotted to it, that too would simply displace its ultimate referential status: the told-story determines what finally is the referent, just as the referent is hinged to nonnarrative units like the interpretant "was depressed." Such predicates have tenuous narrative truth-claims because they impose the nonimaginary or the positivity of "this happened," since "was depressed," raised to the level of a motivation, does not send a reader back through the semic networks but rather on to narrative conclusions (lexias 6–8). This is not to suggest that larger narrative groupings are unimportant; I am stressing that the psychological discourse (told by the imaginary narrator of lexias 5–8) implied as the guarantor of the referent is itself only another level of a coded process—by what rules of the discourse of psychology is "depressed" marked out and distributed as a signified? As untheorized by a reader, *the story is the result of discursive choices effaced by the telling,* the stabilization process already semantically accomplished and being in itself unpresentable as such. The not-chosen predicates are made nearly unthinkable-now and the accumulation of narrativized sentences that also positivizes core and elementary semic materials—"was depressed"—is thus a displacement of thinking. In narrativizing, one can always bypass—or try to—the signifier's status as a conceptual unit.

Moreover, the status of prose stories is not made unproblematical, as some historiographers try to do, by insisting that story is really only a *means* that gives rise to the higher powers of plot, as if story is stable enough always to make possible more elaborate cultural discourse (debate, hypothesis, etc.). Contradictory or contrary or unstatable base semes are deintellectualized by narrating; they do not intellectually disappear even though they are latent. An elementary axiological system, like nature versus culture, is itself always potentially ideological somewhere along its semantic lines and intersections with other sememic materials, regardless of how a story presents such an axiology. Yet according to the historiographer White (1973:6), story can be desemanticized and regarded as a mere enabling condition of plot: the story enables an audience to recognize plot structures, so that semantic units must be superseded in reading a story. Narrativists like White have no interest in story except as it conveys a higher rationality. Thus, we are supposed to encounter a plot:

(9) After Watergate, Nixon was depressed,

requires that the simple stative make use of the reader's implicit knowledge and sense of periodization, here the chrononym of "loss of status" because Nixon had to vacate the world's most desirable position of political power;

(10) . . . he accepted a publisher's offer to write . . .

is an encoding of "accepted" in which to accept (+voluntary, +absence of force and coercion, +agreement) moves "depressed" and "predicament" into a simple immanent transcendence of the latter;

(11) The act of writing so relieved . . .

allows the reader to know that "accepted" was only a means, so that "relieved" concludes the stop of "accepted"; and

(12) . . . to speak out . . .

is the final state, a transformation of the initial proposition "was depressed." This is a plot of comedy and a common story as it is one with the upper-middle-class topoi of pathos. The story is the documentation of the plot and the plot is the answer to the implicit stative that switched on the story in the first place.

But if one regards story as the surface presentation and transformation of often unpresentable imaginary and symbolic propositions, arguments, and predicates, our story can also be rethought this way: (1) "Was depressed" is used as an index of "after Watergate": it thus summarizes all the series of actions and degrees between Watergate and the narrated-now of the story. A narrating voice is not absent at all (how could it be?); it is merely as heterodiegetic as possible; it is negatively implied by the refusal to articulate how "depressed" was arrived at (suppression of inquiry). (2) There is a certain amount of anti-intellectualism, as the reader is implicitly asked to perform the task of "thinking about" and "in" but not "through": the focus is on the new equilibrium, the equation between speech and restoration or "writing equals liberation." One could then say that this theory of the plot really only manifests an (unstated)

Behaviorism which is thereby brought up to date: opposing forces on both the micro- (individual) and macro-levels aim at some form of equilibrium, where the latter is the very goal of self-preservation. This "good logic" of the metaphorical apparatus—"speech equals liberation"—narrativizes a series of implicit interpretations and ideological kernels without the hierarchy of its telling exposed. Plot, as we shall see in chapters three through five, can be decoded into its constituent elements, its discursivity, and not appear as the point of the story but rather as another cultural transcendence, specifically of the story's semic organization. I want to affirm here that categories like negation and contradiction are intellectually presupposed by narrative plot: the latter has no autonomy, for even the naming of an opposition, for example, truth versus lie, despite its binary triviality, is still presupposed by narrating, even when the latter tries to efface its discursive base.

What I now want to stress is that theories of story should be considered strictly in terms of their cultural function and end; whether story is "more like" a grammar (Todorov) or subsumed by plot or is a logic of action (van Dijk), a fabulation (Eco), is of less interest than the manufacturing of the reader of the typical historical story. The ways in which narrative and story transfer "a value or an object from one character to another" (Scholes 1974:103) analyzes the autonomization of the sending and encoding procedures of story telling. There is no strong reason to consider story a form of pre-predicative handling of events and actions or one of the root forms in which intellect itself speaks. I concur with Barthes's de-idealization of story and, by implication, of the entire historiographical tradition, scientific or not, which has valorized story and narration; through story (or the far better term, storification) academic culture encourages a consciousness that is never able to arrive at criticism, for story ensures that

> reality is neither mysterious nor absurd: it is clear, almost familiar . . . the world may be full of pathos but it is not derelict . . . since he who tells the story has the power to do away with the opacity and the solitude of the existences which

made it up. . . . The narrative past is therefore part of a security system . . . reality becomes slighter and does not outrun language (Barthes 1967a:32).

One need think only of the banishment of sources to the periphery of the text, the refusal to "think out loud" (in front of the reader), the reliance upon a central subject (and more, as we shall see), in order to place historical narration closer to what Marx called an abstract signification system where one can mistakenly believe that

the single logical formula of movement, of sequence, of time, can explain the body of society in which all economic relations co-exist simultaneously and support one another (cited in Althusser 1977:107).

Finding the Reader

One should not thereby embrace the notion that historical narration is made at all recognizable by invoking certain negative cultural implications of story or, conversely, that its impact and effect are guaranteed a cultural place on account of forms like plot structures. Both stances miss what is essential (to the former position goes the "scientific" fantasy of a history without a story, to the latter the fantasy of finding the right story to fit the data). The dismissive view, usually associated with "scientific modernists" within the historical profession, tends to assert that story is only a necessary form of presentation which does not interfere with argument, explanation, truth, research, colligation, or any other properly cognitive operation. One can even avoid using the signifier "story"—no less than a president of the American Historical Association prefers the oxymoron "comprehensive narration" (Bailyn 1982:23)—but this usually means that some aesthetics of story telling are all the more internalized. It evidently does not matter that no historian presents research or the cognitive processes of inquiry, the *how* of procedural and analytic aspects, independently of the story form. Nevertheless, one recent and sophisticated apologist for the "modernism" of historical thought notes that certain conditions—notably (1) the increased international "scientization" of scholarship (because academic historians frequently use terms like "binary" or "interface" or "problematic"), (2) a world of imploding events (for example, the speed with which commodity prices rise and fall directly entails surplus or "normal" death in West Africa), (3) Europe's decline (but here one has to note that this is essentially at the military level in relation to the United States, not in terms of capital accumulation (see Mandel 1980:108–109), and (4) the challenge of "communist" societies—have coalesced so that a "new history" utilizes narration merely for a sense of readability. This new history

(13) will be concerned with the study in the widest possible range of different societies
(14) of the perennial problems that have assailed mankind everywhere—
(15) the basic biological urges of hunger and sex, the struggle with a grudging environment for the means of livelihood,
(16) the inadequacies of established social patterns to deal with newly emerging conditions,
(17) problems of power and corruption,
(18) the oppression of the weak by the strong and the reaction of men driven by hunger and oppression to desperation (Barraclough 1978:168).

Farewell to the "old history"? Not at all: it is only here massively recoded. The successive narrative integration of these social scientific "thememes" would result in a reestablishment of the "narrative equilibrium" that obtained in "history's golden age," the middle and the later nineteenth century, for a new "ecumenical interpretation of world history" is now possible (Barraclough 1978:176). The belief that the history text presences immanent reality because there are "perennial problems" (the transcendent) tries to set this kind of historical thought as far as possible from, for example, the aesthetic position of a Huizinga with his notion of "connoisseurship." Instead, biology ("urge"), ecology ("grudging environment"), sociology ("social patterns"), and politics ("power") transmit scientifically accepted codes like the behaviorist syndrome of "oppression-reaction-desperation," so historical narration is to aid in the scientific *management* of the world. One goes from perennial problems—positivized over immanent contradictions—directly to management. The function of this form of historical thought is to depoliticize immanent and local contradictions in favor of the perennial. The new history has the precise function of using story organized by science so as to dampen other forms of thought. Dilemmas that are nonnarrative in their existential status can be shriveled and contained by scientific stories. The perennial versus present-now (transcendent versus immanent), draws in its wake, of course, belief in the benevolence of science, a notoriously naive position.

However, celebratory projections of the story form continue to recode story as a cultural universal. White argues, for example, that story results from the way a narrative that tries to show "the true form of things existing behind a merely apparent formlessness" (1978:58). There is an obvious epistemic impossibility built into the very signifiers used by White; written signs are never visual ("show"), they are successive (Martinet 1972:25); the materiality of written language can only simulate a showing, as the visual channel is independent of language unless reduced by the latter through intellectual/cognitive operations to verbal signals (internalizations, expectations, redundancy factors); the most "showable" telling is also the most silent about how it shows (see Genette 1980:166). Written signs on the primary level (a discourse) are already interpretants (in Peirce's term) of other signs, so it is odd that one would want to retain showing to describe the effects of the mere *successivity* of discourse. White also goes on to provide other notions that design a reader, some of which are relevant here: he argues that (1) narration works by a destructuring of events and information wherein the historian fulfills the role of demonstrating that semi-intractable data (trauma, for example) can properly be made to yield their sense; (2) historical narration recodes events in such a way that the initial story (basic frames, initial disjunctions, statives) is transformed by means of the modality of reversal (the initial formation is undone by the new plot), so that (3) the narrative impact or specific difference of its effect lies in the production of a psychoanalytic effect—rendering the strange and unfamiliar into the familiar (White 1978:58). Intractable data are placed in dramatic forms that deproblematize them for the reader. The plot forms of story—romance, comedy, tragedy, and irony—provide the encoding of "from unfamiliar to familiarity" and these forms are said to

(19) be followed by a reader of the narrative in such a way as to be experienced as a progressive revelation of what the true nature of the events consist of . . .

(20) these modalities . . . ultimately have their origin in the figurative (White 1978:59).

Such "figuratively true" (see Vico) systematizations or structuring by metaphor, metonymy, synecdoche, and irony are valid in turn, because they have their basis in the common "structures" of language and "ordinary educated speech" (White 1978:56). It does not strike White that ordinary educated speech is a fiction, a strict metalinguistic classification that is used to displace these tropes onto a transcendental level of language, there misidentified as a common a priori (a virtual model of cultural hypostasis). After all, because one can identify tropes in writing, it does not follow that such tropes then inhere in language as one of its essences, or as a model of how story is informed.

If stories are prewritten by poetics, one may immediately ask: does it follow that "uneducated" speech is equivalent to those who do not share or participate in these plot structures and tropes? What is one to do with readers who do not care to follow a story? Let me give an example in detail of what is wrong with White's attempt to justify historical thought on the basis of his theory of reading stories, an example drawn from his major work, *Metahistory* (1973), which has been systematically misread by most historians as an attack on historiography (when read at all by historians—one cannot stress enough that most historians will not think about the culture of historiography). The following passage from Tocqueville is cited by White as proof of Tocqueville's emplotment of history in the tragic mode:

(21) In 1780 there could no longer be any talk of France's being on the downgrade;

(22) on the contrary, it seems that no limit could be set to her advance.

(23) And it was now that theories of the perfectability of man and continuous progress came into fashion.

(24) Twenty years earlier there had been no hope for the future; in 1789 no anxiety was felt about it.

(25) Dazzled by the prospects of a felicity undreamed of hitherto and now within their grasp, people were blind to the very real improvements that had taken place and eager to precipitate events (cited in White 1973:217).

White's immediate commentary: "What these passages suggest is a conception of the laws of social change similar to those met with in Greek tragedy, the laws by which those whose condition of life is improving should look to the advent of some calamity, usually a product of the overextension of their own limited capacity for understanding the world or for looking at it and themselves realistically" (1973:217).

The tragedy supposedly encoded by Tocqueville connotes recognition of the limits of one's power and denotes submission to such knowledge; there are epistemic tragedies (the *Critique of Pure Reason* being the most famous), psychoanalytic ones (*Civilization and Its Discontents*), novelistic ones, and so on. In the passage from Tocqueville, White probably stresses the tragic (since he does not say) as the gap, the difference, and blindness raised by Tocqueville's mention in lexia 25 of thought's leap ahead of experience ("real improvement") and the asymmetry between thought and experience, for which Tocqueville uses the sememe "dazzled" and which is opposed to real improvements. "Dazzled" and tragedy here concern what the "people" (lexia 25) *could or could not have known* in the story starting with lexia 21. Lexia 25 is Tocqueville's synthesis proposition, which constructs the people as children/subjects of a process they could not have experienced unless they were thinking historically in the first place. Tocqueville's passage presents a story about contradictions and blindness; but one can also say that the narrator works off a dominant psychological code, that of Desire's refusal to acknowledge reality, which further presupposes an epistemic coding left unstated by Tocqueville, that people cannot know in self-presence their own thoughts and demands, that objectivity is impossible for the agents of a revolutionary process. This has nothing to do with "looking for" the "advent of some calamity," outside of the historiographic consideration that the French revolution manifests a continuous story theme of *excess*. By this scale of narrativizing, one could regard the Viet Cong victory over the U.S. military forces as tragic if one also regarded the current Vietnamese regime as the conclusion of the whole story of the Viet Cong, which becomes, of course, the "focal" story. In fact, Tocqueville's strict correlation between "felicity undreamed of" and "blindness" is storified by reliance upon nontragic elements: lexia 21 closes another, earlier, story line; lexia 22 states an initial condition, that of appearance ("seemed"), which is then dismissed by the narrator's use of "now" (lexia 23) so as to introduce the argument that "theories" were the destabilizing factor in perception (or that intellection was responsible); lexia 24 states that in 1760 the future was negative, in 1789 it was positive, and both representations within the story are covered by drawing the reader's focus onto what people then should have known, improvements. This sense is, of course, in blatant contradiction to the verb "dazzled" ("dazzled" forgives them: they could not have known because of their real past). In short, the overelimination of human desire from thought is not at all tragic unless the tragic is widened to include *modal* forms as well (for example, that what lexia 25 says is both true and had-to-be-true).

Plot structures can be extracted from a reading of Western literature and correlated with tropes, which makes them repeatable and long-lasting formulas, not transcendental types. The reading of tragedy because of what past actors should have but could not have known is something other than tragic (it certainly is moralistic); and plot structures do not just serve to recode the real, even if the latter is simply the initial shape of another story or documents that one wishes to retell. It is preferable to say with Eco (1976:145) that plots function (to inspire, coax) only in relation to the value systems of social groups who already embody a system of expectations about inclusion and exclusion from certain cultural activities. Plot structures, raised to a metalinguistic fiction of the defense of the autonomy of the tropes, require a more basic question, which is properly cognitive: in the leap from plot to history, what thinks in "historical thought"? The culture itself? Or in Sperber's (1977:141–149) terms: *what thinks* insofar as plot structures parallel the historiographical attempt to construct a reader, where thought is provided with *passive* syntheses, an operation that slows down acts of rethinking, renaming, reanalyzing and recognizing? I stress that the historical consequence, the later tragedy of the French Revolution, was presented by means of a theory of relations between desire and thinking, not by means of a plot structure at all.

The transcendence of plot structures is yet another instance of reifying pervasive and abstract academic models. For now, let us consider the reader of such structures in terms directly related to the readers of stories, readers designed to be stitched to the immanent transcendence of the form of story. White can again serve as our shift to this plateau. Thus:

(26) The reader, in the process of following the historian's account of these events, gradually comes to *realize*

(27) that the story he is reading is of one kind rather than another . . .

(28) And when he has *perceived* the class or type of stories to which the story that he is reading *belongs*,

(29) he experiences the effect of having the events in the story explained to him . . . he has grasped the point of it (White 1978:49, italics added).

Note that the model that defines the reader is completely narrativized: (1) the act of reading is virtually an anaglyph of thought, a cameo, as it were, of the form of story. The realization of the class precedes and makes possible the perception of the class; this is obviously a philosophical stance, much recoded from the Aristotelian tradition: what is "in" the plot structure is "in" the mind; (2) "realize" is an act of classification, but since no one, including White, suggests that the reader learns how to classify at this juncture, one might stress that such classification is merely *re-cognition;* (3) if this is the case, then "grasping the point" of the experience is really no experience at all: what "really happens" is that the reader encounters confirmation of what he or she already knows. The reader is not confronted with a story whose "followability" is threatened by the information or its telling; it is neither disparate from experience nor excessively redundant, either of which would cause the work of history to fail. If the story cannot be amalgamated to a plot (by, say, successive abductions), then the genre conditions are canceled and one is confronted by a text whose very name is suspended. However, if each story goes into one or more plots and these lines are kept singularly free from, say, excessive attention to the text's cultural voices (the reader excluded from knowledge of how the text is put together), its reader is thereby removed from any serious consideration of the encoding procedures; the telling overtakes the encoded information as it is read and the reader is actually experiencing identity (of plot, thesis, motif, etc.) all the way through. One could obviously say that every work of history is some sort of Pascalian wager on the genre's capacities (its competency) for combination and selection (difference and identity), but this is too flat and idealizing; instead, it is more cognitively responsible to note that what White really encodes in lexias 26 to 29 is a catachresis of the reader: "to realize," "to perceive," "to belong" characterize the reader as if such readers were well-made stories of cognition. The circuits that connect story, narration, and reader are tautological: story is encoded by plot, plot is encoded by literature, literature is encoded by language, language is encoded by psychology, and the act of reading, since it is always in alignment with its object, confirms the history text as yet another formation of the passive Western subject; it produces the reactive reader for whom the text recodes existing classification systems, keeping the reader's pre-existing subjectivity intact.

Let us call the positivizing performed by the philosophy of story the metalanguage of narrative engagement, in which cultural subjects are ciphers of critical thinking (and see, in this regard, the "necessary story" in Jameson 1981:102). The formal reader is defined as *precluded from disengagement from the story,* a position at the very center of the culture of story. White's stance expresses the epistemology of identity and it is an infectious position. Sartre, for example, in his Marxist phase, went so far in this as to encode Marxist thought in completely homologous terms: "Our historical task, at the heart of this polyvalent world, is to bring closer the moment when History will have only one meaning" (1968:91), where story = a meaning, and history = the meaning, which is exactly what the unabashed professional historians of academe urge when they too call for "an evolving story . . . The drama of people struggling with the conditions that confine them through cycles of limited life spans" (Bailyn 1982:5). Culturally, the story form transcends to the extent that it is homologous with one's nondisengagement from history, which we must now more carefully isolate as a cultural operation. Before passing on to that topic, let us note that narrating forms within stories are not to be thought of as necessarily attached to set grammatical forms.

Mandelbaum (1978:24–45) notes that the nineteenth-century subsumption of explanation and interpretation "to the story" has faded with the professionalization of the discipline, so that no modern historian has to embrace the full narrative form, and, in many cases, is unable to do so. In cases, for example, where a concrete historical text uses formal hypotheses derived from demographic science to reconstruct mobility patterns of a town in, say, 1830, historians obviously exchange among themselves nonnarrative or discursive codes—applications of a metalanguage to a new field (for example, replacement of political categories with urban categories—these category shifts express the internal economy of academic departments, their expansion and contraction). But Mandelbaum does not recognize that historians storify-narrativize at every level of contact with data. Historians often suspend subjects by narrative digression. For example:

(30) "The peasants did not hold title to their plots; to understand this, one has to consider the state of . . . ," [in which case another story is introduced by gesturing to the reader] historians obviously describe and compress:

(31) "The following week, Churchill's impersonator stood before the microphone and in a nervous voice wearily imitated . . . but this failed to outwit the Nazis" [in which the descriptive tags are subservient to temporal markings]; historians employ explanation phrases that fade into chronology:

(32) "In order to continue the war, they had to mobilize because the Germans . . ."; and here is an interpretation that approaches structuralized time:

(33) "European Idealism helped to deaden the working classes' understanding that their own internalization of ruling class ideas blinded them to their own material interests. Only the dominant classes in society reject Idealism as they endlessly propagate its value."

Lexia 30 expands some story laterally and is a mere switch by comparison to 31, which intensifies a character's situation, a focalization that crystallizes earlier statives and arguments; lexias 32 and 33 specify, respectively, necessity as next-later (the causal), and 33 is an answer commentary because it is really a theoretical proposition. Land, impersonation, mobilization, and theory are then inseparable from narrativizing functions, such functions postponing, at best, the reader's apprehension of how the told is said, as well as saturating the reader in thought that is theoretical and ideological.

Subject and Reader

In his magisterial *Analytic Philosophy of History* (1965), Danto made the argument that narrative historians are unlike "philosophers" of history because historians do not make statements about the future: they do not predict. Historians, he went on, may explain, but explanation is not the dominant signification form of the historian's writing; historians can use any and all psychological theories for explanatory frames, but neither empathy theory nor gestalt theory is fundamental to what historians do (Danto 1965:24–26). What historians actually do, according to Danto, is write in such a way as always to transcend a "plain narrative": the historian's narrative must be "true" and yet something more than a report of what happened (p. 130). One of Danto's main targets was to abolish, altogether, the notion that it is necessary for *explicit* explanation and interpretation to make up the historian's primary activity; as he put it, in historical thought,

> Phenomena *as such* are not explained. It is only phenomena *as covered by a description* which are capable of explanation, and then, when we speak of explaining them, it must always be with reference to *that* description. So an explanation of a phenomenon must . . . be relativized to a description of that phenomenon (1965:218, Danto's italics).

Descriptive language, especially language that coappears with desire (see Blanchard 1980:19) is further tightened by Danto. What separates the historian from all other classes of "describers" (novelists, for example) is the shape of a grammar that historians are obligated to respect:

> (34) Narrative sentences . . . refer to at least two time-separated events even though they only *describe* (are *only about*) the earliest event to which they refer (p. 143, Danto's italics).

And here is the canonical formula of this act of description:

> (35) x is F at t-1
> (36) H happens to x at t-2
> (37) x is G at t-3 (p. 236).

When the description is combined with grammatical transactives ("hit") or project verbs, with nominatives construed as temporal wholes (the Age of Anxiety) and with "mentions," the historian is guaranteed that it is already structured as a story. It has "a beginning (1), a middle (2), and an end (3)" (Danto 1965:236). Narrative culture and historical culture are identical since they are linked by the cofunctionality of description and narration. For example: lexia 35 can be rewritten as

> (38) Kissinger was determined to convince the Russians of American resolve,

and lexia 36 as

> (39) He reneged on pursuing any serious peace talks; stopped by
> (40) Kissinger was furious when this was leaked as he was terrified of a possible jail sentence by a future world court, so he accepted the negotiation process.

Lexia 38 is the description in which a singular referring expression conveys a subject, while lexia 39 presents the active argument, the new information, "reneged," which is also coreferential with 38, and lexia 40 ("accepted") is the reversal/stop; in accordance with whether this simple story was followed by n-tuple then-clauses after lexia 38 or is made part of a braiding of narrative sequences (usually signaled by "meanwhile" clauses), story expansion occurs. Danto's model of historical sentences, which are narrative and descriptive at once, is meant to show that a transformation of the type "x is G at t-3" supports "narrative as a form of explanation" (p. 237). On this account, history = a *grammar of change,* a very important position, precisely on account of its nonreduction of transformations (to laws, and so on). One can see that the meanings—determine, renege, furious—fade from the reader's intellect or, what amounts to the same thing, give no indication of destabilizing anyone's thoughts about will, negation, or consequence.

Danto makes grammar the ground of historical narration and his model fits for the most part with more recent grammars, notably Todorov's (1977:108–119). One way or another, all historical narration is a manifestation of a valid grammar that renders intelligible the presupposition of the "unity of subject" (p. 249) and in which, even if one can project general laws as the premises of "H happens to x at t-2," such laws add nothing that is not already lodged in the description. Now *all* of what Danto has to say is very close to providing historians with a prolegomenon of historical reason, and is surely one of the strongest legitimation texts for the modern historical profession. But more important here are supplemental ideations offered by Danto in passages that disclose the *cultural* connotations of his model of "grammatical historical thought." For a certain sort of privilege and advantage emerges during the thinking of narrative sentences, which is to say that the grammar of narrative has its own cultural plane:

> (41) For the whole point of history is *not to know* about actions as witnesses might, but as historians do,
> (42) in connections with later events and as parts of temporal wholes.
> (43) To wish away this singular advantage would be silly, and historically disastrous, as well as unfulfillable.
> (44) It would, in analogy with Plato's image, be a wish to reenter the cave *where the future is still opaque.*
> (45) *Men would give a great deal to be able to see their actions through the eyes of the historians to come* (p. 283, italics added).

Strange conjunctions, of which Rimbaud's symbolist idea, "As for the world, when you emerge, what will it have become?" suggests another rendering than the emphasis above on psychology. Many codes and subcodes provide narrative form with a transcendent cultural function: (1) lexia 41, first, stresses a *space* of knowledge occupied by the historian, which amounts to a knowledge founded against "witness"; hence there must, logically, be some sort of epistemic possibility lacking and absent in "witnesses"; "witnesses" cannot know "later events" (consequences) and "temporal wholes" (the historian's act of giving the colligatory *name*); (2) this "singular advantage" is thus a *metalingual* advantage, established over the inadequacy of "witnesses," the latter's physical and legal status defined as a lack by comparison to the historian's implicit extra-legal and extra-perceptual actantial function of knowledge. The disequilibrium which always surrounds "witnesses," stemming from the over-abundance of perception and experience, enthusiasms and be-lief, or strong thoughts as Nietzsche put it, has to be corrected in favor of the equilibrium of distance and story. The simul-taneity of the extra-legal and the extra-perceptual takes the his-torian right out of immanent culture, so in this sense is a pure cultural transcendence. (3) Lexia 44 is very bizarre: if one rejects the advantage of historical thought, an "opaque future" would occur—but it always occurs anyway, that is, the future is always opaque even for those who embrace historical thought as an institutional practice. Since subjects in time-now cannot, by def-inition, "know" the future (as lexia 41 says), the presence or absence of historical thought does not change at all the status of anyone's present thoughts; (4) *How much* would someone give to see their actions through the "eyes" of "historians to come"? *Who* would ask that question? The very question, again on the grounds of lexia 41, is impossible of fulfillment or realization. Or, to want to know what will become of oneself is hardly a characterization of historical knowledge unless one assumes a prior encoding, that one should become like the historian's roles sketched earlier. Indeed, as a question, lexia 45 is closer to an elementary form of demand and prediction ("I want to know"), so it seems that Danto, in order to provide a psychologically efficient code for history, has projected a psychological question pertaining to someone's present ("what will . . .") onto the past as the historian's metalinguistic code, and then rejected the idea that one can have such knowledge in one's own present. It is natural to want to know the future; but only the historian can know the future—the future of the past. All of which is fine, except: It assumes that cultural subjects live in order to be re-membered in their future. It presumes history to be present all along as a natural motivation. In addition, to try to disengage oneself from history entails that one has made some sort of pact with futurology, the cave, or false power and pure immanence. We can sum this up by saying that Danto has generated the semantic fields of knowledge and existence. Their affirmative combination results in what we can call a *blocking movement:* nondisengagement from history is positively defined as the present's relation to a future when the wish to regress ("cave") is suppressed; insofar as one tries to reach the future or past from the present according to the role of a witness (excessive immediacy), a false or regressive relationship to culture ensues. These connections can be expressed this way:

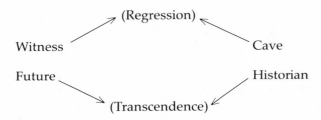

Witness and Cave are complementary because "silly," "disastrous," and "unfulfillment" give them common negative semes; Future and Historian are linked by names (temporal wholes) and advantage. If we try to combine the positions of regression and transcendence as to their manifestation of knowledge and existence, it is apparent that to combine Witness and Cave results in regression, just as Cave and Historian results in an oxymoron, and Witness and Future results in self-cancellation. *Only Future and History release a positive signification:* to think like the historian is to gain the advantage of names that take one out of the Cave, make one more than immediate (more than a Witness) and allow one to transcend the present. Culturally, one can only break from history insofar as one is also willing to annul oneself as a subject with a future. Now who would choose that?

Historical narration is here pressed into the service of an inhibition machine and corrective for supposedly myopic and self-serving images one might form of the present, another case of the devaluation of the present, which, to be more precise, means for Danto a more complete *cave* of the present: because lexia 45 overvalues the extent to which "men" already "think" in the "name of history," and the "thought" of "witnesses" is limited (lacks advantage), the present is reaffirmed in its near zero cognitive status; the present is reduced to a theatrical post, the scene of the *defeat* of thought. The positive definition of the present emerges when knowledge relates to both past and future and is rendered by Danto in this manner:

(46) Indeed, part of the *fascination* of history lies in the *spectacle* of an innumerable variety of qualitatively different actions and passions,

(47) *exhibited* by human beings down the ages

(48) which are for all that still instances of the *same general description,*

(49) and are covered by the same general principles we employ in everyday life, principles which, if enunciated, come in the end to be little more than *truisms* (p. 243, italics added).

The strong correlation between visuality and the positivity of the signifier "history" results from combining "fascination" and "spectacle" with "exhibited," where Actions = Doing (verb) contained by Truisms which = Nominals. The present-audience or reader receives from the historian maximum variety (information) made understandable because the present is already anchored in a descriptive language, truisms, which ensures that past, present, and future are saturated by thinking in which the self-evidence of truisms (Act, Verb) tell what has happened. Saturated by repetition, actions signify the means and transformation of an existence whose meaning is contained by self-evident truisms. This is another way of concocting non-disengagement: only if truistic existence is broken can the subject sever itself from history and, by definition, the future. That is, only by destroying the model of culture based on the transcendence of truistic knowledge can the subject get clear of necessity and arrive at . . . cultural nothingness. The inescapable truisms of existence are indeed powerful, as they signify an obligation to repetition (see Nietzsche 1957:58).

The entire apparatus is then used to justify an impossibility of access in the present. In other words, Danto's implied reader is given to think that the future of the past had to be *the what* it became, but this is performed by a present-consciousness that has no manner of knowing or even of asking about its own future: one would like to know when the discontinuity occurred making present-now a place by which to know the future of the past yet closed as to knowledge of its own presentness. Or, again, and in yet another way since such compositions are so difficult to disentangle: the present-now cultural role of historians is to ensure that there circulates in culture the thought that the present is *deficient* (alienation of the subject, the future is Other, not-now, not-yet). This deficiency, based in part on the perpetual transformation of the "unusual into the usual" as Castoriadis (1984:204) says, is certainly a case of projected sui generis cultural continuity, a thought no one can ever really think out. Moraze (1976:135 ff.) calls all this the "durable" cultural world where "the borrowings of the past are affected by the experience lived in the present for the inspiration of the future," a "common destiny" whose "good sense is perhaps the thing best shared in the world." We thus are returned to the subliminality of history insofar as engagement with history is paralleled by cultural death if one rejects truisms and their force.

Danto, and let me stress again that his *Analytic* is still the only modern *philosophy* of historical thought which simultaneously provides a "metatheoretical" defense of narrative *and* nonnarrative (lexia 48), encodes this deficiency of present-now through signifiers of physical lack and absence, rendered as the historical subject who must embrace and internalize (sublime obligation) and live out the implications and consequences of this deficiency:

(50) Actors . . . are blind to the significance of their actions because they are blind to the future.
(51) Not knowing how our actions will be seen from the vantage point of history, we to that degree lack control over the present (Danto 1965:284).

In lexia 50 the "significance" of action is coded as "not knowable," because such significance is amalgamated to the meaning *future = significance,* an infamous temporal displacement of meaning-now. Lacking control over present-now arises because the future is not present in the present; the immediate effect is that "lack of control" in the "present" is thereby of necessity what one can "do nothing about." The present lacks spectacle because the grammar of present-now falls out of "x happened" and future modals (for example, "if"). Correlatively, to be disengaged from history equals blindness or, better, to be engaged with history equals truncated knowledge. Around this binary, the latter is positivized over blindness; cultural subjects can choose between such blindness or truncated knowledge, a choice that affirms the positivity of the less negative. To use Elias's terms (1978:236), the subject here implicitly arises as a knowing subject from a distance set forth as actually present in existence, not as itself an act of distancing, something performed by a doing of thought.

There are a variety of ways in which such nondisengagement from history has been recently expressed; here we would like to cite two forms of the contemporary imperialist ethos that links the positivity of narration to models of reading history. This is pursued to illustrate the pervasiveness of the positivity of non-disengagement, to show that we are dealing with a cultural systematic of historiography.

Current historiography rarely achieves Danto's philosophical and conceptual threshold about the impossibility of severing oneself from history. Stone (1979:19) has proclaimed that the "new social history" must readopt "historical narration" because the impact of "scientific" history threatens to expel the infamous "lay" reader. It is not coincidental that science is preserved as a mystery while the historian is to replenish the depletion of new passives with deleted actors (see Kress and Hodge 1979:134). Stone affirms that, as a device, narration is indispensable for obtaining

(52) an intimate glimpse of man in the past,
(53) *to try to get inside his head* (italics added)

The historian is to narrate using the imperialism built into academia: nothing is inaccessible. Since "man is our quarry," and narration can provide good reading and good sense, lexia 53 updates Droysen's formula about apprehending individuality: $A = a + x$, where x is open to the historian's insight, projections, enthusiasm, and so on, all of which are sanctioned by the need to tell, to bring back to the present specimens of utter value, that which must not be lost to time and forgetfulness. The historian knows no barriers.

More scientific is the narrative model outlined by Henretta (1979:1319). He argues that contemporary historians should integrate three distinct historiographical dimensions: (1) objective structures ranging from climatics to behavorial constraints (rules); (2) a Marxist variety of moral concern for those continuous in time-present with those defeated in time-past (women, workers); and (3) the experience of past actors or a phenomenological threshold that focuses on the actual lived experiences of the past. Rules, morality, and experience make up the new levels which, of course, can be subdivided as well as overlap. Henretta separates analytic operations or "construction" from narrative presentation insofar as statistical methods do not necessarily allow for "close description of the chronological," and then argues for a "reanimated" narrative in these terms:

(54) This approach directly addresses questions of time, change, and sequence;

(55) such chronological concerns . . . form crucial aspects of the discipline of history . . .

(56) Historians who adopt a chronological framework establish a *basic congruence between the lives of their subjects and those of their audience.*

(57) Narrative history holds great appeal for the lay reader . . . because its mode of cognition approximates the reality of everyday life (1979:1318–1319, italics added).

Lexias 54 and 55 reaffirm that it goes without saying that narrative effect can be reduced to the stability of linearity, the latter some sort of unanalyzable category and transcendent cultural relation. With lexia 56 and the fairly blank term "congruence," an imaginary and symbolic valuation is manifested: the congruence between past (actors) and present (readers) is a situational identity within the world of truisms (the latter virtually one with the everyday). Neither past subjects nor present readers know: reality for both is reduced to the chronic, mistakenly thought of as movement in its own right and not the cultural malaise it actually is. Indeed, Henretta endorses "modernizing" narration, keeping it calibrated to the discursive changes in the social sciences. One finds buried in his footnotes, however, the intellectual construction of the role the historian occupies between past and reader. Culturally regarded, the historian is a version of a narrative commissar, a Kafka-like bureaucrat who insists upon identities wherever one finds gaps:

(58) Although some degree of artifice enters into the construction of a narrative—

(59) in that the author already knows the outcome of the story and therefore

(60) provides a false sense of open-endedness—

(61) artifice alone does not constitute a major objection.

(62) *For the reader's imperfect knowledge approximates that of the historical actor: neither knows for certain how events will turn out* (1979:1318, italics added).

The sketchy figurations between "artifice" and narrative say very little, therefore reveal a lot: a form of writing is manifestly not artificial because of someone's withholding knowledge or not, and the "false sense of open-endedness" (lexia 60) due to the historian's knowledge-post is a pseudo-statement of the actual problem. If historians are genuinely interested in knowledge and getting a handle, once and for all, on artifice, why not publish *pure* inquiry (that is, complete, line-by-line nonstory of the working-up of historical objects)? When lexia 62 blithely and preciously equates the past-subject and reading-now subject through the signifier "imperfect," a straightforward code links them: both share the same lack of knowledge. Once again we are actually in front of narrative authority, as the historian is modeled as metalingual to both readers and past-actors. This is another rigged schema: the historian occupies a place of full presence and is the tutelary-narrator. The historian is not an instructor of what has been presented to thought as learned; the historian is the one who pretends not to know (manipulates through story) so that the narrative can be written (recodes a form). Narratees (of the story) and addressees (of the text) are infantile vis-à-vis the historian's post: readers/subjects are flattened insofar as they are coded to accept existential and narrative suspense (and its implied roles).

The Narratable and the Unstatable

Now I want to present stronger arguments in favor of a systematic critique of story, arguments that parallel my criticism of the historians' rather excessive claims for ascribing to the signifier "history" and its conjugations various kinds of primacy and significance. Starting with Lyotard's note that narrative "certifies itself in the pragmatics of its own transmission without having recourse to argument and proof" (1984:27), or what I have stressed as its reliance upon unstatable discourse, I want to specify why historical discourse cannot present itself as a doing without thereby canceling its reliability, plausability, and cognitive claims.

Again I will start with Jameson's *Political Unconscious* (1981) to illustrate materially how story and narrative thought are sutured, illicitly, to history; then we will consider some examples from practicing historians. With only minor variations from the notions put forth by White, Danto, Henretta, and others, Jameson has recoded historicism by defining it as part of narrative thinking, this because one can no longer postulate that historical thought is directly linked to the materiality of nonthought (for example, Class, Capital). In taking up the semiotic challenge that thought never directly encounters the Real, Jameson keeps the transcendence of history going by also invoking the reader of history:

> History as a ground and as an absent cause can be conceived . . . by attention to what the Aristotelians would call

the *generic satisfaction* specific to the great monuments of historiography . . . the "emotion" of great historiographical form can then always be seen as the radical restructuration of that inert material, in this instance the powerful reorganization of otherwise inert chronological and "linear" data in the form of Necessity: why what happened had to happen the way it did (Jameson 1981:101, italics added).

It is sad that neo-Marxism has to treat the emotionality of necessity as a positivity. In this new-old Hegelian froth, one sees here that story = necessity and, by reversal, *to not tell a story* = *nonexistence,* so that the combination of history and story is responsible for conveying a transcendence of nonnecessity, the history effect cited *answering* a question, communicating to all readers a common culture of satisfaction. The implicit equations between closure = datability = nonregression = engagement of the reader who negates the "no longer" of "not knowing" are quite astounding.

We can immediately give theoretical rejections to Jameson's claims. Genette suggests what can be considered a materialist starting point in specifying how narrative enculturation is built into acts of telling. His argument distinguishes "telling" and "showing" to argue then that both are linked to an overall neutralization of the communicative function of language—narration cannot show necessity unless the latter is reduced to an equation between a discourse that seems to show and a necessity that is identical in thought to such discourse. There is, in brief, no necessary form that shows necessity, the epistemological resonance of which historians cannot hear (they refuse to be the receivers of nonnarrative thought). According to Genette:

the very idea of showing, like that of imitation or narrative representation (and even more so, because of its naively visual character), is completely illusory: in contrast to dramatic representation, no narrative can "show" or "imitate" the story it tells. All it can do is tell it in a manner which is detailed, precise, "alive" and in that way give more or less the *illusion of mimesis*—which is only narrative mimesis, for this single and sufficient reason: that narration, oral or written, is a fact of language, and language signifies without imitation . . . "showing" can only be a *way of telling*, and this way consists of both *saying about it* as much as one can, and *saying this* "*much*" as little as possible . . . pretending to show is pretending to be silent (1980:163–164, Genette's italics).

The conceptual result is that no instance of historical narration can say the way it tells what is shown as it tries to show: this silence of every historical narrative is a semiotic absolute. Narration ceases to be autonomous and stable as soon as a reader is able to focus on how the narration says what it purports to show, as its series of devices of telling are made explicit. These devices are perforce displaced by historians because the primacy of story is hinged to a reader's precritical acceptance of telling the told and not saying the telling; to do so interferes with placing the reader in a continuous alignment with both what is told and the telling, and, as well, to a simultaneous discontinuous relation to how telling is accomplished. As we shall see, historians cannot generically satisfy unless the devices and machinery of narrating also move away from a reader's intellect.

Restated, this "moving away" is nothing other than the discourse(s) historians evade as they transmit a narrative. The term "discourse" specifically refers to conditions presupposed by the effects of messages—the concept covers relations between senders and receivers insofar as a contract is maintained or ruptured, which requires the contact or physical presence of both. In discursive utterances, one cannot privilege sequence and narrator (role). Instead, with the discursive co-presence of speakers, both the unsaid and how what is said are potentially destabilizing; unlike discourse, narrativization maintains control over what it makes inert. Through a series of reductions, historical discourse or even historical communication might appear to be a member of the family of discursive and communicative systems, another monograph of human consciousness (for example, Lukacs's statement that "the living relationship to the present should be expressed by the movement of history itself" so that speech = history, a position with too many implications to take up here; see Lukacs 1972:377).

Historical discourse, however, has very specific textual functions that implode Jameson's "generic satisfaction." As Barthes (1970) has pointed out, historians employ discourse proper in order better to eject excessive discursive manifestations (for example, blocking of indirect discourse). The performative onset, for example, can discursively locate the historian's motivation in an "outside," like the injunction "In the name of God, I . . ." which, as a performative opening (see Barthes 1970:147–155), is incomparable to today's social scientific support "All of history is the more or less imperfect record of geo-political relationships," which performs only the enunciative act of creating an onset by replacing God with "geo-political relationships" (Cochran 1981:3). Take the following sample based upon what Barthes called the historian acting as the *monitor* of "first-order" narrative statements, which guides a reader to a thesis where the second-order narrator (historian) overtakes the first-order saying; I use it to argue that nonnarrative discursive units are systematically blocked from the reader's thought, so that narrative meaning occupies the reader's intellect by default:

(63) Gone are the days
(64) when the leaders of the U.S. steel industry confidently prepared to take over world markets.
(65) "We can't compete when somebody else, particularly a government, is underwriting the competition,"
(66) said Henry Love, President of the NSC in 1977.
(67) Love's observation . . . veils what is perhaps less obvious . . . by far the longest period of the industry's history in the U.S. has been a history of protection—
(68) of artificial interference in natural market processes (Yeager 1980:33).

White would just note the ironic stance of the historian. But consider how systematically the historian effaces signification—another signal, one can add, that narrative empathy must give way to rehistoricization, leaving the participant-actor stripped of existential status. (In our Age of Signs, there are no longer actors, only positions.) This code switch from what the historian is theoretically supposed to provide (empathy) is organized by the past-now report of lexia 65 used to confirm 63 and 64, and thus establishes 65 as a pure *exemplum;* in this sense, lexia 65 registers the passage from "no-longer" to "now," which, in turn, is encoded in lexia 67 as an untruth. This preparation, again in turn, announces a discourse of demystification ("veils") which lays out the story to follow (expressed as the "by far"). What is the precise cognitive status of lexia 68? How can "interference" be "artificial" in the first place and what are "natural market processes"? The intellectual truth values of these concepts, their discursivity, is not raised at all: they are really textual displacers of the discourse they destroy (Love's) and simultaneously a modeling of that which transcended Love's "observation." The historian speaks here through unstatable codings; the presumed reader is someone who agrees with what lexia 68 says. What is communicated are assertions that cancel one plane of discourse and yet narrativize, the latter occurring as soon as the "longest period" (lexia 67) is released from its discursive organization.

The most common argument today in favor of history as discourse or communication was put forth by Berlin in his *Historical Inevitability* (1954). It is worth quoting this piece of analogical reasoning to see just how far historians can go in disclaiming the materiality of the signifier and writing so as to defend common language by way of a theory of the transcendent properties of language itself. According to Berlin, historians employ

(69) crucial terms as "because" and "therefore," "inevitable," and "possible" and "probable," "surprising," and "unexpected," "influential" and "trivial," "central" and "accidental" much the same as in ordinary non-technical thought and speech . . . we explain and elucidate as we explain and elucidate in ordinary life (1954:51).

Like the speech-act theory that this citation prefigures, Berlin just assumes the intellectual validity of language as expression, uncoded, as it were and, by pure analogy, making the historian's language continuous with everyday life. The model of language discourse is close to those conditions postulated by Searle's "normal input and output" requirement, which assumes declarative-enunciations to have world-to-word reciprocity on account of their form. Such reciprocity assesses and judges a state of affairs in one and the same act, a performance where neither language nor the world interfere with the other (see Hervey 1982:124). Here I note that historical thought treated as ordinary discourse has also served, when used for retrospection, as an act of "historical recovery," as Skinner (1974:126) puts it, of the illocutionary force (intentions) of past speakers.

Semiotic theory dissolves such illusions about history-as-discourse. Here is one premise: In either a discursive or communicative situation there must be "BOTH A SPEAKER AND AN ADDRESSEE/HEARER AND WHERE THERE IS A PRESENT NOW" (Banfield 1978:446, her caps; see Banfield 1982:170 for a more complete analysis). In recasting Benveniste's theory of the distinction between discourse and narration, Banfield tightens the criteria in sorting out minimal intelligible differences between written narrative and discourse. To be specific, discourse entails an act of communication in which there has to be the *co-incidence* of an "I and you," so that in a communicative-discursive situation, expression and communication are one and the same phenomenon. By contrast, narration is a form of noncommunication (nondiscursive) and only quasi-expressive because in narration there must be a split between the speaker and self and the present and now. In, for example, "They were lonesome," the manifested subject ("they") is *not* the speaker, which is impossible to perform in a communicative act except insofar as one quotes another. Speaking-with carries discourse along, while narration is marked by transitivity and expunging of discourse (see Genette 1982:139). In Banfield's terms, narration cannot signify without the absence of "I and you," the present defined as a not-now, and the splitting of subjectivity into roles, those of saying, telling, spoken of, and so on. The elimination of pronunciation factors, the nonexistence of direct address (for example, "He said 'I want to . . .'"), and the exclusion of "I-you" shifts narration to the side of a *pseudo-expression* because there is a "divorce in performance between speaker and self, between present and now" (Banfield 1978:445), and this nondiscursive space is the space of narrating. Again, as a noncommunication, narration only knows the self as a third person and never as first or second because direct and indirect address do not rigorously calibrate now with past, and signals like the adverb "frankly" are unallowable in narration that can occur without an addressee/hearer (1978:448). The linguistic presentation of narrative sentences strives to free itself from the taint of subjectivity, interpretation, and evaluation (Banfield 1982:263). Such sentences and texts aim at manifesting autonomous thought, "social speak," the what is not-made presented as an experience of necessity and obligation. Because of this, the historian's prose narrative is not materially linked to a commitment to represent or to tell the truth at all, but rather to the refusal of allowing disengagement from its own narrative form. Once the historical narrative is written, it is culturally first about its own competency and legitimacy as a form. The belief in an *autonomous* temporality, like irreversibility, is sentenced and timed by coordinated sign forms (for example, Jameson's "history is meaningful even if . . .").

Thus I will formally emphasize in the analytic chapters that *a historical text prevents disengagement from its own sentence forms or it ceases to be readable.* The most famous cultural expression of this, but perhaps not the most important one, is the *spectacle effect* where inscribed in the told is what a reader is to accept as a world preexistent to the speaking self and which then "limits," "horizons," "determines," or "causes" the reader's modes of submission, the latter *presenced* by the transcendence of the past realized in an autonomous-appearing discourse. This is what Faye, in analyzing the Nazi manipulation of many different types of story, has called the reader of *reassembling*—who actualizes the spectacle effect—which strikes me as one of the real objectives of the historiographical "discourse" about "followability," "recognizing," and "grasping the point" of the "ideal historical narrative."

Historiography—as opposed to concrete historical narrative—legitimizes historical discourse as a cultural necessity and uses sign forms like the performative onset to ensure effacement of its own nonnarrative constructs (for example, "natural markets" is a thought but it reads as a narrative idea). If Danto and Mink are correct in arguing that narration is the core of historical autonomy, and I think they are, the cultural-intellectual organization of this "doing" is linked to its cognitive severing, which has to preclude thinking from appearing in the same scene or space as the told. The release of the told from both teller and telling, formulized by (F) (x—y) or "someone did something" (Greimas 1976:170), throws into relief the fact that historians work against other sign forms, presenced by such standard categories as definitions, explanations, and the putting forth of complicated semantic networks. Considered this way, prose (truthful) narration is more often than not part of the evasion of speaking and refusal to examine how the "real" is first of all discursively expressible (nameable, categorical, semanticized); in this regard, I note that some historical texts whose discursivity manages to stand out are barely narrativized: allegorical texts, hagiography, while narratives of exemplification, present the historiographical formula "someone did something" with a focus on precedents where the sanctity of authority dominates what is told (see Jauss 1979:219–220). Is it a historical voice that corrects Henry Love or the speaker of an economic ideology?

Re-posed, can historical narration be aligned with an intrinsic anti-intellectualism when it presents the told as the form of the real? By comparison to signification-practices like analysis, definition, and criticism, does not historical writing, as the "utterance for which no one is responsible" (Barthes 1970:151), also promote a surplus-culture in affirming that the "real" is *already narrativized* (historicized) at the level of perception and in the form of story? With Deleuze in mind, is all of this not an "abstract overcoding machine" (Deleuze and Guattari 1983:80), a culture for which no one is responsible? To put this question in the context of the act of reading: the transcendence of language in the ways we have suggested it appears refers to the subliminality of contact between such texts and readers who are culturally reactive. The reactive reader is programmed at the moment the text speaks of some mode of transcendence and the reader cannot think out the text's organization. (On the reactive subject, see Deleuze 1962:160.)

A Concluding Example

As a tentative conclusion, consider the following lexias from one of the more prominent contemporary social-economic historians:

(70) The change in life styles involved in moving from farm to factory was not easy.

(71) In evaluating the many arguments on the effect of early industrialization on the unskilled worker, however,

(72) one must remember the alternatives.

(73) The twelve hour day, maintained in part to keep workers in control

(74) did not appear as a major deterrent to recruitment of farm labor . . .

(75) In general, mill work was less demanding of strength and close attention than farm work. On farms, as soon as children had sufficient strength, they were assigned chores that kept them busy most of their waking hours.

(76) Consequently, the twelve hour day of children in shop or mill did not seem as horrendous then as it does now.

(77) There were also compensations in more varied companionship, participation in social activities, and personal independence in leisure hours.

(78) Twelve year olds who worked in mills when they might have been in school may have preferred the mill with its atmosphere of sharing tasks with adults (Cochran 1981:136).

Leaving out the inessential, this narrative piece suggests an encoding by an overall metonymic transformation: the stative "change" (lexia 70) is rendered as the story of the succession of "liberation"; going from the farm to the mill was an optimization of the "alternatives" ("less demanding"); children were "net gainers" ("compensations," "participation"); the transformation to acceptance and integration (lexias 76–78) closes the set with a verb of attitude, where it subjectifies (a psychological code) the positivity of the result and thus terminates nonnarrative thought, that is, the question of who is speaking the affirmation of the told, which has been given the frame of "must."

The nonspeaking narrator defends the transformation (stabilization after the fact). "Was not easy" (lexia 70) acknowledges the "difficulty" but, instead of being given a full description and discursive working up of exactly how "difficult" the "difficulty" was (that is, a model of fundamental oppositions and contradictions), the reader is blocked from the full semantics of "difficulty" (its unfairness, for example). The implicit intellectual effect is that the reader is restrained by an unstated pseudo-law against such "full" thought, an obligative "must remember" that chokes off the reader's intellect as well as depriving past actors, "mere children" after all, of their desires, choices, and so on. Lexia 72 establishes both past and reader in the logical frame of "progression through necessity"; the comparison is rigged so that the "twelve hour day" is not registered as negative either "then or now" (lexias 75–76), while the "less demanding" of lexia 75 abolishes "from farm to mill" as a negative idea—the narrator saves the notion of progression while getting rid of the negative as such. And this works to diminish all of the possible actual relations between labor and time, the physical requirements placed on these narrative subjects. This mini-summary is overcoded not just on account of its narrative closure and assimilation of past to necessity but also because the historian assumes the roles of apologist, anti-intellectual, behaviorist, and anthropologist (for example, lexia 78 assumes an unspecified kinship tie so that "unskilled" workers might also be subcategorized with the class of "anti-students").

Now it is inconceivable that this piece of historical narration, in the specificity of its material organization, could even happen (enter cultural circulation) without first being a transformation of specific, discursively activated, semantic and cultural meanings. And it is even less conceivable that possible tags of "realism" or plausibility or acceptability or legitimacy, which are already part of this text, could exist without the reader presupposed all along as a supplier to the text of certain acts. Such acts are different from White's (1978:61) belief that the reader "fictionalizes" the "historical text" through an "illumination" provided by poetic forms, or Iser's (1978:140) equation between image building and reading. The acts I have in mind are, in general (they are made specific in the chapters to follow), classified as belonging to the ways in which a model reader of the historical narrative must deintellectualize all of the codes through which the text is formed. As I will argue, the type of reader no historian can "foresee" (Eco's term) is the reader who de-territorializes (Deleuze) the historian's instructions concerning limits, necessity, realism, value, and so on, and so can stand outside of all the normal Western notions about reading in the first place (reader as spectator, passive syntheses, aesthetic response).

To conclude: as Barthes (1977:199) reminded us, the "greasiness of natural language" results from the latter's being constructed so that it may be reused the maximum number of times; the greasiness of the signifier "history" is caused by what even conservatives like Kermode (1979:113) recognize as the historical narrative's opposition to "awkward questions" about its construction and effects. We can say that a historical text is transcendent to the degree that its semiosis is illegible: when its narrativity overtakes its discursive organization. What now requires extensive analysis is how historical narration engenders its own semantic and extra-semantic fields so that, in cognitive terms, mass-ideation is presented, in advance, with historical-pragmatic grounds for favoring narration over critical thinking. Faye, in a remarkable work on the social functions of narration in the Weimar-Nazi period, writes:

> the combined transformations of "narrative" . . . are not action. It was not the contrivance of Saint-Just and Tallien's narratives that arrested Robespierre, but the hands of officers. . . . But then as now, [historical narration] constituted a field of discourse which cleared the way for the *acceptability* of such decisions (1973:106, Faye's italics).

These issues will turn on the following questions: Based upon analysis of historical texts, what exactly does a textualized narrative culture look like? What are the textual material thought processes of those subject to history? How does a concrete narrative allow for the transcendence of the past by means of the immanent transcendence of the telling?

The historiographical rejection of disengagement from the culture of history fails to make good its cultural program because the signifier "history" is an elastic, always connected to underlying nonnarrative sign forms, which appear to critical thought only when provoked. In the broadest sense of the term, all this suggests historical thought to be a structure of defensive signification. Can a nonreactive reader even read a historical text?

Now we must be as specific as possible and cognize full historical texts as they generate historiographical abstractions yet produce certain cultural positions.

3

Narrative Summary As a Reactionary Form

The object text is Peter Gay's "A Short Political History of the Weimar Republic," which appeared as a conclusion, summary, and supplement to his book, *Weimar Culture* (1968). The text is representative of historical works read by an audience as a confirmation of the act of synthesis: it is condensed and scholarly, the grammar never engenders obstacles, its theme is lucid, and it does not raise historiographical disputes. It has an indeterminate extraprofessional audience, a segment of the historian's infamous "ordinary educated public." It is not quite a textbook essay, although, as we shall see, it aims for the status of quotability, and is completely severed from the kind of popularizing associated with a writer like Tuchman. Concepts, not images, are privileged. The text is linked to modern theory through its undercoding of psychoanalysis, in the sense that a very diffused psychoanalytic model has the function of legitimating the narrator's role, as well as the reader's cognition. Among some of the text's implied readers, for example, one could include college students at the upper levels, as well as those who might cite it (or a thousand other texts) in a current argument employing analogical comparisons, which favor the common belief that history does repeat significant problems, which if recognized "in time," can be prevented from occurring. It offers a model of reaction to history, which, as we shall see, dissolves the very claim of liberalism to a discourse "on history." The text focuses on the theme of political and social leadership, and it raises the terror projected by liberalism that there may in fact be a void in society because of the utter lack of plausible liberal charismatic leaders (an oxymoron to be sure), leaders who can diffuse social and cultural crises so that the major roles of classes and individuals are not upset or overturned. It shows the anti-democratic bias of liberal ideology woven into the narrative, the latter in turn controlled by an (uncritical) psychoanalysis that semanticizes the text's explanatory and descriptive formations. We will specify how the historian is able to *theorize while narrating,* and how in the narrating, the theory also controls the telling. So while the analysis proceeds syntagmatically, reading the text's "flow," my objective is to isolate the text's intellectual economy, how it brings about the pragmatic result of issuing forth intellectual use-value in the context of capitalism's competing sign systems over the value of the political.

It is a commonplace among historians that narrative endings are not and should not be perceived as an addition to the story (the best story = seamless = intrinsicality = good style); sometimes there is a dovetailing of the concept of the intrinsic ending and the general form of successful explanation as well. G. A. Cohen (1978:280–292) defines the neo-Marxist articulation of functional historical explanation in terms very close to those that formerly have been offered in support of narrative endings; in describing the increased scale of factories as a result of growth, where it is not mandatory to specify anything but consequences, functional explanations are a way to end other explanation-statements:

> The cause occurred because of its propensity to have that effect: *the increase in scale occurred because the industry was of a sort in which increases in scale yield economies* (1978:281, Cohen's italics).

There seems to me a high degree of correlation between Cohen's defense of functional explanation and the more traditional historiographical position where, in Louch's terms, endings

> confer the aura of inevitability . . . that the different episodes that carry the story forward are chosen in such a way as to

lead to the circumstances with which the historian has chosen to end his tale (1969:69).

In both formulations, endings and explanations are to enable a reader to summarize the narrative safely for further condensation and cultural destination. Endings in fact are bound up with all sorts of mysteries about satisfaction (see Barthes 1970) and usually strive to create what the Futurist Technical Manifesto of Painters (1910) called the "persistence of an image upon the retina," where figural suppression eviscerates what cannot be fit into stereotypical depiction (see Boccioni, Carra, Russolo et al. 1973:27–28). In the quotation from Louch, for example, "circumstances" is nothing but the entire prior description, where the ending is believed appropriate to the description that best forestalls or eliminates entirely inappropriate "subjective generators" of time expectancies, that is, that an ending is simultaneously a middle, a trace, a fragment, and so on (see Jones 1981:571–572). In other words, the historiography of endings is usually connected to the disintellection of speculation and theory, the latter activities generally removed from narrative endings so as not to disrupt the closability of the historical text.

Historiography and historians have paid virtually no attention to the starting up of historical narration.

(1) The Weimar Republic was proclaimed on November 9, 1918, by the Social Democrat Philipp Scheidemann.

Lexia 1 opens the story in the same time as the story was initiated: no one's memory and no other versions co-occur with the start of the narration. There is just the report of the action so that the reader is located at the beginning of the story. The narrator avoids exposure as there is no performance of the narrator's, no "As I hope to prove, the Weimar Republic was proclaimed in order to . . . ," no trace of any historiographical component as, for example, Namier used in opening his *England in the Age of the American Revolution* (1961) when he wrote, "The social history of England could be written in terms of membership of the House," which at least indicates the problematical status of re-presenting others. But the opening here does not conceal anything either. The existence of "Weimar" is established by the identity of elocutio and fact, the verb "proclaimed" one of sovereignty and announcement, performed by the past actor and repeated by the historian. As an existent in the reader's historical lexicon, "Weimar Republic" is thereby disengaged from signification: there is no suggestion of other interpretants that could replace it; the narrator does not write "what was *called* the Weimar Republic by x," which might jeopardize the co-incidence of name and story. So the starting up is one with the creation of an ideal proper noun, a subject and substantive. The signifying channel, grammar, leads directly to passive cognition, which is the same as saying that the reader is blocked from considering the status of such namings. The narrator is an intervenor, protecting the story existent from any sense of arbitrariness; the Weimar Republic is saved from nonnarration (from quoted reports from other subjects who believed, for example, "Weimar was a symptom of the German bourgeoisie's ability to try to do business as usual"), that is, from the discourse of nonhistorians or derisive historians. Why narrate what to, say, a demographic discourse is only a statistical blip? All of this manifests that "Weimar Republic" does not hover near a historiographical quasi-existence but is *anchored* so that its status/name is severed from contention (see Greimas and Courtes 1982:13–14). The opening is part of a double transcendence: the simultaneous separation of entity from language and the narrator's self-removal, the former standing for the transcendence of signification from object, the latter the transcendence of the historian from signs. This opening is both a performative (see Barthes 1970:145) and what Derrida (1976:10) has called a detour for the reappropriation of presence.

This ideal subject is fleshed out by the enumeration of events with varying degrees of proximity from lexia 1; the "bloody war," "disarray of the army," a "demoralized" administration, and "resignation" of the government are summarized in this way:

(2) The country was exhausted,
(3) weary to death of the adventure it had welcomed in 1914

(4) as a relief from petty civilian cares.
(5) Germany had lost 1.8 million dead and over 4 million wounded;
(6) the cost in materiel, wasted talents, maimed minds, sheer despair,
(7) was incalculable.

The overall coding is entirely psychological: "exhausted" denotes a feeling-state of the collective mind which is brought to a physiological reversal of the "relief" of lexia 4. What is striking is the narrator's theoretical assumption: that the motivation for Germany's involvement in World War I had its basis in the *completed* formation of the culture; an "adventure" "welcomed" as a "relief" from the petty can only characterize a culture that is thoroughly decadent, unless of course the characterization is only, in some way, meant to characterize the ruling elite (the Kaiser, for example). Lexia 7 opens up an internal semiotic issue: in stating that the different series—the economic ("costs"), cultural ("wasted"), material ("maimed"), and psychological ("despair")—are beyond description ("incalculable"), the text individuates "Weimar" devoid of markers that might locate "Weimar" in a comparative relation to other equivalent names. "Incalculable" then is a semiotic judgment (it judges the coding process begun at lexia 2) performed with the function of supporting the *incomparability* of "Weimar." Individuation and incomparability are linked by means of the former's overvaluation of a subject and the latter's protection of such overvaluation, what one might call "narrative insurance" or the saving of the subjectivization of a topic. None of this has anything to do with the historian's famous organ of empathy. Subjectivizing the Other is a semiotic act, a cultural decision, with a psychological connotation, rather than originating in some special psychology of the social role of the historian. The downgraded predications (see Leech 1974:149–154) of "weary to death" and "relief from" are only psychological vis-à-vis the function of "exhausted"; but as each one is also a condensation of what, written out, could be another narrative, they effectively serve the analogical illusion that a country has the same predicates as an individual. The reader is already inside a social-scientizing activity.

(8) . . . it had been obvious that the old regime would never survive unchanged.
(9) sailors . . . mutinied; . . . revolution seemed inescapable. The workers of Berlin were in the streets.
(10) some thought Scheidemann's proclamation of the Republic hasty; from Scheidemann's point of view, it was barely in time—
(11) it anticipated the Spartacists who were ready to proclaim a Soviet Republic (p. 148).

Lexia 8 informs the reader that prior to the proclamation of Weimar, there was common knowledge as to the need for a political shift, and lexia 9 is the proof, through illustration, of such knowledge. Lexia 8 indexes a state of achieved knowledge, not a knowledge generated within a volatile situation, and tags the narrator as reporting a common future. There is no requirement to narrate further what lexia 10 raises as "some thought . . . hasty" because this unit crosses into speculation, which is here thoroughly repressed; but what is interesting is the chrononym of "barely in time": the reader is presented with the threat of "how close" to "time's failure" (revolution) was the proclamation? This is an instance of dramatizing time (not a "moment" too soon, familiar to everyone in the film age) so that the "just in time" absorbs the connotation of "defeat of"—the Spartacists were "ready" but rendered impotent by the event that arrived "barely in time." Why, however, did this "proclamation" succeed? Was the Left potent or not? (Today this is a theme of much neo-Left historiography.)

(12) The emperor and his partisans were discredited; leadership would have to come from the Socialists.
(13) But what kind of Socialists?

The interrogative of lexia 13 then opens onto an analepsis which, to use Genette's terms, reaches to a time earlier than the story so as to fill in for the reader enough information about the political groupings; the narrator cites the Social Democratic vote for war credits on August 4, 1914, as having "torn" the party apart (p. 148) and the next date cited is "early 1917" when the "dissidents" formed the Independent Social Democratic Party; nothing "in-between" is recounted, cutting off the history of the Social Democrats. The reader is then brought back to the time of the story's present, which completes the prevention of the past from excessively intruding on the story-now:

(14) . . . the Spartacists found increased support among the radicalized workers . . . they led strikes . . . founded Workers and Soldiers Councils on the Soviet Model.
(15) And so, when Ebert found himself with a Republic on his hands, he put together a temporary government . . . three from the Social Democrats and three Independents.

We see here that the present is dramatized by the "and so" of lexia 15. Lexia 13 raised the question of status, but this is suspended; with lexias 14 and 15 the reader is returned to the story's present, but with a difference: the revolution of lexia 9, denoted as the conjunction of Marxism and a threat, is evaded. "The provisional government actually held intact for almost two months" (p. 148). Therefore, the Weimar Republic encoded as "barely in time" and as the inheritor of the "incalculable" is thus made a subject of focus but not a narrative subject: it has not yet done anything according to the formula of Greimas's model (F) (x—y). An immense passivity thus parallels such individuality and psychology, to which we shall return later.

(16) And on November 11 the war was over, even if peace had not been made.
(17) It was a promising beginning for the new regime,
(18) but the day before, Ebert had concluded another agreement that was to have
(19) fateful consequences for the young Republic.
(20) In the evening of November 10, General Groener had called Ebert, put the army at "the disposal of his government," and asked, in return,
(21) "the support of the government in the maintenance of order and discipline in the army.

(22) The officer corps expected the government to fight
against Bolshevism and was ready for the struggle.
(23) Ebert accepted the offer of an alliance."

The telling quickly rushes past what it has to cite but evades—
the existing control of the political system by elites is not narrated, relieving the narrator from specifying how the reader is
to regard the implied periodization (prerevolution/postrevolu-
tion) and the political difference November 11, 1918, made (and
to whom). Elite power moves made unknowable, the reader then
shifts to lexia 19, a pure prolepsis, a knowledge of the future
known only to the narrator (see Genette 1980:71). The trait
"young" now attached to the "Republic" parallels this sense of
"fate" and both also conclude the "barely in time" of lexia 10.
What starts out as a "promising beginning" (lexia 17) but now
marked by "fateful consequences" registers in the future imperfect (the atelic): here the reader can infer, as a semantic disclosure, that "young" and "promising" will be completed, but
does not know how, except that the completion will probably
be negative (see Comrie 1976:46–48). The grammar of temporality undercodes for the reader this specific amount of fate; we
shall just note that the performance of dramatic fate or the insertion of "fate" in just the "right way" is already practiced by
the narrator. The machinery of this historical narrative says what
it knows mainly by dramatized connotations that are mirrored
in two distinct moods. The first is the optative or the attribution
of desire to a subject (lexia 17): Weimar is encoded as now capable
of progression; however, lexia 23 states that Ebert, the leader,
is passive and, as the empowered agent of Weimar, only "accepted" what he did not initiate. "Was to have fateful consequences," mentioned in advance of the act, is an aspect of the
obligative: Ebert and, by implication, Weimar as a whole, is
ensnared by this mood. Is it interest, expediency, need, or stupidity that explains Ebert's acceptance? If Ebert is to be read as
having no choice, the subject of someone else's determination
(power), this of course would tend to drain the sense of fate out
of Weimar's future, which would evaporate (for example, that
the army would have rebelled unless Ebert accepted makes the

acceptance part of blackmail). The ambiguity of Ebert's acceptance is a way for the narrator to connote Weimar politicians as only marginal to their own future, which means not responsible for causing "fateful consequences." Finally, the quoted report of lexias 21 and 22 shows how documentation is swamped by the narrating. The quoted material does not identify a speaker, yet the verb "asked" makes it seem that this narrator is reporting what another historian has written down as someone's direct address. Did Groener ask or did the first historian in the chain say that Groener asked? There is no way, obviously, of sorting this out, but the quoted material supports the insertion of direct address, which yields the illusion of information that is detached from the story and transcendent to it when, in fact, the information is entirely subservient to its function of standing for a reality that no one can challenge.

(24) The six-man government broke apart on Dec. 27,
(25) when the Independents marched out after inconclusive arguments within the cabinet, in public meetings, and in the streets,
(26) over the future of Germany.
(27) The left wanted all power to the Soviets and a complete reconstruction of society.
(28) The Social Democrats wanted a parliamentary regime and a waiting policy of social and economic transformations.
(29) There was fighting in the streets in December . . .
(30) But on the whole the country supported the parliamentarianism of the majority Socialists.
(31) Accordingly on January 19, 1919, there was a national election . . . ; despite a Communist boycott, over 30 million Germans turned out to vote.
(32) The Weimar coalition had received a strong mandate (p. 149).

From lexia 24 through lexia 32 the sequence is one of a transformation from disequilibrium ("broke apart") to equilibrium ("mandate"), the change one of result ("had received"). The sequence is carried forward, however, by a number of intersecting codes. The reader is drawn into two different forms of desire: the same verb of "want" is used to specify the point of difference between Independents and Social Democrats, but the former "wants" "all power" (lexia 27) while the latter "wants" a "parliament" and "to wait" (lexia 28). Such encoding enables the narrator to connote that the "left" wanted too much, while the Social Democrats exemplify just the right kind of "wanting"; this is overcoded in lexia 25 where the "left" (Independents) "marched" out (the subconnotation of which is "militaristic"), with the further implication that strong "leftists" cannot tolerate the "give and take" of democratic inconclusiveness. The sense then is that this "left" is close to political illegitimacy (the "boycott" of lexia 31) and, complementary, that "elections" were a valid index of political legitimation. Such connotations are the real discourse that stands between the narrative telling and what is told. In addition, the sequence as a whole carries the implication that those who placed themselves on the side of "parliamentarianism" were inherently more "thoughtful," since the semic nucleus of "waiting policy" implies distance from what is to be transformed, while the "left" "wanted" to subvert such thought to a force "beyond" thought ("there was fighting in the streets"). What transcends from the left is its negativity. The narrator thus loans a political and cognitive predicate to Weimar: it signifies those who think over those who act and allows Weimar to be juxtaposed to the unbalanced "want" of the "left." The distance taken by the "thoughtful" government leaders, the Social Democrats, is the equivalent of the distance the narrator takes from the "left." The narrator has overcoded a binary investment in the act of narrating.

That this is so is demonstrated by what the narrator inserts between lexias 31 and 32. Here, there at first appears the historian's inventory of political existents (groups); but the inventory is also an overcoded instance of the narrator's paraleptic alteration: The Social Democrats are said, in the elections, to have "led" the voting, the Catholic Center is given the sole predicate of being a political "amalgam," the National Party receives no predicate at all (the narrator merely cites its antiquated title), but the "left"—the Independent Socialists—is denoted through a change in mode where excessive information is deployed against them:

(33) The Independent Socialists *disappointed* their following with fewer than 2.5 million votes. (italics added)

Unlike other political groups but the extreme right wing, the "hard" left is precluded from narrative significance, where to deprive them of narrativity equals direct control of how they are to be thought of; at the same time, and still within the narrative pause (between lexias 31 and 32), there is an orgy of paraleptic excessive information about another group:

(34) The newly founded Democratic Party,
(35) *rich* in distinguished bourgeois intellectuals
(36) and *progressive* industrialists, did extraordinarily well . . .
(37) it was this party,
(38) abundant in *talent, decent* in campaign methods, *rational* in its program,
(39) that turned out to be "the only party that lost in each election." (italics added)

Unleashed is a surplus of positivity and value: the disclosure of the proleptic "turned out to be" is unobtrusive yet highly coded. *Genuine value belongs to "what lost" and did not happen.* Consider how this thought is discursively manifested: (1) "rich distinguished bourgeois intellectuals" dissociates "intellectual" from "left and right" and places them with "progressive industrialists"; (2) the two groups share the attributes of knowledge, morality and thought. These attributes are not disclosed as part of the narrative of Weimar but as a scale used to measure all the political factions. Since they "lost each election," it is impossible for this group to be narrated, as they did not result in what historiography has infamously called "a record of what people did" (Carr 1967:165), the "record" equivalent to a narrative existence as subject. Hence the destination of this descriptive-evaluative segment can only be the symbolic, the making memorable of the unrecognized and unrealized (which is also attached to the sentimentalism for "value"). On another level, one has to ask how this nonnarrative segment is supposed to be thought. Since its form of telling distances these Democrats so thoroughly from Weimar, the reader's correlative function to that narrative distance is akin to making a judgment: the reader draws the conclusion that there was an ideal "politics beyond politics," an imaginary relation of pure distance. This amounts to noting that the story is given a kind of peak, a transcendence within the story, which moves the telling close to the edge of outright discourse (saying).

Let us here note that Barthes argued that the forward pull of narrative meant that the narrative is constantly recoding its own "already said." "The imbrication of sequences can indeed only be allowed to come to a halt with a radical break if the sealed off blocks which then compose it are in some sort recuperated at the higher level of the Actions (of the characters)" (Barthes 1977:104). Any story whose major functions or sequences threaten to dangle, as Barthes put it, outside of some form of isotopism (summary, for example) also threatens to uncouple the possibility of the *irrevocable* narration, the telling of the story in such a way that it could not occur to the reader that, for example, either the story as told has already been told or that it is untellable (for example, the complete difference between a narrative of monetary relations and the analysis of wage rates as they are used to support ideological forms) (see Barthes 1977:104). In the present story, the narrator has the line of "fate" and line of value (lexias 34–39) narrativized as irrevocable; the former cannot be said directly (fate cannot overtake the narrating) while the latter must not be fully exposed. The story resumes by returning to where lexia 32 ended:

(40) This *first full-fledged* cabinet . . .
(41) But the work of the Assembly was marred, though not interrupted, by disorders at home and peacemaking abroad.
(42) In Versailles, meanwhile, a German delegation . . . sought to ameliorate slightly what they could not significantly improve. (italics added)

Weimar is incarnated in the shape of a "cabinet"—it receives political legitimation—so Weimar is now established on a narrative trajectory that endows its earlier predications with a unified semantic core, but where none are identified as "Weimar," since the "fateful consequences for the young Republic" of lexia 19 still governs the story's expansion. The grammatic-semantic mixture of lexias 40–42 affirms "Weimar" as a narrative subject; in the next series, the narrative of its "existence" quickly returns the reader to a cognitive level once more at the limit of narrative:

(43) The new cabinet balked at only a few provisions,
(44) but the allies were firm: the losers must sign without reservation.
(45) Faced with an ultimatum, the German Government yielded and . . . a new delegation . . . signed the Diktat.
(46) No other course was feasible.
(47) But inescapable as it was, submission left scars that never healed.

The overall sequence is from "resistance" to "submission," the latter resulting in the consequence "never healed." Lexia 44 raises the imposition of an outside will; the "yield" of lexia 45 signifies closure ("defeat"), but lexia 47 is on an altogether different level. "Never healed" is a catalyst in Barthes's sense, a sign of the consecutive and associated with a social-psychological collective "wound." The "must sign" of lexia 44 lays down an obligation imposed on Weimar. This is the image of the law of the victorious society. Lexia 45 suggests frustration, encoding Weimar in the psychological space of a will that cannot enact its interests and desires. The "infant" of lexia 42 tries to "ameliorate" or negotiate like a child, but confronts the superior power's absolutism ("must sign"), the narrative organizing first "yielding," then the "punishment," then the transcending consequence ("never healed"). All of this encodes a passive psychological drama: the political is thus reduced to only a sign of psychologized semantics, "submission" canceling the regime of political action (cabinet, for example).

Lexia 47 serves here as the basis for a later axiomatic switch in the story: it says what the reader is to think as memorable and, simultaneously, it regulates the narratability of the story as a whole. The axis of selection, as Jakobson called it, operates in favor of creating the equivalence between the noteworthy and the sense of submission, a narrative conjunction, organized by a discourse that less explains and interprets the "German perspective" ("incalculable loss," "young Republic," and so on) than it transmits the change from one world to another: the separation of one story from another already traceable within the first (that is, the transformation without remainder of one mode of existence to another). An attentive reader already knows the failure of the political lines of the narrative.

The argument of lexia 47, "submission," denotes a subject at the extreme limit of impotency: such a subject cannot act according to its own desire. But this semantic organization must also give rise to the narrativity of its performance against such submission. The narrator tells what such submission entailed:

(48) . . . heavy economic, political, and psychological burdens on defeated Germany.

The treaty caused this:

(49) It returned Alsace-Lorraine to France . . . split off East Prussia from the heart of Germany . . . deprived Germany of her colonies, forbade . . . imposed . . . reduced . . . put an end to . . .
(50) Most unacceptable . . . were articles that deprived the Germans of that intangible thing, "honor."
(51) article 231 insisted that "Germany and her allies" accept "responsibility" for "causing all the loss and damage" to which the Allied powers had been exposed . . .
(52) While practically all Germans hoped for repeal, some hoped for revenge (p. 151).

All of this then "causes" the so-called negative collective memory of 1919 and the Nazi "success," the future made in the past's-present. The reader is in a position to "speculate" about a "titanic" struggle: "scars that never healed" refers to a profound "lack," in which a society finds itself "thinking out" its self-formation and desire around an ever open "wound." To those "who hoped for revenge," Weimar signifies a "not-the-Father" (force, power) (the "yielded" of lexia 45), so two actantial roles, which allow the reader to "humanize" the story, are implicit: Weimar and its officials are imagined to be the "failed father," the one who "yielded," a psychoanalytic legend, and will gather unto itself the excessive predicates heaped upon scorned objects by a misunderstanding infantile thought ("revenge"); the unspecified actant of the "some hoped for revenge" traces the outline of an antisubject, in the sense of embodying negativity toward Weimar and its narrative projects.

Lexia 7 established the "incalculability" of the traumatic state of "Germany"; the summary of lexia 17 opens the narrative trajectory of optimism, which is then undercut by the historian's knowledge of the future (lexia 19); the exceptional knowledge of lexias 34 through 39 overvalues a group that "lost," a knowledge exceptional precisely on account of the surplus of positive signifiers; the return of "fate" with lexia 47 sets up the "revenge" of an antisubject against those identified with the Versailles Treaty. Now what does it really mean to imagine and symbolize a social system and its antistory in this psychologistic manner? Quite obviously, modern German history is, on the level of information, a vast scene in which every sort of psychohistory can be played out as an interpretive game. But how was "submission" actually transmitted to individuals and groups? How is the reader to "think out" the machinery of such submission? How could one narrate this at all, nothing less than "German life" as "wound" and "wounding," its psychotic roles? Take, for example, Lacan's strong formulation of the experience, entirely symbolic, of the confrontation with the Father: the child is obligated to undergo

> the substance of desire. Desire begins to take shape in the margin in which demand becomes separated from need: this margin being that which is opened up by demand, the appeal of which can be unconditional only in regard to the Other, under the form of the possible defect, which need may introduce into it, of having no universal satisfaction (what is called "anxiety"). A margin which, linear as it may be, reveals

its vertigo, even if it is not trampled by the elephantine feet of the Other's whim. Nevertheless, it is this whim that introduces the phantom of the Omnipotence, not of the subject, but of the Other in which his demand is installed . . . and with this phantom the need for it to be checked by the Law (1977:311).

One can be an "object" of this Other, a "mummy" because of it, or embrace the castration complex with its "Lost Cause" of trying to get back from the Other what one "invested" in it in the first place (Lacan 1977:324). How does one narrate a psychological model of collective actions which relies on signifiers of absolute irrevocability, that is, the repetition of roles that are not themselves narrative but structural (necessary)?

Weimar is made narratable (recountable, tellable)—pulled from the brink of collapsing into theory, and so on—insofar as the narrator puts such discourse in the form of a story which, in turn, gives rise to interrogatives the reader performs: Is the proletariat to be understood as the "mummy" because it did not "rise" against the pseudo-father?; was Hitlerism the "Lost Cause," the "striving for castration" achieved by World War II?; does the encoding of the "best and the brightest" as "losers" mean that the "Law" of the social failed? We can postulate here that psychologizing the narrative is the form that enables these negatives to acquire temporal plausibility. Perhaps the Hegelian mode continues to energize such condensed narratives insofar as a modern audience is played to as itself the site of psychological disaster. At any rate, the reader is in a position to see, as in all large spectacles, a coded opposition, for the reader grows into the story as the story grows out. Historiography has called this growing into the story the necessary shape of reading, which is really the internalization of semantic identities. Later I will return to the question of whether this text was meant to be read at all (see Gallie 1964:227–228 for the classical concept of the historical reader).

(53) Despite all this, the Weimar Assembly agreed on a constitution . . .

(54) Germany became a democratic republic . . .

(55) But Germany did not become a purely parliamentary regime: the Constitution gave it a strong president [who could] take charge "if public security and order are seriously disrupted or endangered."

(56) This was the notorious article 48 . . .

(57) When the delegates came home from Weimar, their Germany was in deep trouble,

(58) but the Republic was launched.

The narrating voice has appeared as the idealizing-symbolizer of the Democratic Party and the speaker of an unspecified psychoanalytic knowledge, the former pertaining to a gigantic lack within Weimar as a whole (this accounts for the distance taken by the narrator toward Weimar), the latter belonging to a discursive code-operator, the semantic channel. For the reader, the connoted subject is the "lack of leadership" within the story, this same lack presupposed as an actant in the liberal social world (of the reader). It is connoted because if directly stated as part of an intellectual or theoretical discourse, the sequencing would be unraveled; for example, "submission left scars that never healed" would require as one of its prior conditions of intellectual validity that collective psychological states are really operative in history. But the justification of such a discursive frame is a nonnarrative issue. The historian's application of this kind of "psychologeme" presupposes a reader who already adheres to the theory of value belonging to liberal estimations of leadership, at the same time that such a reader (or narratee) is already incorporated in the historian's sytem of "and then what happened?" (see Mink 1965:24–47). Here one sees the story pull forward as it displaces its own elaboration.

Is the historical component thus far equivalent to the signifiers of destiny? Is Weimar an exemplum, its actantial character in transit like the golden fish of myth to a future of determinacy? Is the historical in this story an image of fame and noteworthiness achieved through intense experiences that can be used to instruct others, as some historiographers have stressed (see Nadel 1964:297–298)? Lexia 56 carries a political warning as it moves the story forward: a democratic regime incorporated an anti-democratic practice. We will see later how this motif is deeply embedded in narrative practices, but here it is important to recognize that the narrative function of warning calls up an extranarrative imagination, the use of prospection which furthers a sense of the unintended consequences of action. This way of telling has its own message, the circulation of a code: "history happens this way, the future is intrinsically the past." Let us say for now that the narrated story is the form taken by the telling (organization of the signifiers), but this telling only appears insofar as the reader is its implicit cowriter (unconscious symbolism, the imagination of types of conflict, the dramaticized reader), a cowriting able to detach units like lexia 55 from their story function and socialize one's ideation by means of them. Lexia 55, for example, invites comparison with the politics of the readers present.

> (59) The events of the first year of the Republic did not predetermine
> (60) but they did set its general course.

Which really states: Weimar is narratable—not yet reducible to a complete summary—because of the space between "predetermine" and "course." How much space? "Predetermine" raises a historiographical subcode, that of the possible senselessness of telling this story, and dismisses it: the narrator settles on reallocating the realist belief that causes may be, say, generative mechanisms or structures, but society is always an open system, that is, subject of itself (for a discussion of this issue, see McLennan 1981:32–38). The virtually dead signifier "course" means "all-embracing flow" (metonymic) or "immersion" (all-consuming) and preserves the general requirement of modern bourgeois-academic thought to have at its disposal signifiers of change, no matter how flattened. "Course" is really connected to the context of the disavowal of an analytic of causality, which parallels the removal of the causal to the transcendence of privileged social players. The causal is today virtually sayable only within a discourse, but in this story, it cannot be signified, as only the barest image of movement is required. One relies on signifiers like "course" or "movement" or "growth" in order to say excessively as little as possible about time codes and their determinations.

(61) The next four years stood under the signs of domestic violence and foreign intransigence,
(62) the two interacting and,
(63) to Germany's misfortune, reinforcing one another.

Here the issue of selection is again a major problem: what notion guarantees and determines the adequacy and appropriateness of the frames "domestic violence" and "foreign intransigence"? After all, both could be signs interpreted as mere symptoms of other frames (the economic, for instance). The narrator's privilege, of occupying the place of knowing everything about the future of the story, is identical to a displacement of thinking through the unstable hierarchy that frames lexia 61; the narrator has foreseen a reader of agreement drawn either from those who know as much and in the same way (ideological agreement) or those who know almost nothing at all (and are subject to rules of knowledge). These frames are already condensed stories (see Eco 1979:21), interpretants at the level of actants and roles, establishing story pertinence and deintellectualizing other narrative frames (for example, devalue the economic story). Pure determinants of narration, they can be thought of as repressions of semantic contention.

(64) The Kapp Putsch was the first serious attempt at a counterrevolution.
(65) Since the acceptance of the Versailles Treaty,
(66) irreconcilables had made propaganda against the Republic and plotted for a restoration of the monarchy.
(67) On March 13, 1920, the plotters struck.
(68) A naval brigade marched on Berlin . . . Troops refused to shoot at the rebels . . . and the government prudently fled.
(69) But the conspirators were inexperienced and foolish, civilian officials would not join them, and a general strike paralyzed the "new regime."

(70) After four days, Kapp and his colleagues "resigned," surrendering what they never held.
(71) . . . Kapp was allowed to escape abroad, and the great purge,
(72) for which Scheidemann had rightly called, never took place (p. 152).

Lexia 64 concretizes the frame of 61, right-wing violence (itself psychologized); in lexia 65 the narrator now recodes the sense of fate raised earlier, which lexia 66 describes as political opposition to Weimar: the "irreconcilables" are the contrary of the values embedded in lexias 34–39. This antisubject is encoded not in political or social or cultural terms, but through a signifier of pure devaluation: "irreconcilable" makes them incapable of conveying any knowledge about Weimar, they tell us nothing about the social; and perhaps lexia 66 is a distant consequence of the psychology that framed the opening of the story, the notion of the incalculability at the story's beginning now manifesting a result. The omission of an explanation—why did the troops not support the government?—dramatizes the plight of the government, but this contradicts the function of the army previously raised in lexias 21–23. It might be something other than "irreconcilables" confronting troops who were their "fellows" (p. 152). The right wing is not allowed to have a voice in the story, which is part of a liberal discursive strategy of draining extremes of their truth value and restricting claims for the validity of discourse to psychologically safe behavior (see Barthes 1972:151). What expands this episode is the mention of another act/absence conjunction: Kapp "was allowed" to escape and Social Democratic interest ("purge" of the extreme political groups) was not enacted. What is missing from Weimar is the right kind of political will to do violence when confronted with violence (which expands only a connotative plateau, that the legitimate government needed to be overtly violent).

The chronological order is riveted to the political order: the ellipsis from March's "purge" to the next episode, the elections in June 1920, allows the narrator to suppress any frame that interferes with the political story. In this intense story world, the two levels of psychology and politics are not entirely translatable into the other, which enables the narrator to maintain a sense of the irreversible transformation of the political. For if the political were systematically resymbolized as other levels of the social (Barthes's *S/Z* is certainly the most important critical text on how this occurs; see Barthes 1970:139–141), the first thing that would happen would be the draining from the narrative of its sense of motion: if Weimar politics were, say, tied to the speed at which modern capitalism tries to postpone and deflect more basic contradictions, where the political was really only symptom, the political would cease to possess any forward pull. It would then, depending upon the case, be only the function of a symptom or the form of another content. Deprived of any imputation of its own time, the shape of the historical time of the political would force the collapse of the chronological order. For example: if the rapidity implied in the "anticipated" of lexia 11 were, on another analysis or interpretation, strongly connected to the perpetuation and repetition of the "masses' generosity," their letting politics go on in the first place, the narrating of the psychologized politics would lose its status of followability. The success of maintaining the telling here turns on such displacements.

(73) On June 6, 1920, there were elections to the Reichstag;
(74) they were disastrous for republicans.
(75) . . . the Democratic Party declined disastrously.
(76) . . . the Independent Socialists showed great new strength.
(77) Another ominous development was the burgeoning of splinter parties.
(78) The politics of militarism, revolutionary and counter-revolutionary slogans, and direct action was on the ascendant.

The story told at lexia 71 was that the right-wing Kapp Putsch had (unspecified) supporters and "fellows" in the Weimar government; the narrator did not present any information or hypothesis about that possible story. Now, with lexia 78, the reader is presented with a new semantic disclosure which speeds up the tempo of the story. The illustration of this disclosure is quite different from the silence of the earlier one. In lexia 71 there was a plurality of the narrator's silence, in the sense that sectors of the government "allowed" Kapp "to escape" and this was not narrated; now there is the murder of one person, which the narrator overcodes with an absolute voice:

(79) . . . another disaster: Matthias Erzberger [an imperialist turned centrist] was shot to death by two ex-officers.

(80) . . . their accomplices at home were left unmolested or acquitted.

(81) Thousands celebrated openly, shamelessly (p. 153).

Under what conditions in modern society can the death of one equal a disaster? Who experienced this murder as a disaster? Intellectually, the reader is directed (Habermas's "steered") to think of such individual difference *and* not to focalize analysis or understanding on the systematic. This is reinforced with the "masses" completely absorbed by the negative ("shamelessly"), another seme of nonnarrative psychology, here used to encode the collective as negative. The density and unanalyzability of signifiers like "shamelessly" or "ominous" or "disastrously" are nonetheless potent; if the thousands were in fact "shameless," should not some analysis be offered of such a state? After all, it is a fairly radical state by which to characterize a segment of the collective psyche. The ethical judgment implied by "shameless" enables the narrator to exclude the reader from any knowledge of such a collective. The psychological threshold reached by the "disaster" of this murder is part of the "disaster" of lexia 74, so Weimar now acquires the narrative role of victim; and "positive" political systems are especially sensitive to "the fate of individuals." Put another way: the value of singular murder far outstrips any predicates that belong to mass society, which means that liberal discourse is hinged to values that are separable from the predicates of the collective, but this, of course, can only be implied. The important point here is that the masses are only allowed, as the historiographer Mandelbaum unconsciously cast it, to "impinge" on the "central story" and this is the epistemic justification for such narrating: "The original basis for our understanding of societal structures is, then, the experience of the individual" (Mandelbaum 1978:115–116). In narrative terms, the masses are isolated to the role of what Barthes called informants, ready-made "knowledge" which strengthens an actant: the fate of Weimar will be confirmed by the shame of the collective (see Barthes 1977:96). In Blanchard's (1980:86–88) terms, this murder is a disjunctive function within the story's display of roles and actants, a hierarchical/nonnarrative coding, but conjunctive vis-à-vis the reader: the reader can draw the inference that murder is linked to intellectuals and leaders in which the collective is really only a kind of mass that does not refer to as deep a depth of the society. Murder teaches us about value; we expect to learn from negative singularity.

By means of such narrativized psychology, the historical is emerging through the fate and destiny of Weimar; but the future of Weimar and the future of the reader's present are linked, not the reader's apprehension of the pastness of the past. The sense of the historical here is accessed by its presentation as psychologized concepts like "victim" and "collective shame," which establish contact with the reader's accumulation of what was absent from Weimar, imaginary absences. At any rate, it is clearly psychological discourse that is going to convey the historical.

(82) Wirth emerged to succeed himself.
(83) In his new cabinet, Walter Rathenau, that
(84) enigmatic mixture of dreamer and politician,
(85) Jew with a penchant for blond Nordics . . . took a more prominent place. On January 31, 1922, Wirth made Rathenau his Foreign Minister.
(86) The appointment, made to prevent disasters, only caused further disasters.

Lexias 82 through 86 both inaugurate a new motif and perpetuate the individuation-focus on "leaders," inserted within the narrator's creation of an anticipated future (a formation subject to historiographic contention where, as Skinner defended it, the story accumulated its "logic and plot" so that "anticipations are meaningless"; see Skinner 1969:29). Our academic historian operates under a more authoritarian model than the naiveté of those such as Skinner who presumed that description equals recounting, where the chronological order never spun off into speculation or projection of the story beyond what was described (lexia 86 is not a piece of historical thinking to authors like Skinner).

> (87) Rathenau was shot to death by young right-wing militants.
> (88) Pursued by the police, one of the assassins was killed, a second killed himself, the third received a prison sentence of fifteen years
> (89) but spent only seven years in prison—
> (90) The Republic was always generous with its enemies.
> (91) Some hesitant Republicans now repudiated their nationalist, militarist allies . . .
> (92) but the right, unrepentant, continued . . .
> (93) And big industry . . . was regaining self-confidence . . .

Lexia 86 is fulfilled by (87); and both complete the forecast of lexia 52 ("some hoped for revenge"). So Rathenau's death has more than one function: it manifests the removal of another indispensable individual; and it introduces a recoding of violence, raising not the political or psychological planes, but a much more opaque one, that of institutional violence. The narrator engages this motif by accounting for Rathenau's murderers, and slides over the disruptive-interpretant of lexia 90, creating a real anomaly—Weimar was not captive after all, not a victim. Lexia 91 collapses into affirming a certain morality of the Republicans, expressed as "hesitance," another sign of "thoughtfulness." Lexia 90 is a severe distortion; to be "generous" with enemies is virtually suicidal in this story world: this psychologeme thus positivizes—forgives—Weimar simply by embedding it in an unconsciousness. And when did it begin, considered from the angle of its plausibility? If it was co-initial with the inauguration of Weimar, this would undercut every textual carving out of a fate: there cannot be collective fate when passivity denotes a subject as self-complicit. Passivity is not really existent except as the result of some act of doing, which is here blocked from consideration. One can retranslate lexia 91 as stating that the repudiation serves to maintain subject purity of Weimar— protection of the subject—and that lexia 90 thus recodes the narrator's maintenance of distance from Weimar (this distance between the narrator and Weimar may be a connotator of the separation between lexias 34–39 and the political dimension that the narrator rejects, but that is very dimly connected).

The reader is here provided with grounds for speculation. The murder of Rathenau places the reader in the situation where the spectacle is definitely reduced for a moment (see p. 153 where the narrator quotes the thoughts of the "right" about Rathenau), but, at the same time, this contemplation about leadership is accompanied by the disappearance of the reader's ability to think: the reader is to focus on the "right" still as antisubject, that is, unmoral (lexia 92). This is a restatement of Barthes's note about the bourgeois penchant for acknowledging an "evil" so as to forgive it (inoculation); here the narrator mentions an excess ("generosity") so as to diminish it. The reader is not brought close enough to the political right to penetrate their psychological truth or institutional relations, the right restricted to the plural-functions of a narrative mechanism: "threat," unstoppable, without thought, and so on. It appears that both the positive notable (lexia 34) and negative notable values (lexia 81) are linked by *unnarratability*, the implications of which we shall take up later. Here I want to discuss more concretely the implicit reading of "fate."

The reactive subject, in Nietzsche's sense of the term, tries to find significance and value not only in the passivity of ressentiment and bad faith but also through the endless recycling of ascetic ideals that provide the emotions with ideals that drain the subject of affirmative desire, desire that pluralizes without recentering. Nonreactive subjectivity stresses the joy and pain of thought involved through the body: only thoughts saturated by their proximity to sensory excess allow for nonreactive thought, thoughts that continue to be marked by their shock effects. In Nietzsche's framework, the reactive subject is not subsumed by mere repression but by the far more culturally disastrous frame where subjectivity participates in story narrative that culminates in the intellectual death of wanting to be told (one wants to be told by the other). Not only is the narrative-reader held on course when any of its signifieds threaten to open a strong countersense of what is being told, theorized in historiography as the axiom that "narrative must have a unity of its own" (Mink 1978:143), but also narrative and reader generally coemerge, when reactive thinking releases history as an effect of the conjunction of story and thinking. Even ways around such links between "history" and reactive thought will not let go of narrativized thinking. I have in mind here the novel attempt of White, who rejects a cultural or political "revolution" from "above" or "below" and wants to "free" (liberate) "historical thought" by grafting it to a sense of *moral life itself*. White tells us that one antidote to the passivity of "fateful" thought concerning Weimar would be to consider the "historical" and "fate" as deriving from

> the kind of meaninglessness which alone can goad the moral sense of living human beings to make their lives different for themselves and their children, which is to say, to endow their lives with a meaning for which they alone are fully responsible. One can never move with any politically effective confidence from an apprehension of "the way things actually are or have been" to the kind of moral insistence that they "should be otherwise" without passing through a feeling of repugnance for and negative judgment of the condition that is to be superseded (1982:128).

True enough, but White wants to historicize the meaningless: there is true fate in relation to the subliminal goad, the meaningless. He believes that one can resolve problems of narration by this concept, so as to return with a sense of history fully and completely individualized ("to endow their lives") and this would dissolve the bad faith of mere storytelling, which perforce would have to individuate itself by eliminating passivity from its organization. Fate collapses before the subject who internalizes the whole. He does not see that the concept of "meaning-lessness" is still a full narrative program merely subjectivized in the same way that Bergson recognized the "completeness" of the idea of "nothing," for White has merely given a "metapsy-chological" rendering of the usual bourgeois fate (see Bergson 1944:311). "Repugnance" and "negative judgment" are tied to "meaninglessness" by the further presupposition that genuine self-definition itself is only possible through a narrative test with the negative goal. One sees that a Hegelian decision is still proffered as the extreme limit of bourgeois historical conscious-ness. The conceptual distance that separates the encoding of Weimar as subject to fate or the liberation from fate in the name of responsibility is extensive, but both are versions, sides, of the impossibility of real distance from narrative culture.

"Foreign intransigence" takes over as the object of focus, since Weimar must never unwind or be allowed to go flat (become reducible to mega-summary, that is, one line in a textbook). Since "tension" has been canonized as an intrinsic relation to Others within Western Culture, foreign intransigence is fitted to the narrative program announced in lexia 61 so as to move the story forward:

(94) . . . on January 11, 1923, a French-Belgium contingent occupied the Ruhr to operate the mines and the indus-tries in behalf of the victorious powers.

(95) There were bloody clashes.

(96) The German Government counseled passive resis-tance . . . production came to a standstill.

(97) And inflation, *already* a grave threat, now got out of control altogether . . .

(98) . . . in April 1923 the dam burst . . . by October 1923 . . . trillions of marks were needed to buy a loaf of bread or mail a letter.

(99) Farmers refused to ship . . . manufacturing reached an all-time low, . . . food riots, workers hovered near star-vation, millions of bourgeois lost all their savings, while speculators grew rich.

(100) The resulting economic dislocation and psychological upheaval only strengthened the already pervasive distrust of the Republic. (italics added)

The overall action is more degradation for Weimar. Lexias 94 through 96 appear to be straightforward informants, very near pure events, the antithesis of mere signs. The narrator (p. 154) states that the condition for occupation was the German failure to pay reparations "on time." The category "victorious" keeps alive the idea of "Germany's defeat," so what were "reparations" to the victors—economic or psychological? One sees here that the economic is subsumed by the psychological; the reader is once more in the proximity of the narrator's maintenance of both the hierarchical control of perspective *and* a displacement process, which here consists in the narrator's rejection of an economic motif. Through lexia 96 the reader can conjure a quasi-image or quasi-concept of Weimar's ongoing "subjection" by Others. Inflation, however, is an interpolation that is now used to complete such noneconomic thought; with inflation encoded as noneconomic, the one who calls it a "grave threat" crystallizes it as another sememe of fate; the use of "grave threat" thus allows the narrator to segment the economic from all that surrounds it, with the exception of the grave threat itself, whose terrorism is forwarded to the reader as a pure dramatic figure. A morality of the narrator shows through here, taking the side of the little people batted around by inflation. The combination of condemning speculators (lexia 99) while systematically excluding what inflation is (for example, a requirement to prop up the falling rate of value, the protection of surplus value through prices that outstrip wages) is identical in structure to the position taken by Shklar that was mentioned in chapter one: liberalism speaks about excess and extremism while suppressing, through silence and displacement, the stronger irrationality of the systematic; the psychologeme "grave threat" operates as an aspect of a vision of unraveling. The ratio: the maintenance of the narrative's movement by psychological overcoding equals a reader's intellectual *dislocation*, for "dam burst" (lexia 98) is the epitome of metaphor, so filling the reader's imagination that it blots out the retrievability of its discursive organization. *To make inflation a "dam burst" is quite literally both hyperfigurativization and nonsense:* the narratee is required to find a signifier that can satisfy the intellectual slide to psychology. Narrativizing inflation as a catastrophic result, no matter how completely inflation is thought through, causes the economic moment to evaporate. Only "figures" of "dam burst" can be imaged, the economic disappearing as it is narrativized away as catastrophe.

The narrator draws the conclusion: lexia 100, a collective negative psychology toward Weimar. This, in turn, leads to

(101) . . . the government began a ruthless economy drive
(102) . . . Stability returned, though hardships did not end.

The economic motif thus ends or, better, closes, but without any of its implied relations answered. Since the narrator only mentions the ending of "passive resistance, to get production going again" or governmental violence (p. 154), and cites the official empowered to "end" the printing of money and restructure the "new mark," what is the model of the economy for which such steps were the "cure"? Because lexia 102 closes lexia 101, one has to assume that the "cure" worked. At lexia 102, the narrative *returns* to a condition *prior* to "inflation" as a base for the story, so the potential convolutions of the economic are shut off from the reader's mind. All of this manifests a conjunction of privileged codes dominated by a narrativizing-disintellection: the "return of stability" deintellectualizes the economic so that the latter is relegated to the margins of narratability; this is accomplished by making the economic unthinkable by comparison to some other more fundamental "classeme" (see Courtes 1976:49) which regulates the narrator's discourse and the reader's reengagement with the real story. Such mechanisms keep "political fate" narratable by the sign-form of *dramatization,* which reduces the economic to noninterference in the story. .

After "stability returned" the reader is presented with

(103) Stresemann's conciliatory policy exasperated the right,

which is the form in which the economic is completed, absurdly, in its lack of *notability*, the reader again shifted to engage leadership/subjectivity. I do not think it is unimportant to stress again that one is dealing with an instance of discursive liberal social theory where the "economic" (for example, wage differentials, surplus value) has to be recoded into psychological figurations where, as Baudrillard (1981:53) puts it, the "mastery of accumulation" (the economic moment of Capital) disappears into forms of sign exchange that focalize social disintegration and marginality as a psychologization process. In place of defining all of the meanings of a specific level or type of practice, the narrator enjoys the right to exclude significations that interfere with the chosen and privileged narrativized topic. This occurs among new-left writers as well. When, for example, Lasch (1982:31) writes that the "welfare state has turned the citizen into a client," this narrative summary of events is actually a condensed conceptualization that presupposes the acceptability of such a narrative (story) base for action. To contest the asserted hierarchy contained within the "told," one would gain nothing by opposing some counterstory to story. To infer intellectually the pragmatic implication (where does critical thinking begin for "clients" as opposed to, say, marginal members of the Industrial Reserve Army?), the reader has to undo the dictionary sense of "client," which is also to reject the narrative's intelligibility: one has to locate its zone of possible irrelevancy. For example, "client" opens onto a feudal connotation, which is not actualized except in the sense of "to be dependent." Client relations are relations of obligatory reciprocity; so the narrative order here must then pertain to "client" only in the modern sense of one who employs the services of professionals. But welfare recipients cannot be classified in that way at all, since they are dependent on the State. So what does "client" actually signify? Does it signify anything but the narrator's story of "loss" ("citizen") and the conjunction of "loss" with attempts to make present-now *notable* through the invocation of a story?

(104) On the night of . . . Hitler, Göring, Ludendorff . . . staged a putsch in Munich.

> (105) It failed . . .
> (106) Hitler was permitted to convert the trial into a propaganda feast against the Republic.
> (107) His sentence was the minimum possible . . .
> (108) For three years the Nazis fomented disorder, gave inflammatory speeches against the Republic, preached violence against the Jews, and enlisted some sympathizers in high positions.
> (109) When Hitler's rebellion in November 1923 collapsed, and when financial stability returned, republicans breathed easier;
> (110) was Hitler not, after all, just another crank?
> (111) It took years before they were proved wrong.

The narrator here speculates: that which became the result of the future of the story (Hitler's "success") might not have occurred at all; placed within the first-order story, the emergence of the Nazis as a story topic suggests there was a point when the Nazis had no future. The suggestion that the "what happened" could have been prevented raises not only the concept of another narrative possible world but also the real epistemic issue of *who*, strictly within the frame of the first-order narrative, could have, at that time, *thought* along the seme of "proved wrong" (lexia 106)? Scheidemann "thought" just in time (lexia 11); lexia 28 placed "thought" in the frame of "postponement"; the description of "thoughtfulness" covered the Democratic Party, and lexia 96 saturated Weimar in the attribute of "counseled," so that on the side of Weimar considered as a sememic grouping (conceptual) and an actantial destination (a doing, a performance), "thought" undergirds the positivity of Weimar. The absence of links between Weimar and the negative, for example, lexia 108, is consistently displaced onto those in opposition. Lexia 110 raises the supposition that Hitler and the Nazis could be dismissed by the classeme "crank," a recoding of lexias 47, 52, 66, 78, and 92. So the reader must draw the only textually allowable or foreseen conclusion—that the leadership of Weimar only made a wrong guess about Hitler; this, in turn, releases the semantic disclosure "no one could have known" who they really were. By implication any reader would agree or assent to the "realism" involved: in the past "thought" could not penetrate beyond the "historical" (for example, here the sememe "crank" used as a signifier of psychological marginality and opposition to Weimar). Historical discourse here performs an equation between thought and that which limits thought from the outset. The Nazis as *un-begotted* is certainly a primary semic nucleus of this kind of sign display, which plays off the logical code of negative probability and thus once again denarrativizes the negative only to recuperate it, as we shall see.

For lexia 106 denotes that someone gave permission to Hitler to propagandize, partially confirmed by lexia 107, which suggests the judiciary or agents within the government. (One should also consider the range: a judge, some judges; ordered to or not; by some cabinet level officials or not; related in turn or not to big business? Each of these potential agents, also in turn, opens onto more choices, each possible of illuminating the systematicity at work in 1923, and each choice unavailable to the reader.) Is Weimar's historical noteworthiness then conveyable by means of the opposition with "irreconcilables," or are both contained by some other actant that ensured Hitler's minimal sentence? Was some practice linked to those acts of Weimar— its "generosity" with enemies, laissez-faire (lexia 80), and "permission" (lexia 71), which could unravel the status that Weimar was either "subject of" the "will" of Others or "fated" to dissolution? At this point the narration is not ready to disambiguate such thoughts. The reader is presented with the choice of either assenting to the affirmation conveyed by the sign form that even "knowledge" failed before the demonic Right (lexias 110–111) or mutilating, in effect, his or her own previous reading of the encoded story.

When traditional liberal historical narration focused upon presence directly ("history is law"), it relied upon the systematic idealization of codes (Barthes 1977:116) so as to create the effect of spectacle (Civilized vs. Barbarians). Positive content could be emphatically presented as the history of progress or enlightenment. Now, in a situation where liberal historians write about *what did not happen* (game theory, counterfactuals, speculation detached from philosophy and recoded as methodological/ theoretical "play"), which coincides with the failed, the lack, the absence in some past as it affects the collapse of fulfillment and success (what is progress?), liberal historiography has run out of any strong sense of *causal* language. In writing, for example, that "another ominous development was the burgeoning of splinter parties" (lexia 77), the narrating wavers: "burgeoning" might not only be a description of a cause (manifest function) but also a signifier of "incapacity," where its full effect is released in the reader's consent to the hostility of excessive (or the fear of excessive) political groupings. "Splinter parties" is a sign of the feared lack of consensus, which functions narratively but is, to that extent, inexpressible as a discourse. A strong causal presentation of the same proposition would throw the narrative onto the tracks of what its very form prevents—the making of direct discursive statements about the basic arrangement of modern political systems (see Van Dijk 1977:68–81 on the language of causality). One can note the convergence between Collingwood's displacement of causal statements onto the imagination code, where to "know why" occurs once the historian "knows what" (meaning is intrinsic to an act) and the more recent strategy of supposed anti-idealists like Le Goff (1973:215) who argue that the causal is the description of "coexistence and interaction" (causal meaning is the description of a distinctive level), since both suspend causality in favor of protecting an overall narrative impact. The liberal theoretician Mandelbaum (1977:70–75) stresses that as a theoretical discourse, causality is inseparable from the grasp of a "full continuous process," a solution that effectively restricts causation to the naming of occurrences themselves. The "well-formed question" of academic discourse controls the apparatus of "causal" thought (Mandelbaum 1977:79), since the causal has been taken out of society except as relevant to a context. As description must be continuous with the described (an axiom of narration) strong arguments that try to separate "causal signs" from overall description are invalidated, for the separability would clearly threaten the maintenance of narrative autonomy. This is why Hempel's argument for the detachability of causal statements from other kinds of statements was so rejected by historians. For example, the sequencing of the Versailles Treaty as first signed (mass outrage), then exploited by the Right (realized through the Nazis), is formally a causal sequence, based upon the scheme negative action causes a reaction, but to state that "it took years before they were proved wrong," is a forecast (which suggests the signified "erroneous judgment") which abolishes the causal: the causal is made unsuitable for thinking because the narrating cannot relinquish what it says to nonnarrative statements, which are the appropriate form of causal thought. As I understand the "causal," it is not so much tied to the full description of sequentially organized sequences (what Blanchard 1980:211 aptly calls the creation of subjective "object choices" conveyed by sequenced relations of appropriation) as it is the creation of a hierarchically clear presentation of the systematic, that is, argumentation. And this very form is rejected by narrative: the causal is disruptive to academic narrative organization, banished to the level of connotators, where it disturbs neither the flow of telling-told nor the reader's "what will happen next" intellectual expectation. This summary text presupposes all this, especially the causal reduced to narrativized semes (see lexias 106 and 110).

The narrator's sole explicit mention of the historiographical sphere occurs in this manner:

(112) The assertion that happy ages have no history is a myth, and

(113) in any event,

(114) the middle years of the Weimar Republic were far from happy;

(115) still the political events of this comparatively tranquil time can be rapidly summarized.

(116) Sanity seemed to be returning at home and abroad.

Note, first, that the function of this historiographical pause is itself narratively organized: lexias 112 through 116 supply the reader with a historicized rationale for the value of narrativity, the pause initiated when lexia 111 threatened to undermine the story by pushing it into the realm of the meaningless (if the

Weimar leaders knew what the Nazis were at that time, the Weimar leadership of course ceases to be narratable and becomes complicit in another story). Historiography is complicated: linked to the maintenance of the first-order story's variability (its distance and difference from all other similar summaries) from the preexisting plot knowledge of the reader, historiography holds open the first-order narrative for the not-yet-told, as if to deny the summary form itself. As a piece of theoretical discourse, the pause is a device that suppresses repetition. That what historiography has taught is mythic is targeted at the philosophy of history, its promotion of atemporal statements and truisms, so historiography is rejected by restricting it to mythic status. Again, the historiographic pause functions as the stop of the previously read (lexia 111), and enacts a code switch, manifested in the temporal adverb "still," whereby "political events" are recoded as stable enough for narrative processing. The connection between this historiographical intrusion and the capacity to summarize is the attempt to shore up the transmission of a subcode: historiography is rejected while the referent of the telling is reengaged, the latter accomplished by "events and actors" themselves "calming down," moving toward some mythic "middle" (lexia 116). The use of the verb "seemed" (lexia 116) is both inaugurative and indeterminate enough to enable a reader to acknowledge the noninterference of even theory with the telling of the story. So I shall note here that the historiographical "pause" functions as part of its own disengagement of previous historical thought in order to achieve for itself a release from discourse so as to code the simulacrum of an open text (see Eco 1979:49–56).

The reader now passes onto the text's evocation of *continuity:* where temporal relators till now were coordinated with different semes of friction (for example, lexia 10 with its "barely in time," lexia 25 and its sense of dissolution, lexia 67 where political time was momentarily reduced to perceptual time), as signs of rapidity, this is suspended, and the story is governed by its subordination to another atemporal construct, in another mode of leadership/subjectivity, a narrative isotopy wherein identity along the plane of story-time can be presented:

(117) . . . the six cabinets that were to govern Germany between December 1923 and the end of June 1928 showed
sturdy continuity:
(118) each had Stresemann as its Foreign Minister.

The predication of continuity is glued to Stresemann through
the use of "each," so that it is the *frequency* of an individual
figure/agent, and not anything else, which now supports the
ability to think in this longer measure of time, this "beating" of
continuity. Stresemann, in other words, has no function, no
biographical moment of his own, no psychological essence, apart
from manifesting a continuous historical subject. After a mi-
nuscule mention of the setting ("a conservative period"), the
narrator postpones Stresemann to focus on foreign affairs. Cited
are Herriot, the "good European" because he "thought" of Europe and not simply France, and the Dawes Plan, set up to
evacuate the Ruhr and provide for capitalization of Germany,
and both signify the repetition return of the repressed, the past
now released as itself an actant:

(119) The German Government accepted the plan, over fierce
right-wing opposition.
(120) It was always the same story:
(121) the concessions that seemed to implacable Frenchmen
too great,
(122) seemed too small to irreconcilable Germans.

This "same story" overcodes what the reader has already
learned, and displaces the reader to a time before story-now, to
a preexisting quasi-epic opposition (lexia 120). The past explains
the present; history itself is a cause. Psychologistic traits ("implacable" and "irreconcilable") are attached to the physical scale
"great and small" and threaded to the notion of "national character." This indexes "nationalism" as an active factor on account
of the inertia of repetition, and yet it cannot be shown as causal,
since the psychological must, in bourgeois culture, endow
events and existents with density and atemporality (the psychological, with the exception of the crudest Behaviorism, al-

ways leads to the unnameable). And since the Right in both France and Germany are absorbed by this identical full present-pastness (lexia 120), the reader is provided with the anti-intellectual grounds for once again not considering at all just what the Right thought or objected to or protested about. Even the narrator's attempt to sustain a story shift toward optimism (the phrase "golden twenties" frames this segment, conveyed by the toponym of "richness," a comparatizer stripped of its social origination, that is, its mythic signification) is undercut by the psychology of "the same story."

This psychologization of historical thought thrives on modern German history because the story of Germany has consistently remained unintegrable as a historical and narrative trajectory ("Germans" gone awry). The signs of "uniqueness" and "individuality," common to the historian's code of the past's nonrepeatability, have stressed that German society was "unique" in modernizing, that it "lacked" democratic underpinnings, that it never shed its "medieval" heritage of paternalism; and that Germany retained its "traditional" features while it was shifting to a world context where its forms of tradition blocked its own future resolution of contradictions in a nonpathological way. In assessing, in adding up the "net effect" of the Nazi era, for example, Craig (1980:764) writes that Hitler "left the German people nothing that could be repaired or built upon. They had to begin all over again . . . ," which, by discontinuing that era from even its past, promotes the thought that the Nazi "experience" was merely a phase of a story, finished, and not, say, also a form of a far more complete social systematic. Here we see that individuality and uniqueness are also signifiers that can be used to inoculate the Nazi era: it is so specific that comparative ideas are eliminated (for example, the role of the State along the lines proposed by Althusser). Liberal historical education about the Nazi period usually means that it is classified as a period or phase or step or "moment" (the neo-Marxist hedge), but not as an experimental normalization of a permanent possibility of Western Civilization. Even if one grants that Nazism was "aberrational," the nonexistence of tacit knowledge about that period, genuine common know-how of its workings, refers to liberal historiography's collectivized decision to have the Nazi time over and done with, that is, summarizable. It can be made suitable for transmission as a summary once it has been shorn of virtually everything that made it both action and connectable to present-now. In short, the story is grounded in the mode of being a result of its history, which is what the telling naturalizes.

More formally put, summary and intransitivity are intrinsically coded as deintellectualizations: the summary form is a medium of suppressing that which is not allowed to warrant full discursivity as a socio-intellectual problem, summary serving as the sign form of intellectual closure. Within the field of the story, such summarizing is organized by the narrator's ongoing casting into oblivion relations that might unravel the followability effect of reading and thinking:

(123) Hindenburg . . . received the largest vote . . .
(124) Hindenburg acted quite scrupulously, and until overtaken by senility, effectively as a loyal chief executive [President of the Republic].

Lexias 123–124 are summaries of political and ethical processes. But their presentation—as given result—required the reader to bypass another discursive evasion in order to move smoothly onto the program of lexia 124. Between 123 and 124 was this:

(125) And after prolonged maneuvering among the parties . . .

The ellipsis involved here is an index of selection: the historian could have opened up *how* political maneuvering operated or how the political dissolved into the extrapolitical (which are further lines, in turn, to the processes of groups in which the political was at that time articulated), but the foreclosure is complete. One is not dealing with the classical historical narrator, who, as Gossman (1978:38) pointed out, "came clean" in the telling, but instead with a narrator-manager who controls what can be thought in the first place. This further indicates that the ideological cannot at all be correlated with the presence or absence of propositional material (what Macherey calls a text "made of what it does not mention," 1978:132), but with the way(s) in which such purport is organized, the placement of sign forms. The narrator is not interested in the political after all, so here I note that the political is now irretrievably removed from the processes of thinking and telling.

After citing the partial success of Germany in international politics (foreign treaties), the narrator arrives another time at the economic, and unlike earlier dramatic codings (see lexia 101), the economic is saturated in the cognitive effect of the unknowable. The reader is told that by comparison to the disequilibrium of 1923, the economic was "prosperous," and then this moment of positivity is brought up short in this manner:

(126) There was something masklike about German internal prosperity . . .
(127) . . . there were ominous hidden developments
(128) [mergers] on an unprecedented scale
(129) governments . . . wasting funds
(130) Hugenburg . . . gaining control of the opinion industries.
(131) The Communists continued to refuse cooperation . . .
(132) The new army retained its old ideas . . .
(133) And right-wing fanatics never weakened . . .
(134) . . . but things were going too well to make such threats really terrifying.

The "masklike prosperity" of lexia 126 is completed, as before, not by a discourse *upon* the economic but by switching on "ominous hidden developments," a pure temporalizer conveyed by the acts of lexias 128–130, all of which send a line to the reader. The reader can assume the post of being shown—seeing—what was "unknown" about the economic at that time, while the historian supplies a restorative code. "Ominous hidden" is both the historian's special knowledge and a partial access to the semblance of "causal time." Lexias 131–133 reinforce previous mentions of the "isolation" of the government due to the intractable desires of such irreconcilables, a reiteration of the status of nonknowledge extractable from such groups. Lexia 134, however, organizes the economic as if it could absorb the conflict and oppositions of lexias 131–133, a piece of "vulgar materialism." A social model is asserted here—that economic recovery in advanced capitalist societies has the capacity to further the political assimilation of dissident social groups, such groups pertinent only in economic crisis. The materialism of such a society has been, in effect, too successful. The axiom of the "cost of prosperity" is appropriately measured by the loss of the overall steering capacity, which can only be preserved when there is equilibrium of the political-economic, where there is neither too much prosperity, nor too little. In effect, lexia 134 completes the detaching of the economic from this political history, making final at the same time the need for leadership, of the sort called for at lexias 34–39. The economic system will be presented again, but its propositional or cognitive strength will be restricted to a metonymic dispersal, where the economic plays the part of only a difference, a factor, a level. From now on, the economic can be narrated without posing any intellectual problem. The economic, narrated away, is now virtually an inaccessible configuration.

More elections follow, and the Social Democrats are back in office, but "speaking as individuals," not as a party (p. 157). Then:

(135) Stresemann, the indispensable man . . . agreed to serve as Foreign Minister . . .

(136) . . . more and more the Nazi leadership found connections in respectable circles . . .

On the story level, the absence of Stresemann would have constituted a significant difference; the transformation of the Nazis from the status of "crank" (lexia 110) is hinged to the verb "found," which doubly reifies any specification of how the Right created contact with the social. On the one hand, "found" is a grammatical expression denoting a passive completion, which makes it impossible for the reader to think how the Nazis were anchored to the "respectable"; and, on the other hand, the Nazis implicitly initiated such "finding," so that the objects of their "interest" are released from the status of action; one can think there is merely convergence of the right wing. Only the "sinister Hugenberg" is awarded the status of initiating codesire with Hitler; but since this is formed as an "overture" (p. 157), or a kind of "preface" to political behavior, the reader cannot pursue its intellectual force. Still, lexia 136 recodes lexia 111 ("were proved wrong") and lexia 77 ("burgeoning of splinter parties"), so that in story-now the Nazis are a formation of *pure result*, an accumulation of near zero-predication: change itself is told about but changes via action are undemonstrable. For example, the "lack" (nonevent) of the "purge" mentioned at lexia 72 is here recoded as "fulfilled" in a negative manner ("found connections"), which figures the future as an oxymoronic undoing, displacing the reader's thought processes from comprehension of action and then recoding the sense of completion, so that lexia 47 or "submissive scars" is now immanently represented, but without disclosing any knowledge. The narratee must then occupy the post of not-being-able-to-know, a position of nonlearning.

This coding of completion was raised by what Barthes (1970:188) called the narrative "braid," the simultaneity of different actions, roles, ideations, and so on, where the narrated at once precludes a collapse of meaning (the reader snared by the threat of excessive plural meanings [= noncompletion] and the chance that "truth" may not happen [= noncoincidence of telling and told]). There is no exact historiographical equivalent. But something approximating an equivalence is suggested in the new historiographic call for a modern form of "realism," where it is projected that the convergence of the telling and the told *should* entertain the reader with a possible lapse of meaning, whereby the act of closure is both absolute and yet still open to "interpretation":

> History leaves us with a sense that things could not have happened otherwise, because in fact they did not happen otherwise. History is wisdom after the fact . . . Realism . . .

closes the gap between history and the finiteness of the narrative form, by fostering a sense of possibility, unrealized but realizable. It is this sense of might-have-been . . . (Anchor 1983:116).

These assertions positivize the not-possible *sent* by History itself: "it leaves us with," which is an interesting but bizarre mode of delivery. Once here, however, the not-possible is instantly divided into results: "wisdom after the fact" is nothing other than passive knowledge or learning at zero degree of difference; the incommensurate distance between history and any told-story, their possible miss or lapse, is reclosed, for as "might-have-been," any lapse of meaning is restored to the imagination. Compared to this ideal, summary can be understood as an overcoding of completion where an apprehension of the possible past never happens; narrative *resolution*, I might add, the capacity to date and periodize, cannot do more than theorize the possible, and has nothing whatever to do with realism.

(137) . . . the Reichstag finally voted to accept the Young Plan [to settle German reparation payments] and Hindenburg conscientiously signed it.

(138) But then, by mid-March, the architect of Germany's foreign policy, Gustav Stresemann, had been dead for over five months.

(139) In bad health for over a year, harassed by members of his own party, vilified by the Nazis and the German Nationals, he had continued to defend his policies to the end.

(140) . . . succeeded by Julius Curtius . . . but no replacement.

(141) Stresemann should not be sentimentalized;

(142) nor should we exaggerate the power of one man in

(143) the turbulent stream of history . . .

(144) Yet his death was a grievous loss;

(145) it was, if not cause, at least the sign of the beginning of the end.

The "genuine German right" ceases as part of the story with Stresemann's death. Stresemann dies in symmetry with the story's switch in subject; as an icon of liberalism's refusal to abandon individualism, that is, transcendence of politics, Stresemann dies at the moment where the story passes into a black hole, signaled in the absence of rationality from "society." The same subject who within the story was a signifier conveying utter continuity, principle, sanity, and so on, is also the discontinuous figure, a signifier to the second power, a cause or, as lexia 145 provides in its own commentary, a "sign." Schematically, this turning point operates both as what Barthes called a cardinal function which, as expressed by lexia 145, uses *post hoc, ergo propter hoc* as a proleptic de-consequencing of the next story, and as an actant-engagement whereby the next story (Nazis) is already encoded in the unnarratable. Sent to the reader is the coding of the withdrawal of Weimar's story: the intellectual "value" of "grievous loss" and "beginning of the end" disengages Weimar *after Stresemann* as a historical subject. To use a Hegelian mode of expression, Stresemann is an "abstract subjectivity," an "emptiness and formalism of thought," situated at the point of telling where the predicates of positivity give way to story dissolution. In Genette's terms, the narrator has poised the reader at a repetitive anachrony which redistributes the previous lexias that involved Weimar's fate, for now within the same cognitive space there is Subject (realized as Weimar) indistinguishable from subject (Stresemann). The discursive identity between Weimar and Stresemann is the figure of death. The rest of the story will obviously have to present the means of termination, the techniques of termination. But the transcendence of this subject (the needed subject, the required subject, the unpolitical politician) has to be accomplished in accordance with the historian's role of appropriating a further transcendence from this narrated one. The first level is Stresemann's story death; the second level is story consequence, the virtual unnarratability of the temporal unit "after Stresemann"; and the third level is the reader's ability to date, which now takes the place of an ability to think. In terms of textual pragmatics, "Stresemann should not be sentimentalized" says that the category of the privileged subject, here the unpolitical politician, is *less real than History* because the cessation of Stresemann-figure(s), where no other subjects of equivalent value exist, is tantamount to datability itself ("beginning of the end"). Nothing less than the reinforcement of a cultural universal of modern liberal historiography is on display here: everyone is subject to the undated ("stream of history") which flattens all subjectivity (distransitivity). This is the threshold of the "everyone," the release of that which reincorporates all action and difference, where history is real yet unfathomable. The reduction to the level of everyone is directed to a portion of the reader's subjectivity; in Deleuze's phrase, the reader is here a "puppet of the superego," reduced to the performance of the "metareality" of beholding the Same. Behind the subject is history, the backup thought of cultural defeatism (see Deleuze and Guattari 1977:311, 316).

(146) Stresemann's death *dramatized* the dilemma of "bourgeois, politically homeless Protestantism,"
(147) that large number of voters mortally afraid of Communists,
(148) unwilling to join the Socialists,
(149) suspicious of the Catholic Center,
(150) disoriented by the War and its aftermath, and,
(151) on the whole, unimpressed by Germany's rapid recovery and renewed international prestige.
(152) Stresemann had *taught* these millions the virtues of collaborating with Social Democrats . . . he had candidly said . . . an affair not of the heart but of reason.
(153) . . . with his death . . . fragmentation of the Weimar coalition continued (pp. 158–159, italics added).

In the analysis of Braudel in chapter five we shall see how the replacement of focus upon subjects occurs by means of the historian's creation of what can be called *zero-degree interruption,* where time codings are drawn directly from discursive systems, not from models of the subject (see Virilio and Lotringer 1983:33–37). But here, beginning with lexia 146, the narrator's commentary and metonymic rush rely upon another psychologization of an elite social group.

The discourse, basing itself on approved quoted material (cited to authorize the content and the situation) reproduces not some primary interpretation, as its form seems to indicate, but a fully historicized reading of a cultural typification—a social segment encoded as a group whose very history was one of unintegrability. Ostensibly, "Bourgeois Protestants" occupied the space of a dilemma, a dilemma introduced as a temporal-continuator of their social essence. To be "mortally afraid," "unwilling," "suspicious," "disoriented," and "unimpressed," however, depicts a group whose social perspective and distance from their place in society is one of disdain toward their own interests, unless, of course, the contrary evocation is more appropriate, that their interests were only sustainable *when* they enjoyed supreme distance from "their world." *The narration encodes temporal dissolution (lexia 153), while the discourse structuring the narrative accepts their perspective.* The story is propelled by a psychology of caste (lack of leadership) where the narrating implies that this caste lost its very rationality (lexia 152) with the death of its teacher.

The narrating destroys implied connections between the absence of collaboration by this group and their turn to a demand for class protection. Did these "bourgeois, politically homeless Protestants" desire Nazism to arrest "fragmentation," or was it just the withdrawal of this class which promoted Nazism in a slightly longer run? Active or inactive, a transitive or intransitive class? The discursive voice states that without leadership or an active tutelary model, there must be fragmentation (a narrative trajectory of dissolution, where the disintegration of politics is simultaneously another lack, namely that of a pedagogical scene). Stresemann's "death" is encoded to further "bourgeois Protestants" as passive insofar as at this story-now they are disengaged from thought, interest, desire, and so on, concluding a negative process (their "whole" incorporated in Stresemann's death). Can we offer that the implied reader is active insofar as this reader is to internalize a symbolic rule ("scarcity of leaders"), an imaginary opposition ("leaders/nonleaders"), and a social void (riddled with more symbolic and imaginary subcodes, for example, the "social vacuum" draws, irresistibly, disreputable forces [Nazis])? The reader is presupposed now to share a code insofar as Streseman's teaching, presented as the means of this social segment's filiation to German society, calls for the reader's acceptance of the separation of the emotional and cognitive (lexia 152); such political realism requires legitimate schizophrenia. "Reason" is implicitly connotated as "interest" or "self-preservation" or "status," while "emotional" indexes the bourgeois Protestants' distance from society (and perhaps crisscrosses "status"). Is this the way their *collaboration* had been organized, shot through with logical sense, or should one infer that the Nazis exploited the distance between this group and society as a whole? (The narrator suggests their withdrawal from politics, but was withdrawal not also acceptance in that context? If so, how far was it to accept or desire totalitarianism and savagery?). At any rate, on account of their history, "bourgeois Protestants" will not occupy the reader's thoughts.

Within the canonical formulations of historiographical theory, the reader is near the threshold of what history teaches. The contemporary model of this threshold insists not so much upon a restoration of memory (taken to a perverse perfection by the Marcuseans) but upon a *reserve* of judgment or accumulation of meaning for judgment in which the taught is stressed as the seen (see Gallie 1964:136–139; Gallie's notion should be compared to Derrida's reading of "reserve" which is hinged to the notion of deferring "a dangerous cathexis," that is, the allocation of the negative, the painful, which "grounds memory" and sutures it to the real; see Derrida 1978:202). The teachable is manifested by a transfer of value where Weimar undergoes an irreversible shift, the locating of the reader in a position of Final Recognition (see Greimas and Courtes 1982:339–340).

(154) It would not have become dangerous if there had not been a world economic crisis.

(155) But there was.

The Depression has been reduced to an Alibi of modern Western societies: as the sufficient and necessary condition of any number of contradictions and impasses, the Depression is an *incomparable* imaginary substance/ground/reality, whose function within liberalism promotes integrative thought insofar as it has been narrativized and not thought out. The Depression has a status similar to the Holocaust for Jews, the Armenian decimation by the Turks, and the like, which is to serve as a fetishistic rendering of intellectual *devaluation* that is nevertheless always recuperated for summary processes, as a factor of datability. In other words, the Depression can be simultaneously an answer, cause, turning point, absolute, trauma, imaginary Other, production of destruction, object of study, ad nauseum. It is what has eluded common knowledge yet provides discursivity with an original or primary status. Millions recirculate various cultural small stories of the Depression, especially gathered around its presentation as an object of terror: that it might be repeated, that it might not be incomparably historical after all. The narrator uses it to individuate a dissolution, the device of narrative pause used to simulate narrative irreversibility:

(156) The focus of the political debate became unemployment insurance.

(157) *admittedly* a heavy and growing burden on the government;

(158) . . . a principle the Social Democrats dared not touch,

(159) and a grievance to industrialists and conservatives of all kinds . . .

(160) . . . the stock market crash on Wall Street . . .

(161) . . . the Great Depression was world-wide . . .

(162) but it was most disastrous for the least stable regime, that is, for Germany, which had lived off foreign aid far more than many Germans knew or were willing to admit.

(163) . . . on March 27, 1930, the Muller cabinet resigned.

(164) The great coalition was dead. (italics added)

Where all of the lexias dealing with Stresemann gather around the illusion of a primary figurization of the lack, the absent, the missing, the nonexistent (disintegration), the code switch onto the economic is one of utter fullness. The grammar of "but there was" disallows any thought that might undo the sense of supreme reality and negativity about this economy, just as surely as the positivity of leadership was tracked with its various semes of "lack." This is the moment of narrative irreversibility on account of the manifestation of the incomparable. As a concretization of focus, lexia 156 says that "unemployment insurance" was spoken about as a public event, but one does not know how it was voiced, which does make a difference. The voice that says "admittedly" takes the side of Weimar's authorities and is another semantic performative conveying an automatic truth, because all counter sememic positions have been effaced. "Admittedly" is stated as a simulation of telling what one is outside of and different from (Genette's extradiegetic/heterodiegetic narrator), and as positivity is granted to "burden," a sign form of identity, only the State's perspective is acknowledged. The historian speaks out of what is made, as with lexia 90, an *acknowledged thought*. The reader can make the economic cognizable here only in signifiers that belong to the unemployment issue not to the internal organization of Capital itself or any other systematic interpretant. Lexia 157, with its "admittedly," serves to protect the Weimar government by shifting the thinkable onto the connotation of a "beseiged" government, where it is suspended whether that government was incapable or unwilling to resolve its unemployment crisis. The opposition/binarism of the two forces (lexias 158–159) appears eminently rational and appropriate, attached, as it were, to the psychological choice of either-or, a figure of nonthought (since the choice of A equals non-A). The economic is basically completed with lexia 162, the suggestion that the German system of exchange was more unbalanced than other economies because it was subject to factors out of its own control ("aid"); the narrator is thereby released from any strong analysis of the specificity of the economic formation, notably that unemployment insurance is always a marginal aspect of modern Capitalism, especially so by comparison to the collapse of wages in 1929–30 (see Mandel 1975:158).

(165) When no agreement on Bruning's program could be reached, the Chancellor threatened to invoke article 48
(166) . . . on July 16 . . . he invoked it.

Thus the reader is returned to lexia 55 and the "danger" inherent in the political system; this fulfillment of the past/antecedent condition of "destiny" is interwoven with the notion of the *exceptional* (the "substance" of article 48 or the "lack" of a purely parliamentary system; see p. 151 of the story). The exceptional is absorbed within the datable, so the reader here can affirm that a society is subject to its own past: past is present and the present is internally related to past because present-determinations are less actions and interests than results of accumulated antecedents (see lexia 19); the exceptional status or infrequent-singularity of Article 48 made legally possible superconcentration of authority, an extrapolitical configuration; but its narrative role, as the "exception," here is equivalent to the full displacement of how (discursively) such an article was folded into the political system in the first place. The infrequent-exception dissolves into Germany's repetition of "Germanicity."

(167) . . . responsible bourgeois and Socialist politicians, far from blind to the pressures exerted by the extremists, sought for some accommodation.
(168) In vain.
(169) The campaign plumbed new depths of demagogy and sheer violence . . .
(170) . . . the real victors were the Nazis . . .
(171) Among the extremists, it was the extreme right alone that benefited from the condition of Weimar Germany.

Whereas the earlier mentions of the Nazis encoded their social presence as "demonic," "cranks," "flounderers," "denunciators," and "obstructionists," all negative signifiers, the shift in their status is organized around the verb "benefited," which makes the Nazis the *recipients* of the actions of others (or non-actions, if that is logically possible). "To benefit" is a signifier of transmission—to be a receiver of value, to gain from implied negativity. There are different transmissions of value, according to degree and facility, but here it is the sense of the *transfer of value* from the dying Weimar to the negative term (Nazis) which is registered. Apart from the overt blurring of state and change (see Todorov 1977:111), this transformation declares a pure result-fact, a feature of rapid-excessive summarizing. This is coded by an ellipsis that semantically blocks the reader's analysis of the performance of action: the Nazis' "benefit" from the elections of September 14, 1930, is followed by omission of the next twenty months, so that the time between their predicates is one of pure repetition of the last temporal coding (lexia 171). Nothing significant happened, not even a chronicle is enough to catch the historian's interest in the "becoming-victors" of Nazism. Nonnarration again grips the story when the telling calls attention to itself. For between t-1 (September 1930) and t-2 (May 1932) the Nazis did receive legitimation, which is minimally narrativized as a weak temporal marker, so weak as to be barely significant.

> (172) . . . they climbed from 800,000 votes to almost six and one-half million, from 12 seats to 107,

which seems to locate the Nazis in a political frame where they must have done something (or received something). But for the reader, only the *result* is permitted. The reader is screened from the Nazi process. The historian enacts the enthymeme, directed to the reader's *active memorial capacity,* that it is not worth knowing or is unsayable how and by what systematics the "Nazi phenomenon" is to be explained. The extreme unnarratability here or the reader's encounter with the not-tellable suggests that the stabilization of narrative summary is based on the noteworthy (which is not a memory form) once again removed from semic contention.

(173) . . . increasing signs that the Republic was dying;
(174) for many intellectuals Sept. 14, 1930, marked the death of the Republic.

In May 1932, Bruning resigned; the intellectuals are taken as competent to provide the date of Weimar's termination (death), and then the space between the two is filled:

(175) Through 1931, Hindenburg signed one emergency decree after another, controlling the price of food, regulating bank payments, reducing unemployment compensation.

Thus the intellectuals were in possession of a special sort of knowledge: before the Republic died they pronounced its death, an instance of prediction. The intellectuals are awarded the cultural function of signing an authoritative death certificate; and as the certificate of death is signed by them before others knew, they also provide the act of dating significance. As with lexias 34-39, the historian speaks through his own type, the academics. Literally placed before and after the "before and after" of events (the latter the signified, the former the signifier and signified), such intellectuals acquire the role of a full-blown actant: conveyors of the link between event and telling, they are *readers of texts* (lexia 173–174) continuous and discontinuous to story and telling; but they are also encoded as something else besides textual-subjects (see Michaels 1980:185–199). The intellectuals were the only ones who *could* utter such a disclosure because they were the only ones who paid attention to the signs:

(176) The Nazis made no secret of their plans for the future.

This must mean that the Nazis could not be mistaken as to their own interest, desires, and intentions. (So were "Weimar leaders" wrong? See lexias 110–111.) Since the narrator informs us that the nonsecret was knowable at the intellectuals' time of signature, we have to assume further that the intellectuals were the only ones who *could* read the signs, that is, who had the capacity to do so. It is a tiny step to the next thought: the intellectuals were surrounded by all those who could not and did not know how to read ("masses"). In addition, I note that lexia 176 inadvertently demolishes, by connotation alone, the thought that German society after 1933 was surprised or overwhelmed or unknowing or ignorant of "Nazi desire" unless, of course, the remaining intellectuals fell silent after 1933 and so their absence = nonknowledge, which does make them responsible for ignorance (lexia 176 virtually "deconstructs" itself; see Culler 1982:150).

(177) . . . and in October 1931 the Nazis widened their hold on the right at a meeting in Harzburg attended by leading Nazis, industrialists like Thyssen and Hugenberg, military men like Seeckt, financiers like Schacht.

(178) It created a "national" front against Bolshevism—

(179) a fatal, if still rather fragile, combination uniting the power of money, political shrewdness, mob appeal, and aristocratic trimmings.

As the focus on bourgeois and Socialist politicians recedes (one might say disaccumulates), the emergent story is strangely presented: what does it mean to "widen" one's "hold"? The inventory of existent-persona of lexia 177 is offered through the verb "attended," which is a verb of presence; no states, no acts, no qualities specify the modes of attendance, so the emphasis is thrown upon the extension/accumulation of the Nazis, accomplished without any reference to the Nazis' activities. This deprival of their historical subjectivity goes with the refusal to award them a narrative status which, in turn, duplicates the reader's ignorance and nonencounter with the Nazis. Lexia 178 is the simple result-summary of what is presumed a common interest (the "right" has only to gather in order to "agree"); and lexia 179 stresses the minimalist-noun "combination" as the means, the instrument, of death, an unholy blending of the negative. Now was "anti-Bolshevism" really the overdetermined interest that liberal social theory has insisted upon for the last forty years? Let us say that this model of historical process, of the coming-into-existence of the negative, organizes the success of the negative as an inverted Hegelianism. The narratee is manifestly not strengthened to recognize the establishment of a breaking, the perception of an exemplary event, or critically learning to think through; the reader is merely to register the impact of a "genetic" unfolding, as one historiographer has typified one liberal pedagogy of historical discourse (Rüsen 1982:547–551). The narratee is surrounded by a "world" which, as a "machine for producing possible worlds" (Eco 1979:246), solicits from the reader merely the joining of the "wrong" forces and the "misfortune" for the society of such a conjunction. The negative "historical" is the result of an aberration, a construct of disintellective semes.

(180) On May 30 [1932] Hindenberg dismissed the Bruning cabinet, persuaded by his friends and by his influential adviser, Kurt von Schleicher, that Bruning's social program smacked of agrarian socialism.
(181) His successor was the smooth, gaunt, manipulative reactionary Centrist Franz von Papen.
(182) He even looked like an undertaker.

Lexia 180 indexes the political intrigue attending to the personal relationship between Hindenburg and von Schleicher, and the hypersubjectivism of the political context (one uses "context" carefully, recognizing that this seme is shattered by the multiplicity of defining it, each definition signifying its problematic status; see Bruss 1982:127). The reader has crossed over to the simulation of speech, signaled through the verb "persuaded," which makes rhetoric now a momentary actant (of passage). Within this world, the thick description of von Papen is paralleled by the narrating voice's shift to the function of pseudo-icon making (*asiatismus*) where concretized images are embedded in the reader's imagination of an "end," the reader modeled as someone who too can read signs of the appropriateness of the picture and the story, their "concatenation," as Damisch (1975:31) puts it. For nothing whatsoever remains of von Papen with lexia 182, and to state that he "even looked like an undertaker" is to efface the very notion of historical significance, because this "future of the past's present" is so reduced and condensed it can only be the most perfect of illustrations. And the most severe distance between the reader and knowledge is demarcated by such devices of summary; a nontraversable semantic immensity like von Papen's iconic reduction is used to demolish, for a last time, the thinking competency of a reader:

> (183) The rest is a story of fear, terrorism, irresponsibility, missed opportunities, and shameful betrayal.

Comprehension, understanding, answer, full description, complete sense vis-à-vis the Nazis are expelled (which is quite different from the interring function noted by Certeau 1975:116). Historians do not bury, even metaphorically, any narrated past; the notion popularized by writers like Krieger that the "historian is the ghostwriter of the past. He memorializes the deeds and thoughts of others, and he establishes . . . a lasting identity in which his own is submerged" (1977:1) is equally illusionary. Instead, with lexia 183 we are in a place of hyper-disreality, part of the staging where, as Barthes put it, a "code overtakes and destroys the message." This is where coding renders the suppression of the code (a discursive metalinguistic relation to its own signifiers). What is carried to the reader through the elimination of all possible messages ("the rest . . .") is the historian's form of intellectual nihilism, here a void between the reader and Nazis, a case of maximum possible distance which is also the *closest* possible relation between the text and its model of thinking. Liberal historiography here withdraws from the ideology of its own historicism, the "need to know," which has glorified the self-valorization of history as a form of knowledge and shape of existence. For not even the existence of reality (information, data) is enough to require thought. The nonstatable of lexia 183 is not even open to that Hegelianism of the "master's experience of his truth," as Derrida (1978:254) puts it, since the unrepresentability of "the rest" ruptures all exchange and locates the reader next to the "unspeakable," instead of a giving/interpreting of meaning. This (liberal) contemporary historian enacts an ugly game through summary; as text it circulates the sense of the unknowable—there are actions and models and figures and roles and characters which are not tellable in the narrative economy of the historian, a totality of the empty (which, nevertheless, can still serve as the excuse, the problem, the basis for another narration). "The rest" = Zero intellection.

(184) Von Papen's cabinet included the ambitious Kurt von Schleicher . . . and a collection of aristocrats . . .

(185) In addition to Junkers, the cabinet included prominent industrialists.

(186) It was as though the Revolution of 1918 had never taken place.

Indeed, why narrate *between* the same? The enunciative subject— the speculator (lexia 186)—is conjured by the thought that repetition had overtaken all development, all difference, and in advance of the story-as-told, wiping out all sight, vision, significance, and so on. As we shall see, lexia 186 manifests the metasemantic category of *assessment*, a category that underlies the historian's capacity to provide, as it were, the transcendence of value. We note that in this the historian has to evade the "inextricability thesis" worked out by Quine, among others, which holds that each semantic downgearing, each tightening of a sememe that narrows toward a semic nucleus (so as to convey propositional sense), yields no central meaning, only more propositions, more conventions and codings of meanings (there is no line that absolutizes a separation between denotation and connotation); the historian can go beyond—transcend—this wavering of meaning and so extricate (extract) the narrative sense threatened by lexia 186. The implications of lexia 186 are negated by the speed of telling:

(187) . . . Hindenburg dissolved the Reichstag . . .

(188) The Brown Shirts and the Black Shirts . . . went into action wholeheartedly . . .

(189) The Socialists called it civil war and they were right.

(190) But the government did nothing . . .

(190) On July, 31, 1932, the elections . . . ended in a stunning victory for the Nazis . . .

(192) The opposition to the Nazis remained numerous but disunited.

(193) . . . after a clash with Göring . . . von Papen dismissed the Reichstag and called for new elections.

Overcoded summaries of summaries, these lexias intensify the speed of the telling, giving a propulsive force to the accumulation of dissolvants, but as so frequently with this telling, there are no acts that open the story to even the historian's infamous attempt to "set the story right." After a pause that mentions the next elections and the stalled momentum of the Nazis (pp. 161– 162), the narrator returns by means of a Hegelianized code of the "cunning" of "reality" gone awry: the Nazis "rise" to the position of power and authority (but not as subjects of knowledge, which lexias 177–179 have already annulled as an object of thought) is "explained" by the *collective* inability to read (the reverse of lexia 173).

(194) . . . the dying Weimar Republic was experiencing the last and most fateful intrigue of all.

(195) Once out of office, filled with dislike of von Schleicher and the desire to return to power,

(196) Von Papen decided to use Hitler as a kind of stalking horse.

(197) He, too, underestimated his man.

(198) He met Hitler privately and sought to persuade the aged Hindenburg to make Hitler Chancellor.

(199) All of Hindenburg's advisers were confident: Hitler would be kept in check by Vice Chancellor von Papen and other reliable conservatives in his cabinet.

(200) The old man yielded . . . he made Hitler Chancellor of Germany.

(201) The republic was dead in all but name . . .

The "intrigue" of lexia 194 recodes the idea that history is made outside, beneath, beyond the events and actions of public life, and connects, indirectly, the history of elite subjects to the elitism of the historian. The historian has the power to read the documents and monuments of actions not made clear as past doings; the historian can read an "intrigue" because even models of disintegration and death are not disengaged from history. "Intrigue" is a segment Todorov calls "extralinguistic," as it evokes both a "substance" and an "event," a signified and a proposition, a concept and temporality; the sememe is employed to support the notion of an event, but if fully analyzed as to its function within the story, it would result in an unraveling of historicity: was "intrigue" here the last of a *series* of "fates" or the effect of a systematic practice? (see Todorov 1974:115–127). The elimination of all but the internal states of the aristocratic von Papen (who is hypersubjectivized) and the attribution of control (Hitler to cancel and screen von Papen's power), or instances of von Papen's illusions, are rendered as a mode of knowledge—the repetition of von Papen's having guessed wrong too (see lexias 110–111).

Thus, no one had learned; and this is connoted as another sign of absence and lack, as predicative thought itself was not to be found in Germany in regard to the Nazis. The act of undervaluation and the inability to name, the collapse of associational thought and inability to think out, are signifiers of the aristocracy, a pure synecdochic illustration for the reader of the historian's assessment of this elite group. Underestimation definitely connotes the stupidity of the aristocracy, a stance that parallels the overestimation systematically attributed to Stresemann and the Democratic Party. The Nazis primarily then "enter the stage of history" through the implosion and exhaustion of thought, through the incapacity of thinking-then what was specific and unique to Nazism. For the reader, *the path to Hitler is historicized from the inside*—in advance, as it were—as the text manifests a disjunction between past ("aristocracy") and story-present (Nazis), an involuntary disclosure where the past could not know difference (its future) and present (Nazis) knew enough about the past (see lexias 87–93) to *take the moment*. It was the Nazi "sense of history" then which is semantically released as the crucial determination of the Nazi success.

The extreme distance from the reader's thoughts of the organization of this telling suggests that we should amend Barthes's comment that modern "historical discourse" shows an irreversible shift to "intelligibility" (modeling), which negates traditional narration because intelligibility is fundamentally incompatible with narrative-summary. Indeed, the form of historical narration may itself be a model of disintellectualism. Holloway has acutely isolated this narrative point of no return by suggesting that narrative is always accompanied by an internal threat of incoherence, especially when summary modes predominate.

A narrative organization which as it were remains always rebutted, always repudiated, always set at nought, by an organization in the work which both runs parallel to it, and is all pervasive and all-prominent, is a narrative organization which exists under something like a permanent disclaimer . . . either the narrative structure must find a place for that feature [all nonnarrative linguistic or signifying aspects] and enter into relation with it: or the structure of the whole must break down and the work cease to be a single narrative (1979:114–115).

The final act of summarizing asserts another sign form or device of annihilation (disintellection), a synthesizing displacement:

(202) . . . the victim of structural flaws,
(203) reluctant defenders,
(204) unscrupulous aristocrats and industrialists,
(205) a historic legacy of authoritarianism,
(206) a disastrous world situation
(207) and deliberate murder (p. 163).

This inventory has been narrativized—each lexia is itself result and conclusion—but there is no narrative order. This summary of the causal dimension, this attempt to prevent the discursive layer from warping under all that it has dragged along, is close, as summary, to a confirmation of Labov's (1972:366) insight that narratives prevent the reader from thinking "so what?" The inventory starting at lexia 202 says for a second time what was narrated the first time as story, so the reader is to consider again what was organized as story but shifted to the historiographic plateau. These points are, in order: (1) "Structural flaw" is a signification of monstrosity—in the fully socialized world, there are no structural flaws, only jams, contradictions, dilemmas of opposing forces. At best, a victim of a structural flaw could pertain to internal contradictions, but not to Weimar as it has been encoded. Not a single lexia manifested such a display of a structural flaw or victims. In other words, structural flaw belongs to the post of a narrator who has already made the past itself *illicitly* causal (see lexia 166). (2) "Reluctant defenders" operates the idea that those "in charge" and "responsible" were also *elsewhere* in their interests and desires. A subconnotation is the notion that a certain amount of their past(ness) precluded them from entering fully into the present of their own actions. (3) The morality evoked and engaged by "unscrupulous" is only pseudo. Who expected this segment to "play fair"? (4) "Historic legacy" is a piece of mysticism: what is "handed down in tradition" (Gadamer, 1975) is neither historic nor a legacy, for the simple reason(s) that in the forming of the acts of "handing," the "achieved past" (the already-had-happened which continues to happen) is always only present and so legacy falsely suggests the sense that "authoritarianism" was essentially a given (of German-ness). As Lyotard (1977:31–32) puts it, the narrator's encoding of past as a self-identity (internal historicism) is an act of overcoding, a "metanarrative" stance in which the reader is shifted to think in alignment with historians' assumptions. (5) A "disastrous world situation" is simultaneously excuse (the limiting condition, the objective ground, the constant) and a fake context, for it presupposes that the exception of Germany has already been established and so the result (one might say "impact") goes without saying. (6) Only "deliberate murder" (of Rathenau, for example) is topo-sensitive (it did happen), but here another issue is raised: Was "murder" causal (in any sense) since in the story the murders only added to the theory of absence and lack (of value, leadership, and sanity)? Is an "absent cause" capable of really signifying sense at all?

The displacements of this historical narration ought to lead one to reject those interpretations of history which argue that in the modern world we suffer from a "burden of history," a "surplus of the past," a "chaos of plenitude" (Hartman 1970:270). Such ideas deaden one to the cultural illusion of the transcendence of history. The organization of the telling, "code upon code," as Barthes put it, has systematically demolished even traditional liberal notions of "understanding" and "comprehension": thinking has been reduced to receiving the putative importance of the Weimar Republic, which could only "be" what "it was" because of its past, a metanarrative-condition which asserts that, always, story is legitimate because the past is already a story. The phenomenon of Nazism is not even allowed to "fascinate."

In addition, the "Nazi totality" as contained by this historical narrative can be disengaged from its telling and reengaged in the reader's mind as a sublimity of negative transcendence. It seems to me that the overcondensed narrative of the Weimar Republic testifies to both the intellectual grinding to a halt of causality (see chapter two) and its simultaneous replacement by primarily anti-intellectual devices—all the stagings where the nonnarrative leaks into the telling. Each point or place in the telling where the nonnarrative threatened to shatter its containment by narrative devices was met by the narrative-form's expansion of its capacity to subsume the nonnarrative. This expansion has nothing whatsoever to do with either the prefiguration of the text or the prefiguration of the audience by appeal to a plane of (poetic) forms which is transcendent to both (the structure of language according to White 1973:430). The anti-intellectual I have in mind is intrinsic to the contemporary academic aesthetic ideal that knowledge envelops, by reductive sign forms, the strange in devices that close discourse; the episode from lexia 194 through 201, for example, is an aestheticization of linearity *simpliciter* where the kind of knowledge evoked (political intrigue) is overtaken by the form of its presentation, the step-lock of completion and finality. Indeed, the links between narrativization and aestheticization are pervasive in liberal discourse, to the detriment of thinking. Arendt for example supported the liberal fusion of aesthetic form (telling) and politics where political life is said to be, at the outset, excluded from primary knowledge.

> culture and politics, then, belong together because it is not knowledge or truth which is at stake, but rather judgment and decision, the judicious exchange of opinion about the sphere of public life and the common world (1963:223).

The "judicious" is the *correctly made opinion* where the aesthetic, as the form of the signifier, blasts apart the conjunction of knowledge and truth in favor of knowing how to give closure to incompatibles. But for both the reader and the past agent "who knew (and know) not what" (about their respective present), the liberal telling of politics manifests a contempt for politics. Indeed, the narrator all along was distanced from Weimar and overvalued only that political formation that was already the most culturally aestheticized (lexias 34–39).

Negation occurs in the telling of the Weimar Republic, but coded in the modes of what was not there (absence of leadership) and the antistory of the "right." "Lack" replaces causality as a categorical structure, and this is a recoding of the contemporary academic context: with the academization of all signification processes, the bourgeois-liberal historian tries to occupy the territory of a nostalgia for the restoration of presence (see Baudrillard 1983*b*:72). Through the historical profession, the Weimar Republic has in fact been entered into the encyclopedia of modern liberalism as a "victim," and its imaginary status has bodied forth a symbolic law: leadership is the contest between tutelage and murder, where normal politics is thought to depend for its very existence on the balancing of thought and action. Left and right are alike in their being unbalanced. The summary narrative of the Weimar Republic conveys a vast and huge transformation—but the transformation pertains only to the "history effect(s)" of the act of telling itself: the pedagogical narrator has only recirculated a "meta-récit" of capitalist culture itself, the "universal," "common," "normal," horror at the elimination of those parts of value that had transcended Capitalist civilization (lexias 34–39, figure of Stresemann, the "hope" of Weimar). In this cultural division, the historical narrative is not only part of that "spectacle effect" which Debord (1977:155–156) believed was organized around the domination of present by past and whose predicates are "lack of subjectivity" and "false consciousness." Rather than this intransitive shape (which does not exist), the history of Weimar registers the circulation not of a usable past (use-value, need, natural narrative) but of a usable story whose ideological message is subservient to its preservation of cultural exchange (see Lyotard 1977:80), the preservation of narrative form alone, the ideology of form. Weimar = victim, summary = dictionary entry for a reader. End of thought.

For liberal historiography is not concerned with message, theme, motif, content, or even subject. All that has been liberated, made tellable, sooner or later. Unlike White, who postulates that one can criticize historians for the cultural attitude (psychologeme) of excessive forgiveness (their immoderation before the negative), one might better acknowledge their far more outrageous recreation of tutelary narration (the code), the perpetuation of the pair narrative-code and reader-follower, where to the latter pole is attributed the neurotic position of unintellection in reading the political aestheticization of the told. The reader no longer has even a chance to gain "contact" with the past (Dilthey); now, the reader is not even allowed to *think*. In this sense, disintellection, imaginary ideation, symbolic roles, and more are inscribed positions of liberalism, especially the annihilation of knowledge, accomplished by that which passes from this historical text to the reader: the *ability to date when one is* (and is not), itself a sign form of nonengaged thought. "A Short Political History of the Weimar Republic" did not even have to mention the signifier "history" (it did, in fact, mention historiography once) to achieve a "history effect," here the sense that history itself was already at work in the dissolution of the Weimar Republic, "working within," "inside," "internal" to the structure of its acts and relations. Thus while its signifiers arrange time, the history effect only strives to create a *place*, here the lack (fear of the loss/absence) of leaders.

White (1982:26–27) has suggested that narrativity of the "re-alistic" or liberal sort is an instance of a "narrativizing discourse [that] serves the purpose of moralizing judgments," where such judgment emerges from the desire to have "consummation" (clo-sure) of stories that are "open" enough ("withholds" all it can say, according to White) to form the basis of "more story." All of this has its origination in "wishes, daydreams, reveries." Now, what White has to say is interesting, but misleading. The aesthetic, on this view, is the form of the signified (moral), and it is *continuous* with a "deep" psychology. One passes from desire which is precoded as a transcendent writing ("reverie") to aes-thetic form (narrative) without a hitch, this because the basis of narrative ("desire") has already been defined as an aesthetic unconscious ("reveries"). The effect is to deny the intellectual capacity not to desire to think in an aesthetic mode in the first place. I am not intimating that logic, binarism, grammar, the sentence form, or propositions make up "thought." And that the form of such thought is more primary than the aesthetic. I am saying that until there is a cultural revolution on the forms of language, academic forms and programs can only aestheticize thinking, not theorize thinking as nonreactive. Bourgeois-academic writing is never and cannot be about anything other than its self-attempt to transcend itself as thought, in which the aesthetics of summary is but one shape of cultural transcendence.

Finally, the "Short Political History" manifests the historical in conformity with its model of signification, narrative summary. As there can be no history apart from the text(s) of its appear-ance—as an analytic of "temporality," or of the "subject," or of "death," cannot place one in contact with historical reason, the historical is one with its discourse about "lack." The story telling of a "Short Political History" is about the coming into existence of narrativized psychology as the summary form of the "real." In accordance with bourgeois norms which require the privilege of telling (the transcendence of know-how in favor of present know-this), the history of Weimar argues, inchoatively, that the subject does make a difference insofar as the "correct" subject is lacking in contexts of extremism. (But what are these? Seven holocausts in 1982 for those under five years of age.) The master code is organized as the political transformed into a psychological discourse, accomplished, again, as the historian's ideologizing while narrating. The told can be read then as the effacement of its own discursive system, its autonomy being that which equals the nonintellectualism of the reader.

This raises another general problem: can one speak of a "theory of history" without already narrativizing theory? In the next chapter I turn to a neo-leftist example within historiography: an instance of a "master historian" *narrating the Theory* of history, the reduction of Marxist theory to historical thinking.

4

Leftist Historical Narration: On the Academization of Class Conflict

The discourse of bourgeois society, organized by academics, saturates so-called public discourse and folds in on itself; a kind of negative cultural epiphany is achieved as referential discourse becomes, zone by zone, clogged by significations whose reference is their own exchange value. This is where the technicians of bourgeois culture then turn to a writing about writing, there salvaging aesthetic, form, value. No doubt most bourgeois writers, especially historians, still handle only what Barthes called a two-tier language, expression and referent, and in so doing, recirculate the inanity that language is not about its own valorization and functions (denial of the priority of the signifier and recoding). However, the elites of bourgeois-academic culture occupy a permanent threshold affecting language itself (which does not exist) in order to prevent the hemorrhage of signification. Basing itself directly on (at best) a model or (unhappily) a simulacrum of language, academia issues forth programs like de Man's where, after literature is shown to deconstruct itself by culminating in an "anxiety of ignorance," the new shape of aesthetic suspension (indecision of choosing between metaphor and metonymy), literature is still projected as showing "desire as a fundamental pattern of being that discards any possibility of satisfaction" (de Man 1979:19). Deconstruction can reaffirm the best old defeatist clichés, the satisfying ones. Some critics, without a whiff of analysis, currently tell us that we are in some "postmodernist" age, and the valorization of this turning point is hinged to a new function for the new(er) bourgeois-academic: one is now to practice an "oblique style," favoring the "parodic rather than the demagogic," because parody is best suited to the "academic revolution" (!), the recodification of the aesthetic treated as an "erotics of language" (see Ulmer 1983:544–589). Recall the quintessential function of bourgeois-academic treatments of language given by Vico: the "subliminal" form of language must be incessantly recreated by finding appropriate "condensed heroic expressions," which, released by writers like de Man and Ulmer, become signifiers of "anxiety," "erotics," "paradox." The existing linguistic relay system is confirmed even in hypernegative formulations, such as Adorno's dictum, "to write poetry after Auschwitz is barbaric." If "poetry after Auschwitz" is a sign of passing from the conflict of expression versus banality which shaped late nineteenth-century culture, as Adorno believed, when did prose assertion disengage itself from "poetic barbarity"? (See Adorno 1967:224–225.) When was Western prose not attached to all kinds of Auschwitzes (for example, the destruction of twenty-five million Meso-Americans)? Perhaps Auschwitz is a means and instrument for only more normalization of society and language, its "after" positively glowing in the promulgation of new "citations, references, stereotypes" of academic recoding (see Barthes 1977:168). Adorno's attempt to date the value of forms only provides for an expansion of academic moral critique, assuming as it does a slew of "appropriate" times when it was progressive and legitimate to "write poetry." Holocaust studies now blossom in academia.

Again, I assume, if I can, that "academia" is the physical embodiment of "cultural transcendence," the latter springing into existence as controlling, defensive, pseudo-rational, super-symbolic, quasi-logical, and paralytic thought. Despite the most critical intentions (and Adorno's surely were), bourgeois-academic writing must favor the discrimination of language as code (signifiers of boundaries, of acceptability, and legitimation); without this code, there is no stabilized "prose of the world" and hence no semblance of "culture" to be set off from pre, non, or post culture. In effect, bourgeois-academic culture only knows the strategy of replenishment of itself, and does so through signifiers of balance ("tension"), mystery ("forever old, forever new"), spanning "gaps," an endless rhetoricity and grammaticality geared to the proto-narrativity of every conceivable type of phenomenon. I have argued that on the historiographical plane, narrative meaning can exist only so long as a precoded and overcoded "longing" for datability is recoded in accordance with some unstatable discourse: all of society is used as little more than an excuse to rewrite history, so that the past is perpetually returned (recalled, made repeatable), not only as omnitemporal and quasi-universal but also, more disastrously, as a formal institutionalization of obligative-thought. Even recent criticisms of metanarrative forms (see LaCapra's essay, cited in chapter one, where he recognizes that the story of emancipation or truth has dissolved) project essentially academic aims. Carroll proposes a critical but academic cure to resolve the disjunction between formalism and history:

> a truly critical return to history must question itself in the same terms it uses to question the various formalisms it opposes itself to. That is, it must question itself as a particular series or narrative form as it situates and undermines the notion of form as a closed integral, autonomous and self-reflexive entity. . . . Rather than establishing a *ground*, a critical return to history will inevitably be forced to confront not an abyss, total absence or pure groundlessness . . . but the conflictual interpenetration of various series, contexts and grounds constituting any ground or process of grounding . . . an unending process that can never reach its destination (1983:66).

All history is to be reabsorbed by dialogue: thus academia need not undergo any transformation but a code switch. This reworking of Derrida's arguments is merely one of the new shapes of "academic replenishment" attached to what Virilio (1983:43–45) calls *dromomatics*—one gives up the authoritarian "right to tell" in favor of the more stringent "right to accelerate," which is nothing other than the "right to recode," the "right to unending," all of which presupposes the absolute *continuity* of the self-identical means (discourse, texts, all of their *prices*) of academia. "Academic modernization" can "move" toward an "unending process" only because it cannot possibly challenge ("question itself") the future which it already occupies. How could it do away with itself?

One can no longer separate writing/right. One way out might be the systematic application of a thorough neologism to all signifiers; but this too must fail, for in the historians' projected model reader, the ordinary educated public or the reader of identity exchange (reactive subjects), either the neologized text would be hieroglyphic or repetition-identity. In effect, the only resolution is for academia to go. Take every document owned by our universities and reproduce copies so that there is no control at the source. "Academic autonomy" is irrational (see Baudrillard 1975:148–151).

One of Marx's nonhistorical messages was about the hyperincongruity of money exchange (capital) and culture. This was formulated, interestingly, without any historicist bias, under a discussion of "Contradictions of Big Industry: Revolution." Marx had this to say:

> The more the division of labor develops and accumulation grows, the sharper are the forms that this process of differentiation assumes. Labor itself can only exist on the premise of this fragmentation.
>
> Thus two facts are here revealed. First, the productive forces appear as a world for themselves, quite independent of and divorced from the individuals, alongside the individuals: the reason for this is that the individuals, whose forces they are, exist split up and in opposition to one another, whilst, on the other hand, these forces are only real forces in the intercourse and association of these individuals . . . a totality of productive forces . . . are for the individuals no longer forces of the individual but of private property . . . Never . . . have the productive forces taken on a form so indifferent to the intercourse of individuals as individuals . . .

standing over against these productive forces . . . [are] abstract individuals . . . now . . . . individuals must appropriate
the existing totality of productive forces, not merely to achieve
self-activity, but, also, merely to safeguard their very existence
. . . there comes a stage when productive forces and means
of intercourse . . . only cause mischief, and are no longer
productive but destructive forces (machinery and money)
(1977:91–92).

Excepting Marx's tendency to narrativize what is a nontemporal
state ("never have," "now"), "abstract individuals" are those
subjects of society whose very cultural relations reproduce destructive "productive forces." "Cultural productive forces," like
academia, are not primarily a symptom (of "contradictions") or
the material for a "dialectical" opposition/contradiction; Marx
saw that "advanced culture" *is* the means of separation, the
means of alienation, insofar as "cultural" production too goes
its "own way" in the general political-economy of thought. According to Marx, the accumulation process itself, which is endlessly rearticulated around "differentiation" (separability) is
inclusive of both culture and economy, and is destructive in its
basic form, that is, one's subordination to what Marx calls the
"muck of ages," the present configuration(s) of overcoded practices. In this sense, those who labor in the zones and territories
of the university and argue for *any* mode of cultural synthesis
or cultural remodeling (for example, "re-reading" as a systematic
practice) or cultural resolutions of the noncultural, only encode
their own usage as somehow already a social value, and can do
so in the name of projecting some form of cultural transcendence. Any strong evaluation of the "destructive forces" leads
to the conclusion, which is only to say, with Mandel, that there
is now permanent cultural "overcapacity" among those who
monopolize languages and codes of value and destruction for
those subject to the hyperdifferentiation of capital versus labor
(see Mandel 1975:507, 574–576). Put another way, language is
another money, which means: its present material forms and
presences include all the "muck" of capitalism. Language has
equivalent functions to money forms like "discounted bills" (for
example, elimination of a connotation) or deflation (for example,

one conserves paradigmatic signs). The two series are different as signifiers, and in the content of the signified, but not in terms of function.

Marxist cultural thinking also perpetuates "destruction" in Marx's sense when it continues to idealize the so-called problematics of culture by projecting the pseudo-scientific form of a question onto culture, that "we" do not-yet know why or how or enough about all of the permutations of Western culture, so that one must still "discover" elementary contradictions, the people, the exploited, demonstrate the truth of the Other, instead of the viciousness of what-is. Instead of the poly-phonicism of Marx, simultaneously analyst, critic, theorist, scatologist, and so on, one finds, for example, Marcuseans out- transcendentalizing bourgeois writers, or art historians like Clark (1980:38) who "read" Manet's paintings as more ideological (uncritical) than Courbet, because Manet's strategies suffered from not being *finished sentences* (1980:39). Marxist-academics demand completeness from culture. One way of getting at this strange occupation of Leftist, whether Marxist or not, attempts to claim "culture and history" as zones of significance, which parallels their nonexposure of academic institutions, is to focus on the release of signifiers like the "sublime," the "paradoxical," the "dialectical."

Said (1983) protests what he labels the attitude of noninterference in everyday life, which he argues is regularly exchanged as the product of academia. Narrow technical language, self-policing, self-purifying communities characterize an academy which

> represent[s] humane marginality, which is also to preserve and if possible to conceal the hierarchy of powers that occupy the center, define the social terrain, and fix the limits of use functions, fields, marginality, and so on (Said 1983:155).

The antidote:

> a *dialectical* response from *critical consciousness* worthy of its name . . . there must be *interference*, crossing of borders and obstacles, a determined attempt to generalize exactly at those

points where generalizations seem impossible to make . . . breaking out of the *disciplinary ghettos* in which we, as intellectuals, have been confined, to *reopen* the blocked social processes . . . to *restore* the nonsequential energy of lived historical *memory* and subjectivity as fundamental components of meaning in representation . . . opening the culture to experiences of the Other which have remained "outside" the norms manufactured by "insiders" (Said 1983:157–158, italics added).

The exemplary means of the antidote: two "photo-montages" and one "study of early twentieth-century postcards and photographs of Algerian harem women," which, among other values, manifests a subject-author-subject triad, in the person of a "young Algerian sociologist" who "sees his own fragmented history in the pictures, then re-inscribes this history in his text . . . making that intimate experience intelligible for an audience of modern European readers" (Said 1983:159). Said validates, of course, another link: he calls for "connecting" such texts to "ongoing political and social praxis."

Let me rematerialize Said's signifiers and their combinations, in accordance with Baudrillard's demonstration of the ever-false glorification of "use value" over "exchange value," where the former is defended and, as it were, reappropriated from the negativity of exchange (see Baudrillard 1981:137–139). The "negative academy" binds "noninterference," "disciplinary ghettos," "concealment," and "hierarchy" as the presence of its own system of exchange: its intensive force is the product and function of "confinement"; the "negative academy" produces what does not matter to "outsiders," so that its products are really only "about" its own "exchange value." The "negative academy" drifts toward a tautological formation. Opposed to such a signified system are signifiers of "liberation": these are the antidote, and their progressiveness is hinged to the notions of "worthy," "crossing," "breaking out," "restore," and so on, whose center is the "restoration" of "lived historical memory," which is absent from the "negative academy's" representations. The signifiers of the "fullness" of the "negative academy" are in effect empty, while the signifiers of the "positive academy" are filled with the necessary and missing "representations." In effect, Said tries to shift from false exchange to genuine exchange, on the basis of "use value." But the signifiers of this "use value of the positive" also unravel: the "sociologist" and the "photo-montages," but especially the former, are encoded along the axis of the same tautology and identity rejected as part of the "negative academy." To invoke "his *own* fragmented history" some eighty years or so later means that *the object ("postcards") is not Other at all* but already inscribed in a systematic practice of reappropriation of "oneself," a "oneself" *contained* in both the "postcard object" and the academic audience who will benefit from its production. For if "modern European readers" are the audience of this positive "use value," this act of "opening," how do Algerians today benefit? Even to suggest that this sort of strategy is "connectable" at all to "ongoing political and social praxis" (in the West) is to presume that Western (subjects/academicians?) society is somehow significantly modified by such "texts" ("study/ photo-montages"). How can a text already encoded for Western intellectuals "interfere" if it is "intimate"? Which is precisely: how can the apparatus of "dialectic" and "restore" serve the trajectory of "critical consciousness" when it is devoted to "the recovery of a history either misrepresented or rendered invisible" (Said 1983:159), signifiers of pure positivity? The answer, in short, to the lack, the missing, the absences of the negative academy is a practice without any interruption at all of production, the latter entrenched as merely *re*-accumulated familiarity. Such is another "triumph" of present-now "reactive subjectivity," which "thinks within" a newly coded *expansion* of the Signifier.

Much of the melodramatic prose of contemporary Western Marxism is on the trapdoor to intellectual oblivion. Instead of furthering the fracturization of the signifier from the signified (the principle of heterogeneity without identity) and thus *not at all privileging any form of the signifier* (gestural, verbal, cognitive), which involves a demonstration that even "negativity" is another kind of "identity," Western Marxists recoil. Horkheimer, who certainly forced criticism out of bourgeois norms by stressing its "totalism" and "impracticality," nevertheless aborted his own program by also asserting that certain pieces of "idealism" had to be dragged along; "art" has "preserved" the "utopian," one must accept accumulation(s) of "the sciences and in historical experience," a position that postpones what to do with academic privileges and discriminations (see Horkheimer 1972: 226–227, 275). With Western Marxism as a whole, Horkheimer assumed that the cultural future must already conform to some configuration of the past. The projection here is that the "highest of high" cultural artifacts and relations are capable, in some unspecified way, of distancing the subject from (1) destruction that differentiates, the recoding of "use value to the nth power" where, for the subject, as Deleuze points out, consciousness of contradictions is no longer progressive, and (2) undifferentiated destruction where, for example, violence unleashed in one uncoding ("Love Canal") is simultaneous, for those involved as victims, with consequences of a generalized decoding, such as loss of employment and intellectual disequilibrium (see Deleuze and Guattari 1977:247–248). Insistence on such "distancing" is tantamount to acceptance, deferral, postponement, the glorification of the not-yet, the fantasy that reconjunction of the economic-cultural has its own proper time. Habermas, for example, in grappling with modernist "communicational" theories, overcodes "distance" *within* normative theory by stressing the "ideal condition" that an emancipated culture must be one of understanding, not criticism. What Kristeva called "syntactic irregularities," meanings not motivated by "communication" but which instead are "transversal to the logico-symbolic processes that function in the predicative synthesis" are simply unformalizable for Habermas, and so incapable of providing "positive" criterion for "real" understanding (see Habermas 1979: 3–5, 35; Kristeva 1975:50–51). Western Marxism seems to accept academic institutionalization: it is not going to defamiliarize radically its own relations to the academy.

Within cultural leftism, but mainly Marxist, the economic has been replaced, no longer exposed, just as "scientific Marxism" has been dispatched with the positivism that engendered it. According to Jameson, "dialectic" now must make up the internal code of cultural criticism, as both "science and criticism" must yield to the "vocation" of the "dialectic," whose goal lies in the

transcendence . . . toward some collective logic . . . the anticipation of the logic of a collectivity which has not yet come into being (1981:286).

This overcodes literature as the most dialecticized imaginable object of cultural criticism. Dialectics is no mere logico-semantic apparatus capable of rendering the social world more knowable, for this kind of culturism severs dialectic from technique, from instrumental action. Since scientific Marxism has failed— though, let it be added, in (Western) societies which have never collectively decided on science—the Marxist literary critic is now supposed to (1) synthesize the utopian moment of all class thought (its "desire"), and then (2) intellectualize and appropriate the "collective energies" of meaning from the oppressed (see Jameson 1981:286, 296). As Buñuel showed in film that workers' dreams are bourgeois, so Marxism argues that the positive unconscious of the oppressed is socialist. A "mere" demonstration of the repetitions of unpaid labor, surplus-value, super-profits, and the rest of the "only economic" is not enough for a "dialectics" which here leads to another "beyond" ("Marxism as desire"). Indeed, Jameson tries to salvage a philosophical but not an anticapitalist Marxism by organizing literary criticism within the academy as the Final Voice of significance. Here is academic Marxism severed from criticism while it aims at providing access to transcendence:

. . . only Marxism offers a philosophically coherent and ideologically compelling resolution to the dilemmas of historicism. . . . Only Marxism can give us an adequate account of the essential *mystery* of the cultural past, which, like Tiresias drinking the blood, is momentarily returned to life and warmth and allowed once more to speak, and to deliver its long forgotten message in surroundings utterly alien to it. This mystery can be reenacted only if the human adventure

> is one. . . . These matters can recover their original urgency
> for us only if they are retold within the unity of a single great
> collective story . . . for Marxism, the collective struggle to
> wrest a realm of Freedom from a realm of Necessity; only if
> they are grasped as vital episodes in a single vast unfinished
> plot (Jameson 1981:19–20).

The concoction here is equivalent to its codings and hierarchies:
(1) all of the problematics of history are given closure by Marxism, the latter equated with cultural surplus and re-accumulation
("re-solution"); (2) Marxism is psychologized and theologized
into a ritualistic code: the "reenacted mystery"; (3) the narrative
code proper is lodged in the semes of the identity of temporality,
the "one human adventure," which grants narrative a hierarchical, metaphysical, and integrational power against other
thought systems; (4) the "recovery" of "original urgency" unleashes another psychological code, some unstated presumed
need in present-now; (5) the cultural effect is that of Marxism
as a repository, which overlaps with the acceptance of both
"academy" and "book" as the institutionalization of restored
identity (to the "past mysteries") and confirmed identity (subjects
in present-now *receive* identity). School = Totality. Star-Trek
Marxism.

Adorno (1973:33) gives a particularly gnomic and mystical
codification of the "dialectical" replacement of "scientific" Marxism. Even in the "closest contact with objects," he writes,
"dialectics" evades contamination; that is, dialectics is not concerned with acts and action, what Adorno calls "movement itself," but only with how "a movement begins and ends."
Dialectics is precoded as a distance from acts, this to restore the
"speculative moment" of thinking:

> In the unreconciled condition, nonidentity is experienced as
> negativity. From the negative, the subject withdraws to itself
> and the abundance of its ways to react. Critical self-reflection
> alone will keep it from a constriction of this abundance, from
> building walls between itself and the object. . . . The un-

regimented thought has an elective affinity to dialectics, which as criticism of the system recalls what would be outside the system (Adorno 1973:31).

"Nonidentity" can only be "negativity" on the condition that "identity" is "positive," a proposition boggling in its implications; Adorno's celebration of "withdrawal" and "to react" encodes the salvageable "subject" in "distance and passivity," in a thickness ("abundance") and special moment. The isolated and reactive subject is crystallized insofar as its result, a thought-product, has achieved "unregimentation," further subcoded as the ultimate passivity, "recall," the latter merely a signifier of what has already transcended (has-been). Adorno bathes the reader in an imaginary code of distance, which is really only destruction of critical writing, just as Jameson does; the latter does so through future redemption, the former through connotations of awe before the past. Let me add that both kinds of distance are also distanced from another series of time, the approximately one thousand hours of unpaid labor extracted from the average subject of manufacturing in one year's time. Distance is not just past and futural, but also *simultaneous* with its different formations. Academic Marxism, like Capital, is, to use Deleuze's phrase, "continually behind or ahead" of itself, but never out of synch with attempts to either resuscitate or long for value (Deleuze and Guattari 1977:259–260).

In what follows, I propose to analyze Edward Thompson's essay, "The Poverty of Theory: Or an Orrery of Errors" (1978), as to its relations of signifiers and the concomitant imaginary system of historical culture which it generates. As before, I am interested in what can be called textual pragmatics, provided that this is understood to include emphasis on those paralyzing, stabilizing, and immobilizing cognitions that operate for the reader as part of preconscious and thoroughly overinvested ideations that recode "history" as another machine of subjugation (Deleuze and Guattari 1977:364–365). Before turning to analysis of Thompson's text, however, I want to reintroduce certain Nietzscheist notions concerning the naturalization/transcendence axis without which, I believe, academic culture would fall apart.

Analyzing Thompson's work via Nietzschean critical frames shows, I think, the proof that gives the lie to leftist illusions of the basis of "cultural memory." Here it is a question of the intersection of moral signs with the immanence/transcendence system, where academic leftism encodes its relations with contemporary society as *continuous* with the preservation of past moral achievements, and so is only able to critique this society by focusing on and multiplying its lack of complete morality, its unfulfilled history. I have in mind, for example, the formulation by the Tillys at the end of their *Rebellious Century*, where a mélange of forgiveness, "historicity," traces of regret, and more are brought to bear in a constellation that strikes me as illustrative of the dead end of academic Marxism and conjures the great Nietzschean endeavor to collapse all planes of transcendence.

> In this day, when bigness and nationalism are such evident curses, it is easy to side with the localists. . . . Wouldn't it be a better world if they had all lost decisively? Better still if they had never come? Of that, we are not confident. Like Marx, we think a parochial world is a stifling world. Like Marx, we think that the logic of some form of world economy organized around industrial production and large capital accumulations was already in motion before the nineteenth century. Like Marx, *we think that the world knit together in the wrong way but that it had to knit together* (Tilly 1975:299, italics added).

The moral seriousness of this passage generates a narrativized hierarchy: academic Marxism takes the hard road, for after the necessary affirmation of the idea that it would have been better if such "curses" did not happen, one is plunged completely into a massive apophasis; *if* such curses had not occurred, there would have resulted, automatically, a parochial world. So the curses are given, implicitly, less stifling a function and purpose than any other historical telos (with the possible subconnotation of the stimulating effects of such curses). The historicist code pushes back in time to before the nineteenth century, the effect of which is merely to lengthen and complicate "industry" and "accumulation," which are returned to the reader completely mystified: to say that it had "to knit" but did so in the "wrong way" is to assume the combination of an "erroneous must," an "obligatory negative," but also a full and total identity—even the wrong is necessary, full, absolute, the basis for one's moral stance. Recall that "history is what hurts," according to Jameson, which elevates as far as possible the academic Marxist attitude of history as a moral phenomenon. For the Tillys, "history = suffering"; the moral: acknowledge this. Such is cultural madness, what Nietzsche called "a dark invisible burden" which deprives one of the chance to forget culture and by that route subdue the myth of the necessity of the past.

Writing, according to Nietzsche, is yet another instrument one can put to service in the name of becoming "master of reality in a shrewd manner." Thompson's text, for example, is written in the name of the "exploited" as their "moral voice." To do this, the "Poverty of theory" stabilizes the post of a historical and cultural observer—the historian's overview of things—and encodes the historian in yet another angle of transcendent perspective, whose voice then, somehow, synthesizes and directs, summarizes and leads us to cultural necessities. For Nietzsche, the ability to shift between all such transcendent angles, which are embedded in perception, in the unconscious, in the preconscious, in normalized and stable thought, belonged to the Platonic simulacrum of immortality: one writes so that the writing lasts, a sure sign that weak, passive, defensive, already obliterated thoughts are captured in their "fatigue" of "flight" (Nietzsche 1954:611). Moral signs here belong to the no-worldscape of one's not yet being tired of "old tongues," the acceptance of "worn-out shoes," which, despite a positivistic echo, are marks of those with a "conscience in their ears," so short-circuited in their thoughts that thought has itself been dematerialized, where the period of a sentence is digested by the mind bereft of its "physiological breath" (1954:560).

"Written and painted thoughts! Not long ago you were so variegated, young and malicious, so full of thorns and secret

> spices, that you made me sneeze and laugh—and now? . . .
> some of you, I fear, are ready to become truths, so immortal
> do they look, so pathetically honest, so tedious! And was it
> ever otherwise? (Nietzsche 1954:611).

Moral discourse, the discourse of "flags," is linked to semantically "full" but cognitively "empty" imaginary ideas, where in
a society racked by "ideals," the dominant classes recodify their
control around "figures and likenesses," the "inexhaustibility"
of "evasion," ensuring for themselves the role of

> executors of older and higher orders (of predecessors, of the
> constitution, of justice, of the law, or of God himself), or they
> even justify themselves by maxims from the current opinions
> of the herd, as "first servants of their people," or "instruments
> of the public weal" (Nietzsche 1954:489).

In all periods, the ruling forces of academia aim at turning cognition away from an interest in mastery and utility, which are
the sensuous core of strong thought, for by such thought, there
is no longer the "sunshine of a good name" or any device of a
"reflecting mirror," but rather the least expenditure of reactive
and "defensive energy" (see *Ecce Homo*, sec. 8). Supported by
the conjunction of sterile logic, psychological reduction and morality, the forces of reactive thinking take refuge, where to understand is defocused and severed from its capacity to upset
and overturn the discourses of justification and conviction, so
that the refocused subject is held in check by the relay of the
inertia of language. As expressed in the *Will to Power*, what
enables the phenomenal forms of "legitimate" expression to take
hold is the subject's dizzying connections to modes of neutrality:

> we seek the reason for a thought before we are conscious of
> it; and the reason enters consciousness first; and then its
> consequence . . . we are conscious of a condition only when
> the supposed causal chain associated with it has entered con-
> sciousness (1968: sec. 479).

The priority of thought decimated by such reason means that reason neutralizes the "enigma of the stimulus," the "this-ness" or "is-ness" of X; but reason can perform this operation on each and every X ("thought") because the very strength of the "passivity of reason" is attached to forces of neutralization; "executors" is related to "executive" and "execute," functions where reason annihilates the rush, the irruption, the multiplicity of names, for reason is surrounded and carried along by the apparatus of a dead language.

> The whole of "inner experience" rests upon the fact that a cause for an excitement of the nerve centers is sought and imagined—and that only a cause thus discovered enters consciousness: this cause in no way corresponds to the real cause—it is a groping on the basis of previous inner experiences, i.e. of memory. But memory also maintains the habit of the old interpretations, i.e. of erroneous causality—so that the "inner experience" has to contain within it the consequences of all previous false causal fictions. . . . "Inner experience" enters our consciousness only after it has found a language the individual understands—i.e. a translation of a condition into conditions familiar to him—; "to understand" means merely: to be about to express something new in the language of something old and familiar (Nietzsche 1968: 265–266).

"Excitement" becomes: "cause," as there is already "memory," the synthesis of all past "causes," the repetition that enables repeating to reoccur; what accumulates is then a "surplus of causes" by comparison to the remainder allowed each and every "excitement"; and all of this happens whenever language (coded signs) outlives, through academic requirements, each and every one of its own utterances.

Consciousness is protected and distanced from its own "experiences" by the language and involuntary memory that it is; acceptable moral language is precisely transcendent to "moral experience" because moral subjects have also produced their own discourse and forms of evaluation (see 1968:119–122, Nietzsche's list of "moral recipes") which, as "passive understanding," can be activated at the merest trace of an "experience" that goes against the social. For example: before it is a piece of "cultural endowment," the signifier "fulfillment" must be detached from "body-now," as its basis, and joined to a temporal marking such as "later," where "later" has already been connoted as postponement; "fulfillment" can be a signifier one "understands" as "postponement" only because the effort involved in thinking through its sense, its value for exchange, does not have to encounter the shorn-off traces of a fulfillment which is not a "postponement." Moral discourse is a "tool of civilization" wherein the strength of moral terms is in direct proportion to their fusion of distinctive sense experiences, which are killed off by the homogenization of language instruction (see Nietzsche 1968: sec. 506).

As Lowith (1964b:193–197) points out, Nietzsche was able to decipher only the remnants of a "corporeal humanity" over and against the "educated philistinism" of the then current elites. Nietzsche saw that linguistico-cognitive experience, as a "passive force" of language, had resulted in significations through which "transcendence" became one of the elementary codes of victims; the thought content of sememes like "fulfillment" or "genuine" serve as the cultural a priori forms of cultural paradigms where subjects are presented with given sites of passivity and domestication: such significations ensured, precisely because materialized, that one can be enslaved to one's own thoughts, for each sign is a mnemonic, an organization of "sameness." "Empty transcendence," for example, the belief *in* culture, *in* the state, is aided by the security of the linguistic relay. Abbreviation *(Abkurzen)*, for example, is crucial in supporting the exchange value of signs. When a "leftist" critic (Lasch 1982:32) calls for the "left" as a whole to embrace the contemporary issues raised by the political "right" (personal relations, the problem of narcissism, the lack of inter-generational ties), where the "left" is awarded the function of "taking back" such issues and of making them "recognizable," the "left" is enlarged. "Taking back," however, is an abbreviation of the left's expansion, presenting its agenda as a consensus, that such problems are relevant to political action. Abbreviated thought intersects with the series of condensation and re-territorialization, with the aim of closing and terminating analysis, in the name of a semic nucleus which is idealized yet censoring. "Take back" gives, as Nietzsche put it, "security, for quick understanding, on the basis of signs and sounds," but does so by witholding from thought its codedness (for example, its symmetry with the "right"). Abbreviation is aligned with highly dramatized signs favored by speakers who wish to enlarge their field of significations and, through appropriation, create need and interest: "take back" is attached to the cultural atrophy of its conceptual implications (take back = to disclose, to render whole, to solve) as well as to "idle talk," which spreads the concept so thin it can only vaporize when thought out.

In the case of abbreviation, encoding is withdrawn so that the absolute positivity of a value occupies the whole of thought. In the case of synthesis or synthetic signs, transcendence acquires the shape of something closer to a kind of sign hypnosis. A well-stocked conjugated memory required for deference to cultural universals demands summarized thought. Here folded into every social group, thought finds itself overwhelmed by irrelevant and outmoded significations as opposed to the programs conveyed by abbreviation. "Limit," "nonidentity" (the new identity), "dysfunction," or Adorno's avowal that "subjectively liberated experience and metaphysical experience converge in humanity" (1973:397) can be used as supersigns to ensure that one is never bereft of significations of abstraction, simplicity, and possession (Nietzsche 1968: sec. 503). The support of all such synthesis is cultural memory which makes serene every cognition that stumbles across its path. The "silence" of memory "thinks" according to the trajectory of reduction, assimilation, and identity, eliminating the hyperintensity of an experience; such memory is another form of repetition, of deadening (Nietzsche 1968:289). For example, in the act of periodization, comparing each side of a temporal break relies upon memory so as to evade the strong consciousness of severing itself from repetitious thoughts: a proletariat that saved and could integrate itself by property acquisition must passively re-member such a state(ment) in order to stop itself from the thought that even integration made no vital difference in its life. When periodization is reduced to the concrete promulgation of dates that are supposed to create a difference, passive serenity is usually nearby to lead one to anticipate, to long for, to desire dramas entirely removed from consideration of the *means* of action. To periodize = place of satisfaction, insofar as cultural memory is itself turned into a means of cultural performance.

As we shall see, academic-left writing, in its reliance upon such passive forms of the signifier, recreates in its audience (readers) an identity with the objects of its discourse, past vic-tims; by engendering sympathy with the past, it fosters a sense of relaxation *(Spannungsabnahme)*. One can be as animated as one likes about that which makes no difference; that is, one can write about past victims of every imaginable process but the writing only really connects with its cultural functions, notably the sub-ject's ability to blink before the transcendent (history). The left wants to see life clearly, to become that "sensorium that receives a thousand impressions," a "dead fabric of words and ideas," a subject "cogital" (Nietzsche 1957:70–72). In unscientific Marx-ism, authentic and valid knowledge is often falsely modeled on the image of thought as absolute distance from action; as one epigone of Critical Theory has characterized the "heritage" and tradition of Western Marxism, "the dialectic trick is to keep everything in view," which, no doubt, means that thought is not allowed not to stop looking (which is not even thought). The dissipation of thought is the consequence (see Jacoby 1981:126). Said, Jameson, Adorno, and others, despite their re-spective differences, sanctify cultural distance, for their dis-course maintains distance from the regimes of differentiation which eviscerate Marxism. In short, the strategies of these ac-ademic-leftists are not separable from bourgeois-academic ones; both are code systems centered on preventing an "ethnological reduction" of the West, which could be carried out by a critique of what Baudrillard (1975:115) calls the "final privilege" of this culture, its incessant (atemporal function) recoding of the discourses of conjunction. In Nietzsche's terms, "moral" and "historical" codes overlap in Western Marxism where, through education, instruction, and learning, the culture is amortized to a language of "more historical powers:"

> one that studies history for the purpose of recognizing the foolish kind of egotism [that which does not recognize and internalize its own limits]. Their study has taught them that the state has a special mission in all future egoistic systems; it will be the patron of all the clever egoisms, to protect them. . . . For men know well that a grain of historical culture is able to break down the rough, blind instincts and desires, or to turn them to the service of a clever egoism (1957:63).

We must now turn to the "history" signifier as it is textually organized. Methodologically, it should be recalled that a signifier is already a relation; the simplest joining of any two signifiers is already a turnstile of meaning. In the reading of Gay's "Political History," the "history" signifier led its model reader through device after device so as to arrive at a version of historical culture where the story of Weimar was constructed as the lack of the necessary sort of political leadership and the negative transcendence of history understood as the presence/absence of historicity in the various subjectivities and actants of Weimar. Marxism, however, effects a shift to an altogether different level—to the domain of philosophy, process, and concept, which is nothing else than an attempt to locate and stabilize *history as irreducible to story*. This history is a signified—"ground," "basis," "determinant"—and has been rewritten (versioned, one might say) in so many different forms that it is impossible here to summarize them all. But the basic textual-philosophical function of history as signified—to guarantee the legitimacy of *any* story— has received exemplary articulation in Habermas's following characterization:

> With each new evolutionary problem situation, there arises new scarcities, scarcities of technically feasible power, polit-

ically established security, economically produced value, and culturally supplied meaning; *and thus new historical needs come to the fore* (1979:166, italics added).

Philosophically, Habermas calls forth the dimension of learning in order to rationalize the traumas of the "productive forces," which have forced the species to evolve as a cognitive subject (1979:170–177) and so are, as capitalist modes, necessary. Habermas raises the ante against liberal historiography: for there *not* "to be history" (as signified), there would also have to not be "learning," and as this is unthinkable, "history" can be retained as a systemic "criterion of plausibility," a necessary form of all possible thought.

Now for the left, in general, the attempt to project this necessary transcendence—as productive forces, "learning," the rule of law, or class conflict—through histories of such a signified, is something more than simply providing the grounds for the narratability of recorded and documented existents; it is also an attempt to evade and displace any other discourse that argues that history cannot provide intellectual motivation. Left historiography has yet to acknowledge that every actual historical narration in fact cannot show history to be signified, on the intellectual grounds that every historical narrative amounts to its devices (codings) through which history as signified is thrown and projected, inscribed and located, in the imaginary consciousness of a reader. The symmetry between part (a narration) and whole (history as signified) is indefensible. If no actual historical narration can equal history as signified, then history as signified has to be abandoned as a ground or condition. With Habermas (and Thompson), one is confronted by the spectacle of a defense of "theory of history"—a model of the whole— which aims at placing history in the role of some inner dynamic, which then governs the adequacy and appropriateness of a particular historical narrative. Acceptance and belief in such a signified history is tantamount to a macro-narratological ideal post of sending knowledge, another conceptual "unconditioned authority" as Nietzsche put it, with which one then can stop thinking about means (of revolution, of flight, of disturbance, disruption, and so on). We must now examine the massive defensiveness of Thompson's attempt to protect "narrative history" from being reduced to the level of a *story of theory*. Again, where bourgeois historical narrative cannot narrate without presenting negative lessons, leftist historiography aims at producing positive instructions, a way out of cultural impasse.

Thompson is currently regarded as one of the world's leading historians. His *Making of the English Working Class* (1963) is a modern masterpiece, if only because it is one of the most cited works in the postwar historicization of Marxist theory. The significance of his current position is such that he writes both as a historian who has enriched historiographical organization (especially the narration of casualties of history) and as an oracular figure, thus crossing the threshold between rigorous empirical research and political activities. The cultural voices of the moralist, the defender of historical reason, and the political figure are combined in his book-length essay, *The Poverty of Theory*, in which he has tried to establish a narrative program for rational, responsible, civilizing, necessary, and transcendent thought. I shall start with the significations—the materialized concepts—by means of which Thompson encodes what the debate with Althusser is actually about, that is, with the semantics of this rejection of theoretical Marxism, how it is put together. As before, on the plane of culture, neither form nor content is as interesting by comparison to what Hjelmslev (1969:75–77) called the "cleaving" of meaning out of the "nonlinguistic stuff," the "purport," the "amorphous substance" so that the signifier does not waver in relation to a "meaning" base.

> (1) As a mature practice "historical materialism" is perhaps the strongest discipline deriving from the Marxist tradition.

Of all the possible signifiers that could convey the senses of "historical materialism," the reader is placed before these signifieds: (1) the framing code is narrative itself but coupled with a variant of historicism, because "mature practice" is presented as a state of achievement, as already firmly established; (2) "mature" means "completed development," a temporal presupposition, and "continuous use" is the connotation, so that (3) subcoded is the sense of "historical materialism" as itself a historical result, and this yields (4) an implicit decoding vis-à-vis "strongest discipline," through which the latter concept is severed from other sememic values, for example, "revolution." The reader is subjected to (1) the narrative code at the outset, (2) a fact ("mature"), and (3) the inconceivability that "historical materialism" could be thoroughly embedded in another, entirely contrary, system (for example, ideology, a mistake, or revolutionary activity).

> (2) This is not to say that this knowledge is finite or subject to some "proof" of positivistic scientism.

If pursued, lexia 2 could (or would) encounter its limiting sense in "strongest discipline": a "discipline" precisely defines propositions, theories, and rules of evidence so as to exclude non-knowledge and error; but as lexia 2 raises the specter of an infinite knowledge and excludes positivistic proof, there is promised not a "mature practice" or a "discipline" but an entity closer to what Foucault calls a "discursive formation," in which statements, theorems, and hypotheses "multiply and disperse" the very field of their discourse. "Historical materialism" has no future-close, no end. Thus based on a narrativized history (lexia 1), it is not subject to subsequent narrative treatment, that is, it cannot be reengaged by another telling (through another discourse). That lexia 2 qualifies the sense of a "history already achieved" as still unfulfilled announces the transcendence of this (possibly) infinite knowledge; and since such infinity is raised, we shall have to watch carefully for its later textual realizations, how one is to think out what has been achieved and its relations to a critical Marxism.

> (3) . . . one had supposed these to be advances in knowledge.
> (4) . . . And the Marxist historiography which now has an international presence has contributed significantly not

only to its own self-criticism and maturation . . . but also to imposing . . . its presence upon orthodox historiography: imposing its own—or Marx's—"problematic" upon significant areas of historical inquiry.

Lexias 3 and 4 announce respectively the accumulation and extension of "historical materialism." Its becoming more of what it was (mature, scientific, valid, and institutional), however, is interrupted by a story switch where its steady state of accumulation is threatened:

(5) . . . we have been suddenly struck from the rear . . . not "bourgeois ideology" . . . but from a rear claiming to be more Marxist than Marx. From the quarter of Louis Althusser . . .

Now it is certainly an overcoded piece of psychologism to say "struck from the rear" (it raises a number of possible contexts, such as the politics of betrayal), and these signifiers, in turn, intensify:

(6) The project to which many lifetimes, in successive generations, have been given
(7) is thus exposed as an illusion . . .

and this calls forth accusations that Althusserian Marxism is a "freak" (p. 195) of the "lumpen intelligentsia," that its practitioners are "diversionists," "amateurish," full of "imaginary revolutionary psycho-dramas." The voice of denunciation "speaks" directly from a psychological mode to refute Althusser's "challenge" to "historical materialism itself," and the zenith of this psychology sets the tone of Thompson's "refutation":

(8) What is being threatened . . . is the *entire tradition of substantive* Marxist historical and political analysis, and its accumulating (if provisional) knowledge (p. 197, italics added).

By the end of lexia 8 it should be clear that the object side, if there was one, the place of Althusser's theories within the European Left, their intellectual/cognitive value, is but a pretext (literally) for a discourse on the positivity of "Marxist historical materialism." The reader is hence located near what earlier our sketch of Nietzsche isolated as that imaginary field of dramatized signs, riveted to their formation in abbreviating synthesis (here recoded as the "promise" to disarm the threat of lexia 8 and labor for the "infinite" of lexia 6). In Barthes's terms, the real cultural issue is intellectual authority, power, and the invocation of axiological writing

in which the distance which usually separates fact from value disappears within the very space of the word, which is given at once as description and as judgment,

where

writing is univocal, because it is meant to maintain the cohesion of a Nature (1967a:20–23).

To which can be added: because Thompson employs a grandiloquent discourse ("the project to which many lifetimes"), the obverse of intellectual deconstruction (where signifiers resonate with thinking through), his "elocutio" can only be a signifier of its own form, what lexia 8 raises. Tradition is embedded in axiology, a preintellectual formation, and as it tries to suture accumulation and mind, it aims at an audience presumed to share the desire for "normal Marxism."

I shall not make any sort of judgment about the issues that separate Thompson and Althusser except to say that to provoke the most acclaimed current new-left historian to write a "defense of reason itself" (p. 196) makes Althusser's texts invaluable as a means of sorting out the intellectual claims between signifiers of critique and those of defense, the signifiers of both understood neither as allegorical figures of possible thought forms nor as marking a distance between philosophy and narrative; rather, both types of signifiers pertain to sign forms, whether one wants to think without salvaging the detritus of the past and retarding institutions (Althusser's position) or whether one wants to start with projected cultural ideals, the signified, as it is released from criticism (Thompson). By starting with the signified, one inevitably is driven to privilege the fantasy that one is "inside the Real," instead of recognizing that one arrived at the signified through a cultural code riveted to institutions and reproduction of culture.

(9) . . . I begin to find terms for my objection.
(10) . . . evidence does not stand compliantly like a table for interrogation:
(11) it stirs, in the medium of time, before our eyes.
(12) These stirrings, these events . . . seem often to impinge upon, thrust into, break against, existent social consciousness.
(13) They propose new problems, and above all, they continually give rise to *experience*
(14) . . . the mental and emotional response . . . to . . . events (p. 199).

The series beginning with lexia 9 is directed against Althusser's argument that empiricism, belief in the autonomy of the referent, is always borne along by its interpretant, so that the referent is semiotically sutured to the Other, which is simply a signifier's mode of insertion in the signified, where it is instantly given some cognitive value (the relation of "standing for"). Opposed to such intellectualism ("idealism"), Thompson believes he has found "terms" for the autonomy of the empirical-referent of historians: (1) "evidence" is severed from any image or framing of it as a "state" (it is not inert, immobile, a mere document); this, of course, rejects the infamous image of "raw data," its isolation from action, but (2) as "stirrings" and "events," there is no longer evidence—"evidence" evaporates (lexia 11) into "stirrings," so their heterogeneity fades as the latter completely outstrips the former; (3) by lexia 13, one cannot tell if "experience" is the referent of "evidence" or if "evidence" is an experience (for the historian as well as the sense given in lexia 14).

One could call all this a case of reification, but in fact there is a precise coding at work: the speaker (or speaking) presupposes that the historian's initial contact with the real occurs with something animate, and not at all with traces, remnants, and pieces; at the outset, the historian is empowered as occupying an intellectual starting point that emphasizes the inseparability of historical discourse from the things discoursed about. The category of nondisengagement is here recoded as part of the plateau of research itself. Imported into the evidence is the hypothesis of a "theory of life," so understated that it is difficult to discern its Crocean echo.

> (15) Experience arises spontaneously within social being,
> (16) but it does not arise without thought;
> (17) it arises because men and women are rational, and they think about what is happening . . .
> (18) . . . changes take place within social being, which give rise to changed *experience:* and this experience is *determining*
> (19) . . . it exerts pressures upon existent social consciousness, proposes new questions . . . (Thompson's italics)

"Experience" is thus encoded as a nonsemiotic entity—it is uncoded, which manifests the category of the unnameable—and it has a presemiotic signification: on the one hand, as "experience" has this sense of *uncodedness* ("spontaneously"), it provides the historian with something given; on the other hand, models of "experience" are controlled from the inside, as it were, by the predicate contained within this experience—"thought" ("think about") is the "first moment" of "experience." "Determination" takes place after "spontaneity" and "thought" have performed their appropriate functions. Thus, without even raising the topic, predicates of the subject are at once presumed and narrativized (lexia 19). The form of this is set up by what one may call narrativized assertions : a theorized imagination of story makes a beginning of experience, and then, in chronological and linear fashion, "thought experience" generates social being ("results," "pressures"). Indeed, "experience walks in without knocking at the door . . . people starve: their survivors think in new ways" (p. 201), which is another blow for reactive thinking. Metz (1974:238–251) isolated the manufacture of cultural myths when the plausible, drawn from what has already been said (thought, and so on), bases itself upon what is privileged as a first-order system ("experience"), and is thus real to some audience on account of its capacity to reiterate: to say that "people starve" and then "survivors think in new ways" officiates the historiographic claim that it is plausible to begin with a theory of narrative believed to be identical with rational thinking. Narrativized assertion "asserts," as it were, the absoluteness of telling and, thereby, banishes exactly what *is* thought in such asserting (for example, lexia 17 is a semantic misnaming of "rational" for "practical").

The historian thus rejects Althusser's argument that the knowledges of the social and human sciences have no actual cultural starting point other than their attempt, at best, to differentiate between possible means of accessibility to information, their semantic and philosophical organization of what they are "about" (see Foucault's *Archeology of Knowledge* for a full statement of this issue). The historian wants to ensure that "data" are epistemically outside language, released from theory but yet proximate to discourse (a model of domesticated data):

(20) It is untrue that the evidence or "facts" . . . always arrive . . . in an ideological form.
(21) . . . There are extremely elaborate procedures . . . to ensure that they do not.
(22) It is central to every other applied discipline (in the "social sciences" and "humanities") that similar procedures are elaborated . . .
(22) The difference between a mature intellectual discipline and a merely ideological formation lies exactly
(23) *in these procedures and controls.*
(24) If the object of knowledge consisted only in "ideological facts" elaborated by that discipline's own procedures,

then there would never be any way of validating or of
falsifying any proposition:
(25) there could be no scientific or disciplinary court of appeal. (italics added)

White suggests that great historical texts, when their informational core is obsolete, live on as literature; in terms of lexias
20–21, one could say that when great historians write theory, it
is incoherent insofar as they try to tie together incommensurate
modes of thought (reread Ranke's theory of the State today).
The argument that experience was spontaneous and outside the
semanticizations of knowledge(s) about such experience is here
embedded in lexia 23 as "procedures and controls"; the evidence
has been shifted from the plane of life to the plane of a "discipline
beyond the discipline," that is, the "court of appeal," an academic apex-structure (pace Habermas). Lexia 21 tells the reader
that the disciplines have intellectually arrived at the foothold
"ensure," which denotes a negative: they filter or screen so that
predications of evidence which are ideological do not get
through and contaminate "mature practices." Evidently, truth
and ideology cannot cohabit with "mature practices." Now the
sense of lexias 20–25 overturns the attributes of "experience" in
lexias 15–19. Does the historian treat nonideological evidence
because it is spontaneous? And in what ways is historical knowledge susceptible of a determination "by the properties of the
real object" (p. 209)? To put this in other terms: how can one
derive "historical" from (1) the concept of "determining experience" (lexia 18), (2) the signifiers of "procedures and control"
(lexia 23), which alludes to the plane of academic production,
and (3) significations of the Law ("disciplinary court")?

(26) . . . voices clamor from the past, asserting their own
meanings . . .
(27) If we offer a commonplace "fact"—
(28) "King Zed died in 1100 A.D."—
(29) we are already offered a concept of kingship: the relations
of domination and subordination, the functions and role
of the office . . .

(30) *received* by the historian within a theoretical framework which has *refined* the concept of kingship . . .
(pp. 210–211, italics added)

Lexia 26 is a pure piece of mysticism and magic. Only a reader
programmed for the reception of ghosts, the unburied, could
accept the metonymized "voices" (itself a fetishized metaphor,
a cultural piece of archaism which condenses the existence of
the past into "voices," where breath itself is narrativized as an
"asserting") whose cultural strength is forced ahead as a lack:
"to clamor" involves semes of "demand" (for integration?), "recognition" (for acknowledgment?), "outcry" (for justice?). The
form of lexia 28 is a simple preterit assertion; its very form precludes it from being a "concept of kingship" unless there is the
further precoding (overcoded) that the statement "King Zed
dies . . ." signifies "kingship" because "facts" are already concepts (a position which Althusser demolished in his theory of
Generalities). To say that the historian "receives" this "fact" already "refined" is only to say that the "history of the concept
of kingship" is stabilized by accepting *past* historical practice, its
accumulating organization (which assumes utter intellectual
continuity). In Thompson's telling, the very thing argued, that
the historian is in contact (in Jakobson's definition of the phatic)
with experience, is, however, annulled by the insistence upon
the achievements of historical thought. For what the historian
received is some segment of the present selection of some past
concept of kingship; as experience is spoken of, it perishes so
as to become conceptualized. Perhaps here I can suggest a certain
parallelism between such perishing of experience and the activities of the historian's practice. As past is brought *forward* in
thought, not time, the historian's thought moves toward the
past (the historian's desire, training, commitments, and reading)
and toward the future (the reader who can ask, "why am I
reading this text," "what do I do with it?") to a vanishing point:
experience can be reduced to one line or less in a footnote that
may never be read after its publication. Experience is not a stable
phenomenon. At any rate, the historian has overcoded an epistemic theory: another communicational model of dialogue (and

see p. 201 of *Poverty*). I stress that lexias 26–30 should be read as projections of intellectual stabilization, and that they are embarrassing insofar as historians claim to think and not react to data.

(31) A historian is entitled in his practice to make a provisional assumption of an epistemological character:
(32) that the evidence which he handles has a "real" (determinate) existence independent of its existence within the forms of thought,
(33) that this evidence is witness to a real historical process, and
(34) that this process . . . is the object of historical knowledge (p. 220).

Now these lexias inaugurate major claims and situate the reader in the epistemic debates raised in the later nineteenth century by Windelband and others. The three that-clauses mark thoughts grammatically separated from the direct address/discourse of lexia 31 ("I say (believe) that a historian is entitled . . ."); that modalizing assertion is also carried over, transferred, into the semes of the content units of the that-clauses and, as one might expect, the contents are hence judged as they are enunciated, theorized as uttered. The implied reader can only be another historian, a reader without interest that the form of the assertion that is transferred to lexias 32–34 breaks down in contradiction: how could, for example, some practice "entitle" the historian to operate on the basis of "evidence is witness," since "evidence" is always embedded in relations of standing for the interpretable, the symptomatic, whereas "witness" involves some copresence of a speaker and self who interprets? (Lexias 32–34 might be considered then axioms of the phatic code between the historian and Otherness).

(35) Without making such assumptions [the historian] cannot proceed: he must sit in a waiting-room outside the philosophy department all his life.

The interesting question is, of course, how does historical thought really proceed, since it is not a form of thought. But no matter: what happens through this discourse is that the content of lexias 32–34 is simply emphasized, the content absorbed by the function of code maintenance. "Entitled to" means: between the heterogeneousness of, say, "evidence" and "witness," mediation has already occurred, and this occurrence is unsayable. It is unsayable because such semes cannot be combined without leading to their dissolution. The reader who supplies the missing subcodes so as to de-idealize "evidence is witness" would arrive at precluding their very combination; the modalizing assertion ("must sit") asserts once more the supposed autonomy of all "mature practices," which confirms the division of intellectual labor while projecting into philosophy an imperialist ethos. "Evidence is witness" explodes when analyzed because its amalgamation of anomalous semantic markers cannot be unwrapped: to pursue that which is to be interpreted ("evidence") while coding it as simultaneously interpreting ("witness") yields, at best, paradox or its equivalent (incongruence, oxymoron). How is the historian entitled to make these assumptions? It is a fake question because the assumption has already been made. The possible thoughts—"evidence is such that it is copresent with itself" or "evidence is alive"—refer to a code of presencing. In addition, lexia 33 is a piece of unthinkable discourse (an example of academic "word salad") unless one supposes that the enunciator has imported the concept of a "voice" into the syntagm, since a "witness" must ultimately speak; and as "voice" is one of the primary constituents of a narrator, one might suppose (propone) that "evidence is witness" refers to the historian's desire of wanting a clear title to the referent, an unmediation. If one makes that supposition, the conceptual/intellectual value of "evidence is witness" refers only to an interest that preserves the autonomy of historical discourse. Lexia 35 says that historians may use unsayable presuppositions; only the saying of this "saying" (assertion) is the entitling principle.

The Poverty of Theory is filled with dozens of these points where adherence to narrative, to historical thought, is discursively asserted, the discourse receding from the reader as it is uttered, into the unsayable. That Thompson's discourse on history enacts such techniques of writing is the basis for contextualizing this discourse as part of that strategy of disengagement analyzed in chapter two. What I want to show now is how this discourse so completely overnarrativizes its intellectual arguments that one can think of it as little more than an exercise in recoding, here of the new-left's capture of an intellectual realm shorn of critical implications and operations.

(36) By "historical logic" I mean a logical method of enquiry appropriate to historical materials.
(37) designed as far as possible to test hypotheses as to structure, causation, etc.,
(38) and to eliminate self-confirming procedures (instances, illustrations).
(39) The disciplined historical discourse of the proof
(40) consists in a dialogue between concept and evidence, a dialogue conducted by successive hypotheses, on the one hand, and empirical research on the other (p. 231).

Note that the signifier "historical" appears three times: as "logic," as "materials," as "discourse." According to Barthes's reworking of Hjelmslev's theory of the commutation procedure, what difference does the signifier "history" make to the terms in which it is embedded? "History" makes no difference at all until one is introduced at lexia 40 to the significant unit "dialogue." Presumably, the historian works in these stages: once the "materials" are separated into those components in which pure "historical matter" is yielded (procedures having eliminated ideology), the historian can apply "hypotheses" which access a knowledge irreducible to "instances and illustrations" (which implicitly rejects any *symptomatic* reading of "historical materials"). Such practices are epistemically underwritten in the "historians' discourse" because "proof" is threaded to the concept of a "dialogue." The epistemic solidarity that holds these components together is found in a logic that can be demarcated from all other logics (the projection of a "historical reason"). And here we are taken to the matrix-figure of Marxist epistemology, to the territory of "dialectic."

This "dialogical logic" is not itself analyzed or made the focus of an analytic. Instead, the reader is offered for this dialogue and dialectic a heterogeneous series of the historian's requirements for textual production. The dialogue has a *place:* it is conducted within

> (41) a common discipline whose pursuit is objective knowledge (p. 233),

which means academic departments. It is a *type* of knowledge:

> (42) When we speak of the "intelligibility" of history we may mean the understanding of the rationality (of causation, etc.) of historical process;

It has its own epistemic *norms:*

> (43) . . . the real object remains unitary. The human past is not an aggregation of discrete histories but a unitary sum of human behavior;

and this requires its own accumulation *form:*

> (44) . . . historical process: that is, practices ordered and structured in rational ways;

"Dialogue" is a *competition:*

> (45) . . . the arduous nature of the engagement between thought and its objective materials: the "dialogue" out of which all knowledge is *won* (p. 229);

and "dialogue" also absorbs the "indeterminate historical process" and its entirely "determinate pressures":

(46) "history" may only be theorized in terms of its properties (p. 276).

As grouped, "dialogue" dislocates itself: the various signifieds— "discipline," "understand," "totality," "rational," "to win," and "interiority-identity"—initiate a metonymic skid, the center of which is outside any sense of the dialogical. These displacements of an analytic-logic only embed "dialogue" in institutionally determined incorporative signifiers (see Derrida 1978:274–275), and in replacing "dialogical logic" by "discipline," the latter's semic nucleus, especially its military connotation, acquires positive value. This is a characteristic of a discourse anxious in the face of its own nonmeaning. In Derrida's terms, the imperative of lexia 46 ("may only," where the "only" is a sign of utter negation, exclusion and the like) stops the substitution process by sending thought to the fusion of "only" and "history," and this is akin to the maintenance of a meaning-code proper; as lexia 46 absorbs the various semes of "dialogical," as it recodes the Hegelian *Aufhebung,* its plausibility is really tied to a cultural activity,

> the *busying* of a discourse losing its breath as it reappropriates all negativity for itself, as it works the "putting at stake" into an *investment,* as it *amortizes* absolute expenditure; and as it gives meaning to death, thereby simultaneously blinding itself to the baselessness of the nonmeaning from which the basis of meaning is drawn, and in which the basis of meaning is exhausted (Derrida 1978:257).

The Poverty of Theory thus shuts the door on critical thought by trying to detach the "history" signifier from any subordination to another discourse, and embedding "history" in programs of cultural identity (for example, lexia 43, which is also a model of story telling). It does this by projecting an image of narrative competency and performance.

The signifier "history" is then not presented in terms of a philosophy of history, that is, as part of a conceptual design that underlies history as process; the historian ought to forget about "modes of production" thought of as model, rule, law, structure, because "properly" "historical categories" are elastic (p. 249). Such elastic categories are "expectations rather than rules" of research (p. 249) Concepts like "working class," "capital," and "warfare" are not part of philosophy or theory; Thompson severs the "logic of an indeterminate historical process" from the philosophical context(s) of modern historiography. In turn, as an object-referent, "history" defies any and all discourse that could ever be delivered on it:

(47) For it is exceptionally difficult to verbalize as "theory" history as process;

(48) and in particular, no analogies derived from mechanical or organic mechanism, and no static structural reconstitution,

(49) can encompass the logic of an indeterminate historical process,

(50) a process which remains subject to determinate pressures.

(51) In the last analysis, the logic of process can only be described in terms of historical analysis . . . (p. 276).

Again, all of these lexias manifest hard claims but, above all, it is the connection between the hardness of the signifiers and their field of pertinence which matters. Inadvertently, lexia 51 injects the historian into modernist practices, especially the self-reference of cultural activities, each riddled with as much contradiction and dialectic as it can stand, so long as an internal logic is preserved and is capable of supporting further expansion (see Baudrillard 1975:126–132). Wittgenstein's famous admonition that "logic must take care of itself" is, in principle, no different from Gropius's demand for the complete architect, or the monopoly of recoding regularly carried out by the legal profession (a "profession" that is perfectly sited: it decides its own limits as well as the limits of nonlaw). Lexias 47–51 duplicate this "modernism of the code": (1) one starts out from the situation where the historian cannot employ a discourse naming "process" because (2) the historian cannot use "derived" (analogical) terms; (3) so no other sign system beyond the one actually enunciated by the historian (a narrative) can encompass or replace the (4) historian's practice of narrating this "logic of an indeterminate process"; (5) but (enthymatically) the historian can only depend upon historical analysis, which then culminates in complete self-reference: the historian embraces what already belongs to the historian.

Thompson severs "historical thought" from any discourse of the adjacent "human sciences" the better to defend its internality, its identity, a position that should be thought of as part of the modernist notion of the autonomy of forms. One can expect from concepts like "subsistence crisis" only the chance to interrogate evidence, and one can never uncouple evidence from the processes that are "present within every moment" (p. 240). Only "determinate pressures" remain as "results for every human experiment that has ever been conducted" (p. 240). Now all of this is really the discourse of Law, in Nietzsche's terms: the historian assumes that all existence becomes real only when interrogation goes to work across the zones of (1) the real, (2) concept formation, and (3) narrative implanting (explanation), until evidence is fully integrated; but as evidence is always potentially more excessive (pluri-coded) than the possible telling of it, the "history machine" is permanently "determinately pressured" only from inside, by the historians' suspension of plot ("indeterminate process"), which thus gives rise to the same validation of description and narration as bourgeois positions. This is what lexia 51 refuses to say as it says it.

The "history" signifier may not be unbolted from the "object" side and theorized and it must not be geared too tightly to one's use of concepts; "historical reality" cannot be changed (which means "process is objective," p. 234) and one can judge the past only after its full recovery, which means one must be a historian in order to think about the past. Even significations pertaining to moral value (of the past) are narrativized, that is, they can only appear as valid within the domain of the historian who is encoded as a social actant.

(52) we may not attribute value to process . . .

(53) In recovering that process,

(54) in showing how causation actually eventuated
(55) we must, insofar as the discipline can enforce,
(56) hold our own values in abeyance.
(57) But once this history has been recovered, we are at liberty to offer our judgment upon it.
(58) Such judgment must itself be under historical controls . . . appropriate to the materials.
(59) What we may do . . . is identify with certain values which past actors upheld and reject others.
(60) We may . . . vote for Swift . . . and . . . against Walpole.
(61) If we succeed, *then we reach back into history* and endow it with our own meanings:
(62) We shake Swift by the hand (p. 234, italics added).

As one of those abbreviated and summarizing series of "super-signs" criticized by Nietzsche, we can first of all note that "process" is used, again, to distance the historian from "theory" (model, invention, construction) because "process" is strictly tied to "evidence," and, simultaneously, one should not think too much (in an erroneous manner) about "process," as to do so calls up some "philosophy of history." The concept of *"process" functions as transcendental to both subject (judgment) and object (evidence),* in the sense that it makes possible "evidence" and (evaluative) "historical thinking" in the first place. In another place (p. 279), "process" is equated with the "involuntary results" of "human agency," but only if it "occurs" in the form of a "collision of contradictory class interests and forces." When verbalized as evidence, "process" slides into "events"; when verbalized as "theory," "process" equals class conflict. We note that "class conflict" usually means for leftists (and rightists) the full presence of the "revolutionary reality principle" (Baudrillard 1975:154), which is not intimated here.

By not being able directly to attribute value "to process" (lexia 52), "historical materialism" (see *Poverty,* p. 300) generates "history" as the tie between "conflict" and one's possibility of process evaluation. It spans Otherness—the futureness of the past and the pastness of the present. In addition, "process" is to be thought of in terms which, with "class conflict," further and perpetuate its autonomy (lexias 47–48). "History"—as process—also makes possible moral thought (lexias 57–58), for not to "attribute value to process" until "this history has been recovered" (lexia 57) and then only under more "historical controls" (lexia 58) and yet still, as reader (one supposes), being oneself subject to ongoing "process," means that the form of process—"class conflict"—is mirrored in the knowledge of the historian. Thus the historian alone has access to and knowledge of legitimate morality. And in (textual) fact this is also overcoded, for notice what the shift introduced at lexia 59 initiates. After one accepts the stability of the signified ("process"), one can then transcend the "interrogational": the verb of permission ("may") grants one a right to access, achieved through retroaction, with those values that can now be seen as metahistorical or superhistorical. Present class conflict takes its bearings between repetitions of Swift versus Walpole ("good and evil," "just and unjust," "fair and unfair," *ad historium*). Swift was waiting to shake someone's hand; he has been waiting in-between visits from his future, and will wait until that last visit which, of course, never occurs. As with Jameson and others, complete historical thought—this body of distortions—of the "historical materialist" variety installs itself as the continuum of existence, crossing over into that Heideggerian region (or historiographical version) where "authentic futurity" alone makes possible an "existential of history."

That is to say, the text has inadvertently slid back into "theory of history" or "philosophy of history" in trying to make "process" transcendent and hence open only to "discipline." One must (obligative) make oneself worthy of history, according to this dialectical version of the sublime. This sliding too is an expression of the overtaking of discourse (criticism, theory) by narration: the movement initiated at lexia 52 starts as discursive—because it does not efface an interrogative, the "who is speaking"—but by lexia 62, a narrative success has occurred, a destination. The "reaching back into history" (lexia 61) raises the theme of a narrative existentialism as it is linked to the meaning of the idea "to reach back." I mentioned Heidegger earlier and must explain here the full imaginary/symbolic scope of this mode of access to the past and its intellectual effects in the present.

This concerns, above all, the sense of retrieval and repetition around which much of the modern defense of historicity turns. The complete enunciation of lexia 61 can be considered a theory of historical subjectivity if we try to supply to lexias 52–61 their presuppositions. Fully stated, lexia 61 can be expressed this way:

> If present-now actors "succeed" in realizing (concretizing) progressive values, their choice of a progressive future gives them the right to step into an identity between past, present, future. The recovery of past in present-now (full narration/ retrieval) in the name of the future entails repetition, the latter implied by the relation of identity or passage as such. Present negation of nonprogressive values (as acts of choice, decision, commitment) is intrinsically coded with past and future; hence, there must be atemporal *identity within the negative* as much as there is within the positive, within what Swift "negated," the present-now negation, and *negation in the future, too.*

One cannot stop negation when/where one pleases, even when it passes into the continuity involved in this projection of genuine subjectivity. Heidegger's solution, which underwrites most existential varieties of the autonomy of "historical being," can be used to show the model of the relation between discourse and narration in lexias 52–63. For Heidegger, as here, the solution to "history" was to hinge the internal continuity of history to one's present disclosure of every past choice/consequence ("fate"), released to subjects in their present-now choices, so that there is identity between past/present *and* the future "called" into "being"; in choosing a possible future, one's "possibility" erupts as "anticipatory repetition," retained in consciousness as that future is made-present, and then itself made-past, so that past and future are always identical. "In repetition the Dasein which has-been-there is understood in its authentic possibility which has been" (Heidegger 1962:446), which, given Heidegger's prose, means that "history time" is generated by future-past conjunctions, where the present is reduced to a switching station, a pure relay, a genuine "in-between." Nonnarrative present-authenticity is narrativized away:

> a steadiness which has been stretched along . . . which Dasein as fate "incorporates" into its existence birth and death and their "between," and holds them as thus "incorporated" so that *in such constancy Dasein is indeed in a moment of vision* for what is world-historical in its current situation (Heidegger 1962:442, italics added).

The present is a "steadiness" because it "holds" and "incorporates," the latter actions of suspension (of action) and integration, *actions at zero-degree of presence in change/motion*. At the center of historicity is a discourse that belongs to self-maintenance (preservation). Present-now "steadiness" is equivalent to the preservation of the diminution of transformation/motion in present-now. Negativity of the present (about the present, within the present, through the present) is indeed encoded by Heidegger as the very point of historicity, within "resolution" of "being-towards-death," of weaning one from the present (p. 444). One must be "monumental" or embrace the not-yet-death in order to live "fully", the present devoted to repetition-preservation (authentic future entails an authentic past) (p. 444). Historicity is constituted by "detaching oneself from the falling publicness of the today" (p. 449), wherein subjects-now make-present past authentic "fateful repetitions," and this is the only way in which a subject (self, etc.) can reckon with his own time authentically, that is, by negating disconnected and dispersed time. "Authentic historical thought" aims at nothing less than the identity of negativity and the negation of false identity in the name of some model of authenticity; it dreads dispersion and multiplicity, the hurling of temporality to a place beyond the subject. And narrating leads to the discourse of death:

> (63) In the end we will also be dead . . . inert within the finished process,

(64) our intentions assimilated with a past event which we
     never intended.
(65) What we may hope is that the men and women of the
     future will reach back to us,
(66) will affirm and renew our meanings, and make
(67) our history intelligible within their own present tense
     (p. 234).

To live in order to be told by someone else: here is the body of
academic history; take of it, eat, and die (pace Gottfried Benn).
     The old center of historical materialism, class conflict, thus
co-occurs as entirely *secondary to a discourse of resurrection:* a model
of subjectivity overtakes class conflict, just as the plane of history's value supplants the present-now of such conflict. The full
force of practical class conflict is thus recoded as subservient to
its academization. There is a sharp divergence between what
Nield (1980:499) calls "historical analysis" and the "present con-
juncture," or what I would term the transcendence of process,
the dilution of what class conflict is, and present-now, diminished by what spans and stretches out a present. How is it
possible that historical materialism is hinged to class conflict
projected as identical across the span of all presence (past, present, future) unless, as with lexia 65, class conflict is *eternalized-*
historicized and so, pathetically, drained of its force and material
determinant relations-now?
     The speaker is not very removed from a kind of mystical
variety of historical materialism, the one most strongly associated with Benjamin. The "courage, humor, cunning and forti-
tude" of those who struggle against exploitation possesses a
certain "retroactive force and will constantly call in question
every victory, past and present, of the rulers . . . by dint of a
secret heliotropism the past strives to turn toward that sun which
is rising in the sky of history" (Benjamin 1969:255). It is statements like Benjamin's and lexias 46 or 61 which no doubt confirm
Mink's (1978:137) contention that "Universal History" lives on,
today, only in such Marxist writings, unable to jettison notions
like a "single story" or that some preexisting form like "untold

stories" must be held as a presupposition. We shall return to this later.

The signifiers "historical materialism," as we have seen, are defined in their specificity by the conjunction of the signifier "history" with a code term: "historical materialism" requires "historical controls," "historical dialogue," and so on. Tautology runs through such designations. This tautological plane is now correlated to an academic program when narrativized discipline replaces class conflict as the conceptual center of focus:

(68) Historical materialism offers to *study* social process in its totality;

(69) as a total history of society, in which all other sectoral histories are *convened.*

(70) historical materialism, must . . . be the discipline in which all other disciplines meet.

(71) It is the unitary discipline,

(72) which must always *keep watch* over the isolating premises of other disciplines . . .

(73) "History" *must be put back* upon her throne as the

(74) Queen of the Humanities . . . and

(75) "History," insofar as it is the most unitary and general of all human disciplines, must always be the *least* precise

(76) Her knowledge will never be . . . anything more than proximate (p. 262, italics added).

The highlighted terms return one, as it were, to that Nietzschean space of reactive thought. Lexia 68 says that "historical materialism" is a part (of knowledge) able to enclose the whole. But if one really thinks this out, the starting point has to be: since "historical materialism" is *already a knowledge* (of class conflict), *what is left to do as knowers, what remains to be known?* Lexia 1 told us "historical materialism" was a "mature practice." How does the study of, say, "center" unemployment as compared to the "periphery" (Paris and Bogotá) further class conflict, in the West, as a revolutionizing practice (third *Thesis on Feuerbach*)? Put another way, how does a study of past pertain to revolution at all if class conflict is both the continuous identity of process and cognized as not-yet known? The codes begin to jam one another here. Lexia 68 supplies its own answer: the connections between "historical materialism" and "class conflict" are disconnected in favor of "totality," a synecdoche for the "whole," and the postponement of what one already knows now about class conflict (for example, that it is founded on the same mechanism, the internalization of necessary labor and modes of extracting unpaid labor). The "historical materialist" here wants to, in Sartre's terms, learn what the very concept "class conflict" already specifies as the necessary and sufficient objective condition of Capital. With lexia 69 an academic code operates in a systematic way: shorn of the critical-revolutionary connotations of class conflict, the apparatus of historical materialism can be imagined devoid of temporal markings (transcendent). Lexia 69 absolutizes a place ("in which"); lexia 70 recodes this place as a discipline, the sense of which is fully rendered in a military code (lexia 72)—to "keep watch" places the historian in a symbolic role defined by the defense and preservation of whatever finally makes up the substance of the "unitary discipline" (lexia 71).

Here we must further specify how this academization is concocted, and what its intellectual implications amount to. Lexias 31–34 were enunciated by an epistemic speaker, a someone who asserted that the historian is in possession of "entitled to" assumptions, but once the assumptions were stated, they were displaced: the discourse no longer made itself arguable as discourse, its effects taken over by the thought content (for example, that there *is* a "process"). With lexias 68–76, however, the discursive ("historical dialogue") is given a narrative task so as to reestablish the discursive in its true priority and force. Presumably "class conflict" and knowledge of "process" make up the form of content in lexia 71; at that point, our historian-speaker could say, following Mink, that "historical materialism" has been validated by means of all the evidence narrated by all past "historical materialists," and so "class conflict" is *true*—the future will look like the past unless class conflict is aggressively taken up by the working classes, so "workers of the world, unite." This could be said because if the past is an untold story (what lexias 41–46 and 52–63 *perform*), how could there be any central subject but "class conflict," which *has not changed*, except as displaced (to the Third World?). Now what holds that proposition silent, opaque, distanced is nothing but lexia 72. To "keep watch" is temporality at null-state: "keeping watch" is "looking" once the latter has been militarized, a "time" that draws together fragmented other times ("isolating premises of other disciplines"), and as a "keeping watch" (indefinite progressive in its temporal function), it links up with that Vichian strategy of finding some "sublime form" which, like "poetic wisdom," enables "historical knowledge" to transcend each of its own "historical moments." "Historical materialism" thus specifies the propulsive force in history (class conflict) and is, as a knowledge, continuous with that force, its "watch" ensuring that no *Seinsvergessenheit* overtakes the social order. Instead of narrativizing semes, lexia 72 excludes all temporality-knowledge linkups by comparison to the permanent presence of guarding the center of its own knowledge.

As encoded, "historical materialism" is finally severed from other knowledges; the call made at lexia 73 should be understood not simply as a desire of the historian but also in accordance with those codes that support such a desire. Here we must analyze the enunciator's notions about narrative thinking. If there is in fact a "logic of process" that can be demonstrated as operative in history, then to put history back on her throne (!) amounts to nothing less than a defense of historical reason insofar as the latter can itself be reduced to narrative form. One wants to think out how "keeping watch" is tied in with narrative as a mode of thought, how "history as process, as open-ended and indeterminate eventuation" (p. 276) can be made intrinsically probable as a knowledge form.

The helter-skelter topic switching of *Poverty* is halted when the difficulty of "verbalizing history as process" is textually— need I say materially?—manifested in an example.

(77) Instead of interrogating a category, we will interrogate a woman

(78) . . . Structures . . . get on top of her . . . depression . . .
      the psychiatrist sees her . . . as . . . a structured neurosis
(79) She is indeed the carrier of these roles
(80) . . . But she is not "over-determined," she soon bounces
      back.
      [The sociologist categorizes her as "subject" to the roles
      of wife, mistress, mother, and she undergoes therapy
      which she "thinks" a besetting upon by structuring lan-
      guage, so that even the telling of the example organizes
      the Althusserian discourse as a *victimizer.*]
(81) She gets headaches . . . Beset with the contradictory ex-
      hortations of psychiatrist, priest, husband, lover . . . Her
      depression deepens.
(82) We will leave her in this sad state . . .
(83) none of the disciplines or categories have done her any
      wrong. [i.e., each has "correctly" described her]
(84) But not one of these definitions affects the fact that she
      remains a woman.
(85) Is the woman then no more than a point at which all
      these relations, structures, roles, expectations, norms
      and functions *intersect,*
(86) is she the carrier of all of them, simultaneously,
(87) and is she acted by them, and absolutely determined at
      their intersection?
(88) . . . not . . . an easy question, for many of these roles
      are not only imposed, they are internalized, and
(89) they have gathered up like a knot inside her head.
(90) To answer this question we would have to *observe her
      history.*
(91) I don't know how her history eventuates.
(92) *I have two alternative scripts* (pp. 342–343, italics added).

Starting at lexia 77 "interrogate" is supposed to manifest the
sense of "dialogue" (see lexia 40), and for now we shall register
that "interrogate" is a code verb, an aspect of the phatic "contact"
which the enunciator assumes holds between "interrogate" and
the referent (context of the "woman"). The historian has bor-

rowed "interrogate" from its, one assumes, already achieved enunciative field, a certain segment of the "social scientific" domain where it has been legitimized that "to interrogate" has a singular function—"asking"—a "strategic choice" without which no "scientific" knowing could get out of its own statements and hence "pass through" to an object domain (see Foucault 1969:150–154). But because lexia 77 cannot be part of the historian's "strategic choice" (mode of procedure)—because, once again, "dialogue" cannot really pertain to "past"—its own practice is thereby pertinent: the historian is placed on the side of full and complete positivity, possessing the capacity "to ask," which, in our culture, is already a sign of + expert, + knowledge, + distance, + law, the "we" of "will interrogate" here empty yet linked to an ideology of the shifter "we," a missing actant, the one who profits from an investigation. (The one who profits from "interrogation" is mentioned only once [p. 282] as someone who requires concepts so as to proceed with the "purchase" of historical analysis—see those assumptions at lexia 35. How strange that such proceeding demands a "purchase" or guarantee.)

The "woman's" states (lexia 78) establish different domains of activity, presented as an inventory of roles. But with lexia 79 a story utterance takes over: in passing onto "structures" as "cause" of "depression," the theory argued against (Structuralism) is made, obviously, negative (as "weight," "burden," subconnoted many lexemes later perhaps as "beastly"); "depression" has the temporal status of "past determined," but "limited" ("pressures" are not absolute); after "bouncing back," the "social sciences" "cause" an intensification of her "depression," then: suspension. The reader crosses over, back into assessment, where the historian emerges as allowing that each "discipline" was right yet none of them is appropriate to what the historian "treats," the remainder: what was continuous *before and after* the "structures." Now it is simple to point out that the historian is here imagined as having contact with a role so situated that it transcends every other discourse—*what "no one else can say" belongs to the historian* (autonomy-function). Lexia 85 says that the predicates about this woman cannot be stopped without reduction ("no more than"), and lexia 86 is similarly discarded by a hypothetical statement grafted onto the imaginary dehumanization of her as a disease ("carrier"), as is lexia 87, which conjures "relations", and so on, as actants, which they could not possibly be. All the dramatized ideations perform a series of rejections and openings for the historian's activity, engagement with the subject; the historian's sign system can now span instances (crystallizations of "time"), forms ("carrier") and systems ("acted by"). The historian's moment happens with the *occurrence of past subjective response to* structures, at the point where the *next* is disengaged from what makes it then-now (lexia 90). What is subject of is also subject to: as the subject of the story is subject to "structures," "headaches," and the like, that subject is subject to the historian's narration. The historian's post is imagined as one who tells if the next is *suitable for* more story, as "I have two alternative scripts" now makes *story* a presentation form:

(93) She is carried off to a mental home.
(94) She goes back to work . . . the mortgage has to be paid . . . She calls out the workshop on strike . . . leaves her husband . . . rejoins the orchestra . . . fancies the conductor . . . all her muddles are, once again, about to begin . . .
(95) [this] analogy will serve . . .
(96) we find intersecting determinations, which they are always trying to handle and reconcile . . .

What are these "scripts"? The first (lexia 93) is "eventuation" which results in overdetermination: the "subjectness" of the subject no longer is anything but a mere experience. The second (lexia 94) posits a "historical subject" as reaction to obligations: this repetition-process is processed by the "subject" by "to handle and reconcile," the Subject of the subject's activities. The modern "subject" is so thought of that its very source of activity is purely reactive and so is the historian's—the "scripts" about her narrative essence, to be muddled, which is a line of commonality to the middle-classified "masses," project story telling as the bulkhead against the "disintegration of the full historical process" (p. 282). That it might also be a sheer waste of one's time to "muddle" in practice, that it might be, as Nietzsche put it, "mad and spasmodic" not to stop the "once again, about to begin" (lexia 94), does not occur in this version of academic new-left historical thought. Indeed, the radical connections are stripped between "class conflict" and nonrepetition; the historian steers (pace Habermas) thinking to a transcendent thought which confirms a clear image of passivity:

(97) . . . no worker known to historians ever had surplus-value taken out of his hide without finding some way of fighting-back (there are plenty of ways of going *slow*);

(98) . . . by his fighting back the tendencies were diverted and the forms of development . . . developed in unexpected ways . . .

This makes (1) a pseudo-heroism out of "slowing down" process, and (2) the historian an actant of the social world insofar as "unexpected ways" returns the reader to one core of narrative thinking, its illusion that narrating/story is a negation of repetition. Historians have to account for variation as well as continuity. Because repetition is too horrible to be fully thought out by our academics; because they will not loudly proclaim how insane it is to pump drama into each and every partial narrative (but "whole story") while process is made "unknowable" and out of cognitive reach, the historian can focus on "unexpected ways" as both negation of repetition (annulled by its own non-difference *once* integrated into another more inclusive narrative) and as a link to the masses' so-called desire to believe that history is an *open* process. In the void of no "substantive" idea of Marxist historicism (see McLennan 1981:7–23), refusing a "theory of history," and where "experience" is precisely modeled in ways so as to reproduce the idea of the reactive subject, what remains is the historicism of narrative thinking itself:

(99) . . . if we return to "experience" we can move . . . into an *open* exploration of the world and ourselves.

(100) . . . within that dialogue of conceptualization and empirical engagement . . .

(101) One can only return, in the end, from these explorations
       with
(102) better methods and a better map . . .
(103) a certain sense of the whole social process;
(104) with expectations as to process . . . (p. 359).

Now the signifieds beginning with lexia 99 establish the *cultural*
figure of the historian and provide him with roles. The historian
is safe (from thinking) to assume that present-now is entirely
distant from a scene of rapid mutation (the present), so that, in
Aron's terms, it is safe to practice "history as usual," because
"we know" what the "drama" of "history" is made of, "we
know" what to expect from the narrative proper, because the
academic already knows the "plot" (see Aron 1961:26–32). The
result of narrating is to return (but from where, precisely?) with
a map of time (!). Lexia 103 calls for a reassembling of specific
narrative modes: for example, the signifiers of "affirmation,"
"renewal," and "shaking Swift" belong to prior narrating, because the "historical text" can have an impact, we were told
(lexia 61), only if the future "results" in some "success" around
the continuous term "class conflict," so the prior and posterior
are by definition presupposed by lexia 103. Where the narrating
affects the story, the function of "keeping watch" would dominate insofar as the historian must ensure that in the narrative
transmission, the "other disciplines" do not destroy the narrative's "ensemble" (see Genette 1978:217–223; Mink 1978:144).
What lexia 101 whittles down to "in the end" and "expectations"
(lexia 104), a performative category of what one does with "historical knowledge," amounts to nothing less than the transcendence of the historian from contentious claims of other
knowledges. In addition, the "better method" and "better map,"
thought out as possible positions of cognition, are the intellectual
ideals of an obsession with "access," "opening," "integration,"
("method"), and time, each an aspect of the collapse of "class
conflict" into the myth of social scientific discovery. With "historical materialism" encoded this way, it ceases to be connectable
to "class conflict" except as academia is also relayed to the
masses. Indeed, as liberated, "historical materialism" comes into
its very own time:

(105) What remains to be done is to

(106) interrogate the real silences

(107) . . . and as these silences are penetrated . . .

(108) we find it is necessary to reorder the whole set of concepts.

(109) . . . interrogation and revision.

Lexia 106 returns us to the idea of an "untold story": "real silences" has nothing whatsoever to do with socio-political effects-now of class conflict, but with the extension of the historian's "scripts" onto the not-yet told. How does one link "interrogation and revision" (or *rewriting*) to something other than the institutional practice of the historian? At what point in the interlaced sequences of either the historian's "revision" or society's revisions does such "interrogation and revision" pass from the historian to the nonhistorian? Who is the audience of these lexias? "Our knowledge may not satisfy some philosophers, but it is enough to keep us occupied" (p. 242) tells us that what the historical materialist fights for is repetition and autonomy, the right "to revise" precisely *what* in everyday life does not happen among the masses. In life, *singularity* dominates: the work permits not received, the money never borrowable, the land dioxined out of life; and these are singularities with negative repetition: once such events occur, they cooccur without "reorder [of] the whole set," but as death, dying, deprivation, and the like. Is it not strange that a "historian of the moral left" could encode the profession in signifieds—imaginary relations of legitimacy and necessity, requirement and need, knowledge and morality—completely contradictory to "the people"? *The Poverty of Theory* manifests none of the contemporary forms of what broadly can be called critique of "discursive formations"; it generates no capacity to perform the minimal function of radical discourse, that of refusing to repeat the language (break off contact with the same). Rationality, here "interrogation," evidently includes and subsumes all symbolic/cognitive distortion. Its existentialism reeks of tenure. Is it too complicated for the historian to entertain the script that more victims than ever are produced precisely as the professions go forward? This question is "materialist," but "vulgar." When Thompson denounces "elitism" by affirming the "proper work" of the historian as "driving out" writings and thoughts of "theoretical practice" (pp. 381, 384), is this not desperation?

Is it "vulgar," in short, and to conclude as well, to ask about a last imaginary, the form of thought, that dialectic where one today encounters the "always historicize" (Jameson) as its support system? Dialectic safely sews the historian to the unsayable: our historical materialist informs us that as a practicing historian

(110) I have . . . come to bring "dialectics" . . . as a habit of thinking and

(111) as an expectation as to the logic of process,

(112) into my own analysis (p. 306).

As the basis of "historicization," dialectics sustains the belief that the real can be signified by means of a form of thought and presentation which already includes subject (teller) and object (told) *and* subject-object (telling-reader). The history of dialectics—why dialectics is real, necessary, and reliable—is not appealed to in support of its status as a "habit." This is another "real silence" of historiography. Perhaps lexia 111 is based on the truth of the assumptions presented at lexias 31–34 and so is just an abbreviated/synthesis of the historian's special mode of thought. As a supersign of continuity, however, "dialectics" is first presented as part of the field of "paradox" (p. 306), where a political group (Soviet Communist Party), once based on "progressive" values, now represses "rationality." It represses "dialectics" insofar as the latter denotes the "apprehension" of "flux, conflict, decay, and becoming" (p. 305). But "dialectics" cannot be spoken of at all, not in the "process" (the Hegelian "heresy") or "within" the "subject"; "dialectics" allows no theorizable presentation of its relation with "the real," and, like contradiction, "dialectics" cannot say its dialecticality without thereby ceasing to be "itself." Our historical materialist, using the same procedure as before, narrativizing "historiography" at the outset (overcoding), only allows "dialectics" to emerge as knowledge (knowable) within the space of "discipline." There is no discourse on "dialectics" since

(113) it was not written because
(114) it could not be written,
(115) any more than Shakespeare or Stendahl could have reduced their art to a clue.
(116) For it was not a method but a practice,
(117) and a practice learned through practicing.
(118) So that, in this sense, dialectics can never be set down, nor learned by rote.
(119) They may be learned only by critical apprenticeship within the same practice (p. 306).

The condition of "could not" (lexia 114) and "was not" (113) are reversible in narrative thinking, on account of the fact that "was not written" is the "effect" of the cause "could not," enabling one to affirm first the "effect" and then its "cause." But the cause here is excessive: one can easily imagine the case where, say, Marx decided to formalize "dialectics" but simply did not do so; the claim is much stronger than Marx not "having done so," because lexia 114 insists upon the *impossibility* of "dialectics" as a sayable discourse. This, of course, imposes an anti-intellectual coding on Marxism, that is, "dialectics" transcends what can be said. The passage to lexia 115, where "dialectics" is equated as an "art," code switches one from the "unsayable" into the "aesthetic," and this, in turn, is entirely and completely narrativized because once "within practice" (lexia 116), the one who wants to "dialectize" must submit to a practice *defined* by narrative organization (lexia 119). "Dialectic" as "art" is not encoded near any trace of the "negative" (opposition, contradiction, etc.), but is entirely positive: "critical apprenticeship" means *institutional ego* (and it is not far from the semic evocation of a precapitalist "experience," the artisanal mode of "academic production"). In other words, "critical apprenticeship" is the *metaphorical* equivalent of the closest one can get to "dialectical" thinking; "dialectics" is a pure mark of the historian's quest, and as such, is not attachable (as attribute, predicate) to "historical process" ("we may not attribute value to process"), yet somehow incorporates the "unsayability" of the historian's assumptions (see lexias 31–34). What the historian writes is "dialectical," and nothing else releases a "dialectic." Only those who write "dialectically" are thus privileged, implicitly, to think at all about "history."

This text which has tried to "defend reason" places itself on the side of those reactive forces so carefully analyzed by Nietzsche; the historian is a functionary of the negative who promotes the "value" of deriving positivity from negation, and who ceaselessly promotes the sense of suffering as a necessity arising from the innermost core of the world. It is symmetrical with conservatism. The historian is deliriously self-encoded as a cultural operator incapable of being transcended/overthrown by other discursive systems ("3000 years of practice have taught us something," p. 231), the "discipline" of academic "history" invoked for the "keeping watch" over the tendency of isolation: "historical materialism" is empowered as the political function of a vast containment—no one should "think" himself outside of the basic forms of narrative "thought."

The rejection of a substantive "philosophy of history," which is today a reflex among historians, is an illusion; for those scripts carried around by the historian (see lexias 63, 90, 98) are a philosophy of history displaced into the realm of the historian's direct attempt to stabilize thought processes. The narrator of *The Poverty of Theory* who valorizes the "knots" and "muddles" of the "people" and focuses on the "working out" of what has been "internalized," shows not simply a case of the historian's making familiar the new unfamiliarity of the contemporary (see White 1978:56). What our historical materialist has encoded is the total relaxation, in Nietzsche's sense, of class conflict, for the example of process given, the "woman," is nothing but the diminishment of such "conflict," and the historian who celebrates this is the actant of decadence, furthering the "obliteration of extremes," their nonnarratable aspect (Nietzsche 1913:89–90).

White would no doubt argue that *The Poverty of Theory* is an ironic discourse about narrative and the "historical": "class conflict" cannot be the organizing device of "commonplace experience" and yet submit so easily to the integrating, mythifying strategies of the historian. Instead, I have stressed the nonindependence of the "tropes" because the figurative aspect of discourse is a secondary functioning. *The Poverty of Theory* is not just anachronistic/ironic in relation to "class conflict," (substitutes its own time, its own logic, for "class conflict"), but the thoughts of its ideological practice work by abstraction and substitution to the benefit of a generalized privilege of the "historical code," here the autonomy of the "historical" in the cultural role of the historian. These relations of the signifier, through which defensive, protective, distancing and recoding postures are created, are not just linguistic or even cognitive; such positions are cultural forms through which the historical discipline articulates its fundamental ideological practice, providing academia with legitimations of its exchange of significations (see Baudrillard 1981:100–101, 155–159). Recall, again, the force of the example given to render intelligible the distinctiveness of the "historical materialist": the "woman," who is described (narrated) as "muddled," provides the historian with a *means* for narrating, nothing else. "Her" participation in socialized dying (to be "muddled" is "not to know," "not to be able," etc.) is the result of the academic cruelty that, regardless of the modes of socially acceptable destruction, there must be "enough time" for narration ("3,000 years have taught us . . . "). Thus, historical narrative as organized in *The Poverty of Theory* is little more than a projection-defense of the historian's institutional time, which is also an aggressive rejection of the nonnarrated, the latter included under Marx's great analysis of the time of the "destructive forces."

There is no significant distinction between *The Poverty of Theory* and bourgeois historiography at the level of critical thinking, and this is sad. Just as contemporary bourgeois historical narration employs psychologized signifiers of "lack" in order to maintain its hierarchical plateau, this historical materialist employs signifiers of "limits and pressures," the language of capitalism, to perpetuate the myth that there is some collective, but unnameable, "process." What corresponds to the bourgeois narration of what is "lacking" (missing, etc.) is the new historical materialist stress on placing the historian in the cultural role of moralizing thought so as to perpetuate narrating against critical thinking.

Yet what is, in Barthes's terms, ex-nominated, what class conflict means, is precisely that which is never narrative or historical, since class conflict constitutes the repetition-presence of exploitation, no matter how displaced into "muddles" and "joining Swift." With *The Poverty of Theory,* academic Marxism comes into its own and takes charge of that which the academic system never wanted to integrate in the first place, but now does so knowing that leftist historians reach the exploited through story telling passed off as critical thought, which is to say, without initiating difference.

5

Historical Narration As Intellectual Recoding: On Structuralist Historiography

I have argued that in the case of Gay's "A Short Political History," the "historical" is formed by the interpretant of a "sense of lack," where what "did not happen" organized the telling of an "absent proposition"; and that in the case of Thompson's *Poverty of Theory*, the "historical" kept reappearing as a "process" ("class conflict"), the sememic nucleus of which was made antithetical to the negative cultural implications of such class conflict. In both cases, the culturizing role of the historian is one of recoding (a discourse) and then overcoding the historical as that which one is "subject to," from which no "true cultural subject" can be disengaged. The distinctive force of "historical narration" (*what* theories, propositions, symbolisms, hypotheses, etc., it employs) is made unrecognizable by narrating (a story, a theory of story), so that not only is the discursive channel parasitical upon other discourse (the validity of which is then presupposed) but also the actual text is not intellectual: the imagined reader must not be allowed to think out (decode) how the told is told. A historical text is a closed-semantic world. In the same intellectual space the reader cannot both "follow" a "story" and think through each and every sememic choice, connection, and so on. The historian presupposes and reproduces the anti-intellectual:

that what is said, defined, and characterized by "language and concept" is closed to any further analysis of its symbolism and effects. The historian has to presuppose that the act of narration "works over" (literally) stable semiotic entities on the plane of what the story "tells" (for example, definitions), redeployed from the major discursive system reemployed by the historian. The model reader is presupposed by Gay and Thompson (and almost everyone else) as a subject who does not know how to think about the present apart from history made *into the form of the present*. The reading of such history texts is determined by the reader's making-present the narrative program, trajectory, oppositions, and the like, and reproducing what is thought as "signs" of the present-future, as *axiomata* of the existent. White (1980:91), in his most critical essay on modern historiography, where the organization of *Metahistory* is momentarily dropped, suggests that the "history effect" is achieved by "master his-torians" (such as Marx and Croce) when their "discourse" constitutes:

> an image of a current social praxis as the *criterion of plausibility* by reference to which any given institution, activity, thought or even a life can be endowed with the aspect of "reality" (1980:91).

White interprets this to mean that such a "criterion" takes the form of a "circle of moral conceptions" which "defines," "leads to," and "impels" the "subject" to identify with the "Law" bodying forth a "model of discourse" which is "realistic." "Thus it is" is the common motto of such "realism" (see Cohen 1978:178–179).

The problem with White's view, which is otherwise a strong recasting of Althusser's notion of an "ideological state apparatus," is that historical thought does not operate on the level of an image. If anything, a historical text is a systematic antidiscourse; it engenders what the semioticians call a non-transformative "subject," the reader who enacts the nondoing (immobility, paralysis) of the discursive plane. The nontrans-formative subject in Gay's piece is the reader encoded to "desire leadership" as a guide, standard, norm, model; while in *Poverty of Theory*, the reader was organized as someone who must reject the adequacy of any "discourse" that does not *defend* "process" itself. Instead of pursuing how a historical text "endows" such "criterion of plausibility" *on* the "real," I prefer to ask how such a text both recodes one or more discursive systems and also perpetuates the stability of that signifying dimension along a narrative line. A better question is how does a historian cast "historical effects" so that the "real" appears to be discursively and narratively part of some reader's encyclopedia, sememic constructs available and suitable for application to his or her own present-future? The "real" should be considered not as "images" but rather as "arrangements of markers," transmitted from one semantic machine (text) to another (reader). The historian reproduces the competence of making a narrativized "world" overlap with a reader's, the ways this is accomplished comprising the sign forms of the "historical effects" (see Eco 1979:221–222; 1976:91–114).

Recall the historiographical requirement to protect the strategy of rejecting disengagement from narrative-history. In April 1982, the *American Historical Review* published an address by Bailyn in which the profession was given this anamnesis:

> Narratives that once gave meaning to the details have been undermined and discredited with the advance of technical scholarship, and no new narrative structures have been constructed to replace the old (Bailyn 1982:22).

"Sad historicism": "narrative" belongs with "details" but "technical scholarship" "undermines" and "discredits" the linkage; one can no longer "pause" over contextual items of a "past" because the framing devices of *tableau* are not calibrated with the new technical models, which demand their "right to the past" (access). Psychoanalysis, systems analysis, and mentalité studies—the new "substance" (signifieds) and methods—are required today, but such "technical" zones are too explicit, too discursive, not yet "aesthetic" enough to mesh with "reality effects," those semes of description which say "we are real" (von

Papen, the "undertaker") (see Barthes 1968:84–89). The historical profession has to avoid "obscurantism" (excess of the model) and "modernism" (excess of the present) and "re-tell, with a new richness, the story of what some one of the worlds of the past was, how it ceased to be what it was, how it faded and blended . . . how we came to be the way we are" (Bailyn 1982:22). Beyond the obvious mystifications (for example, narration is really a spatial matrix if it includes past and present), note that contingency or "being-able-not-to-be" and impossibility, "not-being-able-to-be," are both expunged in favor of the identity between present and past; it would seem that it is necessary for the profession to utilize new research models ("technical scholarship") insofar as they recode (reinforce) narrative necessity according to some long view of temporality.

I have chosen the first volume of Braudel's later masterwork, *Capitalism and Material Life,* precisely on account of its instrumentalism for the historical profession. The text has been an unqualified success among historians because it has amalgamated theories, models, strategies and the like, and narrativization; its use as a textbook in the United States is frequent, as were reviews in the journals which awarded it the status of a "masterpiece." A full analysis should yield a strong example of how historians continue to establish contact with a nonprofessional audience and, simultaneously, how the historian recodes conceptualism into narrative form. We shall analyze the decoding of Structuralism by *Capitalism and Material Life* and its reconstitution as a "filtration process" whereby readers are bolted into place as that infamous "ordinary educated public," the latter an idealization of reactive subjectivity.

> (1) Let us assume then that there is a material life or better still a material civilization . . .

"Then" indexes that argument or analysis or discussion is closed, this closure performed by the "let us assume," the latter a sign of some collectivity. The perfective "better still" demetaphysicalizes "material life," reducing the connotation of "material life" with its suggestion of philosophical or biological meanings. "Material civilization" is an existent suitable for the historian, whereas "life" announces a metaphysic.

(2) mingled with—although by nature distinct from—a more full-blooded, often dominant economic life.

The assertions draw a line: "by nature" asserts that there are contents (categories) without "history"; but "mingled" establishes a connection between these contents, a certain "strength" of the "economic" over "material civilization" (or "power," etc., since no semantic markers or subcodes are as yet present), "full blooded" a "natural force." So the signifiers specify the *state* of combination ("mingled"), perhaps an implicit recognition of the priority of relations over other models, but at any rate the suppression of the historian's usual appeal to *res*—not events, but the copresence of different series is raised.

(3) The distinction between this life—more passive than active, repeated for centuries on end—and
(4) an economic life that benefits from it but implies calculation and demands vigilance, is not immediately apparent.

Lexias 3 and 4 are part of placing the enunciator in the cognitive place of the social sciences: a "distinction" not "immediately apparent" but already defined as consciousness/unconsciousness will have to be justified and given extensive articulation. The subject of discourse (simultaneous with the *mise en discours de la langue;* see Greimas 1976:10–12) is manifested now as the operator of all the discursive operations that could hold between "distinction" and "immediately apparent" (for example, that it makes sense, can add to knowledge, etc.). What this discursive operator says is that the "by nature" of lexia 2 and its logical essence (what is "by nature" cannot be otherwise) gives way to what it makes possible: "material life" is not a "force" and "economic life" is of the order of a system that can "think" according to "means" ("calculation") and self-protection ("vigilance"). "Economic life" is already a proto-actant, positioned as receiving an advantage from "material life," while the latter manifests "life" without thought. The reader is "inside" of a scientized discourse, its framing devices.

(5) However, the core of the problem is not the distinction
. . .
(6) we are concerned with a mass of history barely conscious of itself.

With lexia 5 the problems of taxonomy are displaced; now "material life" reappears as virtually undifferentiated in lexia 6 ("mass of history"), the signifier "barely" granting it the status "mere consciousness." This is very strange: one is moved from a discursive handling of "distinctions" to a definite historiographic question, "how can history be barely conscious of itself?" The "however" of lexia 5 acts as a program for what the enunciator has-to-do: to not treat distinctions but answer a question (what is material life?) (see Greimas 1976:34–35). Lexias 5–6, we shall say, raise and then disengage the narrator (and story) from thinking (lexia 5), the positivity of lexia 6 settling on the stabilization of the historian's job.

(7) If man usually remained within the limits of the possible it was because his feet were sunk in clay.

The cliché "sunk in clay" raises the image of material life both as form (inertia, repetition, nontransformation) and the "depth" to which the historian must "penetrate" in his "concern." "Sunk in clay" is performative: it brings about the conceptual zone the historian wants to establish; it manifests the semantic field of a historiography of the combinations raised in lexia 2. It also proposes to answer the strange question of lexia 6: "material life" is not "on the side of history"; it does not provide the conditions for transformation, speed, action. We shall only register here that the discursive arguments associated with Structuralism and Lévi-Strauss's famous comparison between "hot and cold history" (metonymy and metaphor, syntagm and paradigm, conscious versus symbolic, signifier and signified, etc.) have been recoded onto "material life" and "economic life," "freed," so to speak, *for the historian*: the narration of a "mass of history"— cold to hot—replaces the "logic" of the distinctions, their possible combination. So the "movement" from lexia 1 to lexia 7 is nothing other than the historian establishing an overcoded "onset": the sememic value of "sunk in clay" plays off the "history" of the imagination of preindustrial society, and gives a "natural floor" to narration; at the same time this onset gives a "floor" to the inchoativeness of contact with "history," to the strong discontinuity of the lexias, their alternating generative schemes (elocutio).

(8) Let us also assume that man's whole life is restricted by an upper limit, always difficult to reach and still more difficult to cross . . .

(9) An examination of this limit will be the subject of this first book, starting at the bottom level with material life,

(10) the ground floor (as it were) of history . . .

(11) It has gentle slopes along which the whole mechanism slides.

Lexia 8 tells us that "material life" is determined by a spatial figure, a "roof," this "upper limit" *there in advance of the action*. This does not merely signify the presence of the priority of the "system." Indeed, the sense of "difficult to reach" and "still more . . . to cross" implies the "upper limit" as infrequently achieved, this being its temporal coordinate. (I read "upper limit" as "place"; a connotation is thrown to "sunk in clay," which must be interpreted as a "social gravity" and an "origin," devices of embedding. The means of "reaching" and "crossing" as well as the belief that not-being "sunk" is neither "common" nor "often" indicate some narrative program.) The narrated story will be attached to a spatial coding, the "rise" ("up") from "floor" to "upper limit." There is also a trace that the story involves some "rise" in "consciousness" as well (lexia 6). There is a "going up" through "time," from "material life" to, perhaps, the "machine" on "top of" "the ground floor of history." A philosophy of history is still recognizable here, but eviscerated.

(12) . . . The frontier zone between possibility and impossibility barely moved in any significant way, from the 15th
to the 18th centuries . . .

(13) It was the following century that saw a violent breakthrough, revolution, upheaval of the world.

Lexia 12 introduces the modal category, possibility, for the period
covered by the story; the "base" and its "upper limit" are saturated in a type of morphostatic diachrony, where social contradictions are contained by an equilibrium that absorbs
paradoxes and violence. The rigidity of what "barely moved"
refers to a context in which social control is highly efficient (see
Wilden 1972:354–356). By comparison to the nineteenth century,
(lexia 13) the reader is located in a de-sequenced framing, a
"system" whose "process" is highly spatialized. "Barely moved"
stabilizes an object-complex.

(14) We are going on a long journey, far removed from . . .
the normal part of present-day life.

(15) It will take us to another planet, another world of men.

(16) We could, of course, visit Voltaire at Ferney and (as fantasy is free) have a long chat with him without any real
sense of surprise.

(17) The men of the 18th century were contemporaries on the
level of ideas. Their minds and passions were the same
as ours, or at least near enough to prevent total
disorientation.

Lexia 14 tells us that the historian is able to travel twice—the
first time as a researcher and investigator, the second time with
"guests"; to follow a historical narration is a tour, by comparison
at least to the "machines" of research used by the historian the
"first time." The second machine, the narrative one, must be
constructed so that in it one can experience maximum difference
("far removed") at the same time that such differences are prevented from, by excess, generating nonrecognition of that
"planet." The narrative illocution, the "promise" of being
"charmed" by the "journey," implies a reader more like a tourist

than not (for example, "affecting and picturesque," in Macauley's phrase). Such readers usually have to pack something for the trip; in this case there is no need to tell the reader what to bring (no monitorial code in Barthes's terms), for the packing is precoded: one can stop in that past and have a "conversation" with Voltaire because thought and ideation are not subject to "the normal part of present-day life" (lexia 14). The reader's mind is already protected from "disorientation." This strategy encodes the contemporaneity of the reader as a member of a discursive community ("chat").

> (18) All the details . . . of material life . . . even his personal hygiene, would shock us.

Thus, the simultaneity of past-present occurs along the axis of discourse, while nonsimultaneity or "distance" is parallel to "details," which amalgamates "personal hygiene." Does "discourse" equal "nonshocking" while "shocking" equals the nondiscursive (continuity/noncontinuity)? What the reader can simulate is a difference between seeing and talking, which requires a rupture on one level and absolute continuity on another:

> (19) To make the requisite journey back down the centuries
> (20) it is essential to discard all the facts of our environment once and for all,
> (21) in order to rediscover the rules which enclosed the world in stability for such a long period . . .

Let us arrest the meandering of the lexias. A historiographical coding has determined that past contents divide as to their accessibility in present-now according to "discursive continuity" (ideation) and nondiscursive discontinuity (details-hygiene); the latter system requires that the reader expunge ("discard") present-now, or duplicate what the historian has already accomplished. If this were all that was demanded of the reader, we would be in the classical domain of historiographical "engagement" where the reader is to be plunged into a past-world of difference. What is announced in lexia 21, however, is a level of taxonomical composition: the aim is not to "experience" past "details" but to "rediscover" the structure of a period. The object of such a historical narration is manifestly not the representation of transformations but rather the *isolation of the code itself:* what makes "possibilities possible" in the first place. The "existents" and "occurrences" of historical thought (classes and acts) are, with lexia 21, already subject to a system of exchange ("enclosed"), and the "historical" is posited as perhaps identifiable with "structure" (see Greimas 1976:162–164 on some of the epistemic issues). Where one sort of bourgeois historical thinking seeks to locate the historical as a necessary act of imagination (symbolics of "loss"), here far more extensive claims are semantically raised. That such rules (metonymically linked to "limit," "restraint," "impossibility," etc.) were in fact operative as a "profound" enstructuration of "stability" is one thing, but the implication is another: Do "rules" equal "historical structure"? Is "historical consciousness" a knowledge of structure?

(22) A general history always requires an overall model, good or bad, against which events can be interpreted. "No theory, no history," said Werner Sombart.

There are two strong readings of lexia 22. The first proceeds from literary classifications. The indifference in speaking about models ("good or bad"), the incoherent shift to "theory" as a necessary condition ("models" design relationships, "theories" are already a relationship) while asserting the "need" for "theory," indicates, according to Kellner (1979:204, 219) a Menippean satire because of the "undecidability at the heart of it . . . systematic self-reflexive doubt . . . a book that is built upon its own contradiction at every level" (he is referring to Braudel's *The Mediterranean* but his argument, *mutatis mutandis,* holds for lexia 22). On this view, the indifference ("good or bad") is a sign, a syntagm of its literary saturation and cultural choice; hence the referent of lexia 22 is the rhetorical plateau. The view I adopt, however, is that lexia 22 belongs first to an intellectual/cognitive program; what it performs is a *neutralization* of "scientific history," this because lexia 22 goes no further than to "nod" at the "scientific tradition" (Sombart) while it actively refuses to force into the open the precise status of "scientific history." The evocation of science in lexias 2 and 5 is here diminished as a strong code, a wavering between the story and structure.

(23) The model in the present case suggests itself:
(24) the lives of men certainly progressed, from the 15th to the 18th centuries,
(25) as long as the word "progress" is not taken in its current sense of rapid and uninterrupted growth.

Lexia 23 is a complicated syntagm; a "model" can be either homeomorphic or paramorphic: "In the first case the subject of the model is also the source; the doll is a model of a baby and is also modeled on a baby. In the second case subject and source differ; the double helix is a model of the DNA molecule but is modeled on a simple mechanical structure" (Pettit 1975:40). According to this division, what is offered in lexia 23 misfires with lexias 24 and 25. Neither 24 nor 25 has anything to do with models. Instead, these lexias plunge the reader directly into a substantive "philosophy of history," which reads: the historiographical tradition of an "idea of progress" still holds for the period, as long as it is shorn of its connotations of speed (lexia 25) and sheer linearity. As the semantic impact is routed to the narrative lexia 24, so lexia 23 evaporates as a problematical contention.

(26) The right road was reached, and thereafter never abandoned, only during the eighteenth century, and then only by a few privileged countries.

"Models" and "theories" are blasted away by such a "right road"; the latter is a straightforward allegory of direction and telos, of the irreversibility of a history. In addition, this is also a moralized irreversibility: once established, it could never become the object of negation ("never abandoned"), so perhaps (it is too soon to say) a "moral road" is connected to that "upper limit" of lexia 8. In addition, the "limit" and the "right road" "know" only a select portion of historical subjects, those associated with the ascendancy of Europe's worldwide expansion. An elite is traced with lexia 26.

(27) We have tried to find a model, an overall view; not a general theory. We do not claim to have done so.

One negates "general theory" because if it were fully articulated, it would require intellectual decisions or, better, step-by-step articulations of the metalanguage by which one can define more elementary functions (what is required of "historical material- ism" or Freud's working up of repression or, more limited, il- locution theory). Recall that lexia 23 came out on the side of affirming a homeomorphic code which, filled in at lexia 26, has its own message. This simply means that the historical text is continuous with its sources. Lexia 26 returns one to lexias 7 and 8 and says that "a road was cut" or "scaling" equipment was involved, and now lexia 27 absolutizes the historian's disen- gagement from science, the latter rejected as a metalinguistic basis of narrative telling.

The lexias that present statements about the discursive ma- terials and forms are highly elliptical, weaker in what they sug- gest than the substantive lexias that definitely establish the story. There is some wavering between the types of sign forms, be- tween keeping open lines to another discipline, to the past, and to the reader—to a discourse, to the referent, to the interpretant, one might say. These lines are tenuous: for discourse there corresponds the paradigmatic, the metaphorical (perhaps), the discursive, the theorizing, the defining, the subcoding (second- order connotations); these codings include the reader and the past. The referent of the past—progress—is tagged to telling and to the reader. The referent is not a sign to the reader but the center of the narrative (the story of "progress" but not "growth"). So the reader, the third line, like all interpretants, is riveted to understand (decode) by acquiring, in Eco's phrase, "the habit to act according to the prescription given by the sign" (1979:194)—that is, the reader can presume "progress" and dis- course on it to be identical.

Let me note in passing, the "overall view," which replaces "general theory," indexes the historian's access to these lines. For overall view parallels emergence of story: it registers the tracing of the visual channel, a well-worn historiographical subcode generally employed to separate the historian from dependence on modes of access to data studied by the natural sciences. In Windelband's classical phrasing:

It follows that in the natural sciences the bias in favor of abstraction predominates. In history, however, the bias in favor of perception [*Anschaulichkeit*] is predominant (1980:178).

The denial—"we do not claim to have done so"—affirms, however, that the historian is not promising the reader the usual associations with the visual (individuality, scene, thick description, with characters at the center). There is clearly here far more ambiguity of the historian's relations to discourse and narration than in usual liberal or Marxist historiography, but the ambiguity is contained by the framing of the performative onset: it is harder merely to start narration going after the historian tries to think structurally.

The historian/narrator continues to break free, now laterally, from science:

(28) What advice would a modern economist retrospectively give to those economies which broke down so often— genuinely underdeveloped countries before the term was known—

Lexia 28 invites the "other" into historiography, a gesture of intertextuality. But the economist is not in a better position than the historian regarding the past:

(29) If the problem were solved, this book would be remarkably clear and simple. But it is not solved.

The economists have failed, and behold—once more the historian steps into a cognitive-semantic absence of knowledge, a lack, the nonaccomplishment of a scientific discourse. The historian is to answer why those past economies "broke down" so often, why nonprogress was the rule. The missing answer to that kind of question (of which "broke down" is already a partial answer) is repeated in all the relations between the historian and the adjacent disciplines:

> (30) Moreover, not one but thousands of problems are involved, varying with time and place.

The marker "varying" indicates an interest in the idiographic tradition, but with this difference: the historian must deal with variations on the level of logical types, not "concrete" particulars, with "structural" individuals, not actions of subjects.

> (31) . . . the difference between the Indians of the St. Lawrence and the France of Louis XIV is as great as, if not greater than, that between the United States and a newly independent state in Black Africa today.

For such contrasts refer to synchronous contradictions (of space) and

> (32) activated the coherent life of the world . . . but they were, in effect, external distinctions. They are only part of the story.

These contrasts are pairs of oppositions: they are sememes (for example, "advanced," "natural") which account for the copresence of contrariness in a social system. Alas, these contrasts also symbolize the limits of the historian's interest in pursuing their hierarchical status, among other aspects; in narrating an account where the difference between Indians and Louis XIV's France are functions of a story (for example, allow a reader to isolate the forms of conflict), no historian can bypass this domain of oppositional values ("external distinctions"); but the historian would be a mere classifier if this activity were primary. Contrasts would yield effects at the surface (in the same way that the semantic units of, say, "good" and "evil" provide one with an inventory of possible roles and functions); indeed such classificational activity is written off and transcended in favor of grasping a logic of the Social:

> (33) Every economy, society, and civilization is a world unto itself, divided internally and shared unequally amongst its members.
>
> (34) Each of these individual mechanisms must therefore be taken to pieces and put together again to bring out the resemblances, similarities, recurring features, and hierarchies among their components.

Now we see that the object of the new historiography is a recoding of the famous "phonological revolution" employed by Lévi-Strauss in his reading of myth. The shift at lexia 27 takes the reader to the threshold of a dephilosophized Structuralism while providing the historian with a project. To posit the past as a "world unto itself" is also a recoding of Ranke's famous dictum; instead of axiomatizing the "unto itself" in the Rankean fashion, the "equivalence of each era before God," the stress falls directly on systems as a transcendent/permanent scene of "unequal exchange." This contemporary recoding of Structuralism into historiography preserves the right of the historian to affirm the specificity of the past, only now access to "past" is riddled with forms of the "phonological revolution" (in Lévi-Strauss's terms, "all meaning is answerable to a lesser meaning, which gives it its highest meaning"); the "economy," "society," and "civilization" (specific systems or "individual mechanisms") are the vocabulary of history, and so are reducible to "pieces" which are themselves meaningless ("economy" must be decomposed into an object of knowledge and becomes "land," "money forms," "technology," each, obviously, reducible in turn). Because "taken to pieces" yields what the "model" is to do—the "resemblances," and so on of lexia 34—one is here as close as possible to the discursive joined to the narrative: the historian is going to evoke a differential semantics where attention has to be focused on the relevance of contrasts ("Indians" and "Louis XIV") but which are themselves analyzable only in terms of their noncontiguous relation to a system, their significance a function of generative rules (lexia 33) (see Pettit 1975: sec. 23). The historian claims to narrate what kinds of rules and structures there must have been in the past which enabled a *road* (path, route, highway) to function as an *out*; lexias 26 and 34 will have to be combined and shown to be subsumed by lexia 33.

What is interesting about this historiographic opening is the possible subversion by the discursive of the narrative lines: that the story to be told has no autonomous status. This preface and introduction withholds any strong presentation of historical process (but absolutizes irreversibility) and practices a recoding of the discipline of history's lateral relations to knowledge in general. It remains to be seen whether story and telling are in conflict. At any rate, the reader is presented with an intense alternation: when "story" receives signifiers of a narrative program (lexia 26), the discursive recedes; however, when the saying veers into signifiers of "model" and "theory" (lexia 33), the reader is presented with zero-transformation, the historian's nod to Structuralism. We shall say for now that Structuralism here has the status of romanticism for Michelet, or "laws of mind" for Buckle, or alienation for Lukacs: what is radical in the posing of such theory is systematically dismantled. For Lévi-Strauss, after all, Structuralism was merely the myth of myth, a stance refused here in favor of giving the historian a legitimate narrative post.

Immediately after the announcement of the semantic model (lexia 34), narrative propositions again take over. The "present-day human sciences" require a "precise vocabulary" to rethink the past, a vocabulary now encoded in narrative signifieds:

(35) Material Life, . . . old routines, inheritances and successes, is there at the root of everything. Agriculture goes back thousands of years . . .

(36) material life will therefore be deliberately used . . . to denote repeated actions, empirical processes, old methods and solutions . . .

These already positive accumulations are given the status of a primary competence ("at the root"), which includes all that has been amalgamated "in history" (lexia 36). This is "deep time," "historicity" at the level of affirming the depths of what is. Later:

> (37) Economic Life . . . a higher and more privileged level of daily life, with a wider radius and involving constant care and calculation . . . born of trade, transport, differentiated market structures . . . rich and poor, creditors and borrowers, monetary and pre-monetary economies . . .

or "contrast" proper. How "economic" acquires the predicates "higher" and "more privileged" while serving as a binary grid (antagonism and antinomy) will have to pertain to the story, not to the nonstory of lexia 35.

> (38) Capitalism . . . if we use it so much it is because there is a need for it . . .
> (39) it points to certain forms of economic life in the past that are already modern,
> (40) as though oriented to the future.
> (41) Capitalism, with its rules, attitudes, advantages, and risks,
> (42) has betokened modernity, flexibility, and rationality from its earliest beginnings.
> (43) *It is in the vanguard of the economic life of the past* (italics added).

Capitalism is sizzling by comparison to the simultaneity of the signifieds earlier/slower/cooler/old/root/binary. It has the semantic markers of a fully practical system, an imaginary ("attitudes," "flexible") and symbolic machine, and the codes attached to it as predicates (lexia 41) refer to fully activated antinomic semes. Rule/transgression (law and nonlaw), attitude/subversion (skepticism), advantages/disadvantages (loss), and risk/securities (?, we shall see) are structured in the sense that they mutually imply a narrative program, a combination of both the linear order and the order of thought (lexia 42). To go from material life to Capitalism is a journey from minimal differentiation to hypersubjectivization, from the order of the binary (which is "economic life") to the super-binary (from "roots" to over-determination; see Deleuze 1983:8–9). As the "vanguard" of the past is the present's norm, the reader is given Capitalism's systematics: it is an index ("points") of itself; it is historically old/new (we shall return to this); it gives off tropistic effects (lexia 40), which may or may not involve "fulfillment" (of destiny) and satisfaction (completion). Aspectually, it is unthinkable that it could not happen because it has happened (lexia 43). And to suggest that Capitalism (lexia 42) "betokens" only those properties foreseen by its "positive" critics (and does not, hence, entail negative semantic markers) omits, radically so, contradictory sememes (for example, with "modernity" is omitted "mass murders"; with "flexibility" is omitted "determinism"; with "rationality" is omitted "waste," "uselessness," etc.; see Eco 1976:292–297). One can say that with lexia 42, Capitalism is positivized because its progressive features are built in (at its beginning, no less), which already downgrades the Marxist treatment of its history.

On the level of story viewed as a container (of sense, referent, structure, continuity) Capitalism—the reader's present (lexia 40)—which "encroaches on all forms of life" (p. xiii), is thus fitted to a narrative sequencing *while* it is conceptually presented as an intransitive resulting in nontransaction (see Kress and Hodge 1979:41–42). "Encroaches" absorbs the semes of lexia 41. Capitalism must be shown to "emerge" from the lower levels of material life/economy and at the same time engulf these plateaus of the social; the causal is suspended because lexia 40 tells us that capitalism was irresistible: *it is future in any time*. It is important here to note that this continues that intellectual process we earlier specified as the "academic advantage" in obscuring lines of causality. The form of such causality, well established by Olafson (1970:286), stressed the manipulability in the past of a "contingently necessary condition," and was generally nourished by its reliance upon some "operative desire" or "ultimate function" (Peirce's terms), a construction that focused on an agent's ability *to cause*. *Capitalism and Material Life* bypasses the causal in completing, one might say, an intertextual shift where the historian joins up with methodological socialism, set out by Danto (1968:277) that "insensibles" (institutions, etc.) explain individuals, who are consequences of macro-antecedents, not only by affirming the aims

(44) to catalogue, classify, pinpoint reciprocal interplay and distinguish recurring-features,

but also by affirming the priority of a story organized in terms that abolish any traditional notion of cause:

(45) Man was locked in an economic condition that reflected his human condition. He was an unconscious prisoner marking the inflexible boundaries between the possible and the impossible.

A lot of historians would go to the mat over lexia 45 while accepting the implications surrounding lexias 33–34, which asserted the priority of the code, machine, system, norm, language, model, and so on. Many historians would like to narrate in Structuralist categories without being seen as determinists. It is important to stress that this "preface and introduction" overcodes the story dimension and disengages itself from science *while* it employs a Structuralist discourse. But lexia 45 is an extreme position for a historian. While the predicates of the past are outside science, as we have seen (lexia 29), lexia 45 pulls together and spatializes a macro-sequence, a "period." It says: at x time in y past there obtains some S ("human condition") and some P ("locked in") where S and P are null-time and bound by a strict material equivalence (identity); the "human condition" is a *nonnarrative* state, omnipresent, and this flattens usages of "cause." The switch at lexia 27 creates a metonymized, spatialized "historicism": every moment ("condition") of history is the "human" condition, the repetition of "condition" in both S and P serving as a signifier of metaphysical truth and coherence. In addition, "reflected" (lexia 45) is ideological: such notions rely upon a "mirror," which presses into service the fantasy that a description is a relation, that it can be used to "model" subject/

object without any difficulty. "Reflected," then, encourages a sort of silence of the reader: the writing suggests visuality, the "seeing" ("making") of the simultaneity of scene and structure, or the "showing" of a logic (the modal raised in lexia 45). The historian is marking/organizing the past as describable because it is capable of being brought to a standstill, one of the more esoteric forms of narrative pause (see Genette 1978:95, 100). "Reflection" theory, we can say, is a necessary coding of the "chance to narrate," because it lets the historian present a state as an achieved result to be transcended by subsequent narrating.

The historian can now plunge the reader into a supersign of the historical, a cultural space where the future-as-result is diminished in favor of dramatizing the motivation of Capitalism disengaged from its actions:

(46) Those who succeeded [became nonprisoners] usually did so ruthlessly at the expense of others.

(47) [to] step over a line . . . was possible only for individuals, groups, or civilizations peculiarly favored by *circumstances.*

(48) For this advance, though always limited, *required an infinite number of victims.* (italics added)

Those who "desired" to "advance" (lexia 38), to "reach the right road," to, one might say, change logic and structure, are here awarded a psychology at odds with the quasi-collective predicates of Capitalism (lexia 42). What "happens" at the micro-level of the subject, "success," the consequent, results from the positivity/negativity of subjects who were pitiless and without compassion; the sememe "circumstances" indexes a past series of overcoded practices and shifts the reader away from "ruthless" and onto the semantic field of the given ("circumstances" denotes "past context" controlled by one or more "necessities," located in any number of possible functions: physical, psychological, perceptual, etc.). Does "ruthless" belong to "capitalists" or "capitalism"? Better: can one characterize a system ("Capitalism") in which there is "progress" (lexia 28), a signifier of "improvement," *by means of "nonimprovement"* ("ruthless") *at the level of actions?* One can obviously judge "capitalists" without judging "capitalism" (an inoculatory displacement from system to subjects). The story will have to provide an explanation for "ruthless," since it is a sememe embedded in the historian's presentation of action, positivity, future, and so on. "Ruthless" has to reemerge later, inserted in a discursive structure (the moral?) which will unfold its micro-propositional sense, allow it to be articulated (see Eco 1979:28).

Lexia 48 is historiographical, philosophical, theoretical, an "answer" and an assertion at once. But since its ideological function is so strong, let us start there. The lexia virtually closes the "introduction" and is not recuperated or reassembled on another intellectual level, so it is on the level of a macro-proposition, a narrative framing of transformation. Lexia 48 is nothing more than the frame of common "violence," treated as a collective experience, figured forth in a passive manner. The "advance" refers to "success" as the result of "ruthless." So one can say that "victims" is a strict material condition of entailment, because it is analytically included, already, in the ideas of "advance" and "success"; in this sense, "victim" is a "structural feature" of world-past for this role is always also "human condition." It remains to be seen whether lexia 48 will recode the Hegelian classification of "historical subjects," whether "capitalism" can be made homologous to world-historical "heroes" and so a marking "on history" just as surely as "victims" has no discernible marking, on account of its very extension ("infinite").

As a subset of every "unequal world" (lexia 33), the sememes "capitalism," "vanguard," "modernity," and "ruthless" encode a narrative isotopy, a story with a narrative subject—"victors"—while "victims," "prisoners," the "unconscious" make up a semantic unit (a "classeme") but not a strong narrative one ("victims," "enclosed" in "stable rules" and "barely conscious" are heavily overcoded semes of nontransformation, nonsubjectivity). Because of this, I shall argue that the text is organized as a "history of" the "logic" of the "system" itself, the "logic of inequality," an unusual blend of discourse and narration. In fact we are dealing with a "meta-récit," whose center thus far is nothing but the presentation-translation of a pseudo-logical structure of the social into narrative order. This "logical structure," recall, is "naturally" unequal (lexia 33) an ideological projection; thus the story's claim to realism must be accomplished (or fail) if the reader is placed in contact with the story, the latter then a signified, on the level of thought, of the natural logic of history itself. The implicit claim made in the introduction, insofar as narrative form is never explicitly raised, is that such form—or telling itself—is unaffected by logic; that connections "logicized" by the telling (the asyndeton of the omission of connections between "victors" and "victims"; the *dicaeologia* of "required"; euphemism; the incessant undercoding of sememes like "succeeded" and "expense,") create no interference with transformation (either in real time or story time). This narrator is so committed to the essential "truthfulness" of its "structuralist" anchorings (metaphysicalized) that the story of the "naturally unequal logic" in the period of the transformation to "capitalism" *is beyond thought*, especially since it is coded that "capitalism" is itself only a form (matrix) of the metaphysical (lexia 33). But why narrate what is, after all, only an example of the nonstory (lexia 33)? What is left to narration, how can it perform "knowledge effects," if the story to be told (lexia 33) is an example of what shapes all history? Too much action, indeed, dissolves narration. Thus the reader engages the nondiscursive (action) because the story promises discontinuity as part of its intellectual interest.

(49) How could it decay and break-up . . . this *ancien régime*
     . . .
(50) How did it—how could it—break the barrier?
(51) And why, once this was achieved, was it only to the advantage of a privileged few?

The role now granted to story is to combine a mechanism (to answer how) and the logic of society—a narrative of *means*. "How" can be reformulated as a capacity-to-do (being-able-to-do), and, combined with the "logic" of the social (hierarchy of the "few") this intellectual plateau can be called the reader's capacity-to-know (which answers "why did it happen?," accepting the necessity of result). This shift to the level of means, in which "how" and "why" codetermine the historical, is nothing other than the dramatization of the structure(s); the temporal units—"decay," "break up"—are signifiers of "no longer," while "advantaged few" is the signification of "result," and both are linked by the telling. The space between such temporal order and its "logical necessity" comprises, then, a claim as to what narration can show. In this sense this "new" and "total" history is also a new and total attempt to recast the very genre of historical discourse, since it presupposes that the "logic of capitalism" and the form of story (transformations, syntheses) are not contradictory but complementary; and since this presupposition is made (what the preface/introduction yields), it makes a claim to locate what the historical must be for "logic and story" to be connectable, how the reader must think/not-think in the simultaneity of the text's time.

To summarize: (1) Despite the presence of so many lexias with theoretical, historiographical, and epistemic presuppositions and connotations, the achronicity of these display-operators, these moments of paranarrative (see Blanchard 1980:129, 146), do not jeopardize the historian's fundamental arrangement of the wholly traditional need for narrative. (2) The connection between the discursive and the narrative is here arranged as the identity between a recoded Structuralism and the story of the "advantage of a few." Now we shall pursue: (3) how story is the concretization of these shifts (the historian relaying Structuralism); (4) how, as "logicized," the story is coded for a model reader; and (5) how the historical itself is separated from its textualization, how it somehow is made to transcend story and narrating so as to achieve the status of a contemporary basis of cultural knowledge and identity.

It is an important change when historians abandon interest in focalizing on individual characters and instead turn toward an inventory of actants where numbers, technology, towns, and so on, occupy the nominative position. The shifting of possible actants such as "towns" or "technology" from setting-markers to macro-frames and roles involves a complete reshuffling of the entire semantic space(s) and oppositions available to the historian. The title of the first chapter, "Weight of Numbers," initiates the story with an index of a material determination:

(52) What has changed entirely is the rhythm of the increase in life.
(53) At present it represents a continuous rise . . .
(54) previously it rose and fell like a series of tides
(55) These basic facts make almost everything else seem secondary.

Like everyone else, the historian has to stabilize signifiers as to their expressive, conceptual, indexical, and illustrative values (recall that the analysis of stability = critique of hierarchical inequality insofar as one isolates ideological premises buried within sememic selections). The reader is presented with number/past/tide/discontinuity, all of which mark pre-1800:

(56) everything was in a state of change
(57) When the numbers increased . . . cultivation . . . manufacturers spread . . . ,

and the reader is encouraged to overvalue "number" as some decisive condition:

(58) . . . everything is bound up with the numbers and fluctuations of the mass of people
(59) When a population increases, its relationship to the space it occupies and the wealth at its disposal is altered.
(60) It crosses critical thesholds and at each one its entire structure is questioned afresh.

Lexia 58 asserts that "number" is a meta-semiotic system (makes signs possible); with lexia 59 "number" plus "increase" results in lexia 60, a syntactical function: population increases manifest the state of disjunction between "need" and "capacity" (to be fed), shown in the enlargement of "the underfed, poor and uprooted" (p. 2); as the initial set of the possible "rules of structure" of past, "number" acts directly on the whole of the system:

(61) A balance . . . is reestablished by epidemics and famines.
(62) These extremely crude adjustments were the predominant feature of the centuries of the ancien régime.
(63) But the main point for the observer is that everything takes place within the framework of vast and more or less observable movements.

The connection between lexias 61 and 62 is an ideological invention which can be paraphrased as "there is no society between overpopulation and disaster," so that the conclusion reached in lexia 62 is enthymatic: "society did not exist in relation to natural disasters." "Crude adjustments" is the ethos: the present is not as crude, and so on. The quick-cut presented at lexia 63 is the scientific (historiographical) monitorial code: the historian gets to apply Darwinistic rhetoric to the past *and* displace the application by saying, in effect, that "disaster" is a function of "balance," the latter a primary mechanism of recuperation. The "vast"—the object of the "observer"—quite literally absorbs the first-order predication "disaster," its framing ("balance," the topic of the ideological mechanism), by shifting the reader back to the code proper; and the grammar of the clause "but the main point" registers the close of semantic wavering (lexias 61–62) through the ideation of "size," which downgrades intellectual constructions. The structure here is manifestly asyndetonic: in the world of the historian who must say what happened ("disaster"), interpret/explain ("balance"), "vast" enables the narrator to work out to the maximum conceivable context (see lexia 10; and see *Capitalism and Material Life*, pp. 204–206). (Each chapter is organized in the same manner, the effects of which will be taken up later).

(64) Every recession solves a certain number of problems, removes pressures, and benefits the survivors.

(65) It is pretty drastic, but nonetheless a remedy.
(66) . . . Man's very progress became a burden and again brought about his poverty.
(67) Man only prospered for short intervals and did not realize it [overpopulation] until it was already too late.

One should be thankful those days are over. These "long fluctuations" establish a paradigmatic norm, the truism of a negative "remedy," a sort of "historical medicine" which the narrator does not hesitate to extend as far as possible. And the "pain" of European demography acquires its significant contrasting "value" when "vast" is described. By comparison to Europe, world demography for the period 1500–1800 shows that it was

(68) as though all humanity were in the grip of a primordial cosmic destiny that would make the rest of man's history seem, in comparison, of secondary importance.

This is proved by citing the views of an early modern demographer (!). The early "scientist" is quoted within the story for a knowledge effect: as a "witness" to the "truths" *now told,* the past-scientist is a figure of continuity, what we can call a narrative-relator, since his function is clearly to provide the story with a source that confirms what is told, a source supposedly unmotivated by the narrator's own context or time (see Wojcik 1970:272–275 for a concise inventory of relator functions). Indeed, so keen is the narrator to establish this "cosmic demography," this history of number, that the nonnarrative report of early modern "knowledge" (lexia 68) is also a narrative prolepsis, a heliotropic figure aiming, all along, toward now:

(69) "The development of population," wrote Wagemann, "must be attributed to causes very different from those that led to economic, technical, and medical progress."
(70) Obscure, yet prophetic in its way, it will help towards a better grasp of an authentic history of the world.

(71) It is tremendously important to work out this global figure . . . to determine the biological evolution of humanity considered as a single entity . . .

(72) What about the rest of the world? There is nothing or
almost nothing, on India, *careless of its history* in general,
and unconcerned with the statistics that might shed light
on it. (italics added)

Lexia 70 lets the historian-narrator now introduce a morality of
numbers: the historiographical subcode that *inauthentic history is
not numerical,* which is a possible intertextual polemic aimed at
histories of events. One can say that with lexia 71 an internal
historicism is fully present: the scientific historian can grasp
evolution with the armature of the "global," a recoding of Buckle's (1973:126–127) requirement that the historian submit story
to the demonstration of "universal order." Between lexias 71 and
72 the narrator tells the reader that the population for 1500–1800
is not documentable, so the record is an obstacle to knowledge,
the past returned, as it were, to the status of "barely conscious."
Lexia 72 is so strange that it is immediately startling: it answers
a question never put—and the question is answered by attrib-
uting the seme of "careless" (– thought, – interest, + oblivious
to science) to a country, so that history is now confronted by
the rejection of a sense of "history in the past." Wagemann, the
Western demographer, is then a positive precursor, a metadiegetic operator for the organization of the story. Professional
history never relinquishes its rights over history: for positive
and negative history appear at once insofar as someone in the
past had enough prescience to ask the "right" question, and
there are those in the past who throw history away. Professional
history always sides with its ancestors.

The syntagmatic trajectory of "number" is finally rendered:

(73) Nonetheless, the population of the world probably dou-
bled in this immense period of time.

(74) Neither economic crises, nor massive mortality prevented the upward movement.

(75) This is indubitably the basic fact in world history from

the 15th to the 18th century . . .
(76) Everything has to adapt to the general pressure.

We noted in the first chapter forms of the "lure" of the transcendent created by the stability of the signified; such cultural discourse creates tactical simulations that displace language (Baudrillard 1983b:122). Lexias 73–76 are such a simulacrum: (1) "nonetheless" plunges one into the "it doesn't matter" about the evidence (abolished, "real figures . . . do not exist," p. 7), (2) manifested as a "pressure" (spatial-social physics) which is indistinguishably effect/cause; (3) the totality of all possible actions is then semically contained by "to adapt," a macro-Behaviorism (the "to-have-to respond"), providing the reader with access to a continuous process (see Holloway 1979:68). The overall sign form manifested from lexias 73 through 76 is that of the primacy of number and its force, which is an intransitive cause linked to innumerable consequents, and saturated by a psychology, the terrorism of magnitude, an abstract force unmediated in delivering itself to the social. As a syntagmatic device, "number" provides a first trajectory, "upward," which, no matter how thin a temporal marker, provides a temporal line. We register that such imaginary narrative progression is also canceled by nonnarrative ideations like lexia 76.

Links between historiography and story often turn on a narrator's systematic rejection of previous stories; here, the telling of the increase in European population as the result of improved sanitation is annulled, as are numerous other prior stories (see pp. 9–17). It is as if every past story had colonized "the past" (pace Hayden White) and is now recolonized by a telling which, as in Broch's *The Death of Virgil,* "divests itself of all symbol and yet containing the seed of every symbol," must resymbolize everything. The overcoded aspect of historiographical sememes is meant to ensure that the reader never confronts an unmonitored story. Moreover, like the Behaviorist coding of "pressure," "number" is linked to a pure metaphysics of history:

(77) history is fundamentally the realization of these vital differences deriving from number (p. 20).

Amalgamated, "history" as "number" can be used to absorb the impact of social physics (climate) and biological and social phenomena ("uprisings," p. 19), and so history can then also manifest that which

> (78) is common to all mankind . . . [and] would give the globe its first unity well before the great discoveries, the industrial revolution or the interpenetration of economies.

Lexias 77 and 78 rearticulate the "promise" of lexia 21, only now they manifest a certain corrective value to the mind: how can anything really matter by comparison to number and this vast and inert unity? One can readily see that lexia 78 presents what we can call a historiographical program—all possible stories that could be told about discoveries, revolutions, capitalism should be thought of, in advance, as subject to the nonhistorical, for number is the discourse of the whole, paramorphic and homeomorphic at once; it governs what then can be relegated to epiphenomena. This historiographical threshold is consistently little more than the construction of distance: the projected real model of comparative thought, number, is that scale of the real over which no one has control; the cultural expression of this coding is the naturalness of reaction, the greater necessity—to adapt—which precludes internal comprehension of the social. The social, political, and so on, can thus be explained away, downsized to the level of fleeting and fugitive significations, Structuralism made the distancing device for these thoughts.

> (79) . . . it is difficult . . . to discard and break away from our obsession with present-day perspectives unless we continually refer back to some scale of reference.
> (80) . . . at Pavia (1525) . . . 10,000 mobile, furious, and pitiless soldiers represented a far greater force than 50,000 or 100,000 men would do today.
> (81) The victory of Pavia was the triumph of the arquebusiers and even more of empty stomachs.

Even "empty stomachs" are allotted a certain semantic space in the metaphysical; ratios govern history. "Face-to-face" combat in 1525 is more "intense" than that of 100,000 soldiers today; one does not know whether this means that today face-to-face combat occurs less frequently or that its very frequency is common and so drained of its force beforehand. Lexias 79 through 80 are figurized, logicized, and psychologized at the same time; we will call this kind of unit a story-comparer, which belongs on the story-narrating line because of its intradiegetic organization (the supposition that past-present are fundamentally continuous), and which is sent to the reader as a trans-temporal psychological force. The narrative impact here overcomes everything else: the injunction to "discard" (lexia 79) so as to proceed with knowing (lexia 79) aims at introducing in the reader a tearing away—the past requires that the reader submit to a scale of measurement so as to reach the past, this scale then used to recode the content of a psychologized decline in the value of force ("force" is less forceful today). It is clear that such discursive registerings cannot be expressed except as narrativized functions of a story or as a theory of story; and that the heterogeneity of signifiers—"number," "force," "empty stomach"—results in a homogeneous enthymeme: "number" shows how "history is produced," just as past numbered relations are more "forceful" than present now ones.

The "basic fact" of number (lexia 75), then, is both part of a narrative trajectory ("rise," "pressure") and a historiographic scene. The reader is encouraged to abandon false stories, so that while the narrative runs forward, the historiographical function runs, as it were, backward. For example, on the basis of an if-clause used to recalculate France's population, the narrator shifts from the hypothetical ("probably overpopulated") to this conclusion:

(82) France . . . was encumbered with too many people,
(83) too many beggars, useless mouths, undesirables
(84) Brantome was already saying that it was as "full as an egg" (p. 23).

Forward, "overpopulation" leads to "emigration," but conceptually, which means historiographically, social marks ("useless," etc.) correct the earlier stories (other versions) that France in

1600 was "underpopulated." After noting that famine often had more disastrous effects in the countryside than in the towns, "number" explains Europe's "attitude" toward the poor and offers a contrast with the rest of the world:

> (85) The problem was to place the poor in a position where they could do no harm.
> (86) This "great enclosure" of the poor, mad and delinquent . . . was one psychological aspect of seventeenth-century society, relentless in its rationality. But it was perhaps an almost inevitable reaction to the poverty and increase in numbers of the poor in that hard century (p. 41).

Lexia 85 speaks through the voice of the bourgeoisie; we shall later take up the various academic sectors the narrator speaks for in the story as a whole. Once again it is important to note that lexia 58 is still in force here: the seventeenth-century bourgeoisie defined their understanding as a "problem" that was an "inevitable reaction" to the "increase in numbers," the "rationality" placed as the sufficient condition occurred, if that is what it was, in philosophy and literature and politics as Descartes and Racine and Richelieu. The inference is: the perception of "poverty and increase in numbers" was thought out by the bourgeoisie as a suppression of the body of the poor, the latter with zero-psychological traits, the former already having rationalized their psychology or psychologized their rationality. Now an analysis of *that* would be interesting here. What the narrator next says is:

> (87) This was Europe.
> (88) Things were far worse in Asia, China, and India.

The reader can now form the conclusion that Europe was subject to "number" and so psychology, rationality, thinking are reduced to forms of closure, registered when the telling shifts from what Genette (1978:195) calls a lateral ellipsis, a paraleptic omission, to a frame that shuts off the spread and reach of lexias 85–86. Instead of opening onto what was involved, the narrating

swerves out to that "widest perspective" where maximum ideology is found: distorted comparison. All of this is a case of
"explaining away," so perhaps we can invent a category for this
and call it an instance of the discursive *protection* of narration,
since it employs a surplus example of horror subsidizing the
comparisons used to keep the story on track.

(89) We return hardened, consoled or resigned to privileged
Europe as if from some nightmare journey (p. 41).

Kracauer, unhappily under the spell of "history," nevertheless
accurately pointed out how "universal history" (what can also
be called pathological comparatization) has to try to mobilize
some sort of "Chinese gadget . . . a hollow ivory sphere which
contains similar spheres of diminishing size, each freely circling
in the womb of the next larger one" (1969:104), so that focalization upon what no one could ever know or see is stabilized
(explaining away = approximation of God). Lévi-Strauss
(1966:257–259) also had something to say about the comparison
= explain away = protection of the story syndrome of historians. He called it "a spurious intelligibility attaching to a temporal internality," which collapses as soon as selected existents
are made discontinuous (recognizable), because to totalize in-
comparables (Europe, Asia) ends in a sort of tautomorphic race
for the historian. X is bad, Y is worse, X + Y = "inferior," but
X is still = to "less inferior" because Y = "more inferior." In
highlighting "this was Europe," by means of the "far worse of
Asia," the comparatizing (linked to what Mink called "aggre-
gative" history) establishes a *contrarium* in favor of a reading of
Europe. Perhaps now the "journey back" of lexia 19 can be
understood as a journey whose destination is the reader's arrival
at the acceptance of "this was Europe" (what lexia 89 supposes).
The negativity forgiven by lexia 87 is a case of "it could have
been worse."

   We will not enumerate all the paradigmatic contrasts the narrator mentions along the syntagmatic route of "number." "Number" is ultimately intended to provide the reader with a sense
of some "world scale" (p. 65), but the section on epidemics (pp.

43–56) is not even calibrated with a numerical scale. A line direct to the reader, however, is clear:

> (90) The plague . . . multiplied what we would call dereliction of duty . . . in France whole parlements emigrated,

as is a pretext for what the narrator really wants to convey—

> (91) No disease today, however great its ravages, gives rise to comparable acts of folly or collective dramas.

The same tactic: the disaster of disease then was universal and saturated the social system, a full scene; today, in the most intensive of enthymemic conclusions, death by disease is no longer dramatic—today disease must not be thought of globally, which is precisely the view of Westerners for whom such places as Bangladesh are never part of the scene.

Again, the comparisons aim at establishing the priority of a system over the transformations of the system: this historian, who contrasts so as to compare, places such narrative joints within the discursive, as in lexias 57, 64, and 87. Situations absorb actions, in Segre's (1979:17) terms. The descriptive passages are mostly scene setting, action discounted to the point where almost nothing happens. In theoretical terms, there is so far no narrative test, no narrative contract; there are some disjunctive events (for example, "rise" in population and implicit desire, the parlement's "emigration," which, however, are restricted to the status of examples). Earlier and later have not yet been distinguished in any strong manner, at least by comparison to the achronic relationships, so that narrative operations (antagonism, alliances, existential convergences of characters) are essentially thus far the merest inferences. Deep history = near zero action.

But there is a narrative line *within* the paradigmatic: it goes to the reader as the distance between present-past, a distance so far defined or constructed as realizations of that program set forth in lexia 24, "progress." This suggests that continuity is so absolute on the level of "structures" that story is dehistoricized while structures are rehistoricized (the inverse of Lévi-Strauss's texts). We can call this the voice of accomplishment, made out of the reader's internalization of an aspect of reactive-subjectivism (all of the stresses placed on what cannot change), which strive for the extra-dramatic (neither ironic nor tragic) on account of the predominance of statements that encourage the reader to confirm and conform (lexia 46, for example). Thus, after a few more scenes of "number," the reader is presented with this summary/ideology:

(92) The world is divided and organized according to the force of numbers which gives each living mass its individual significance and fixes its level of culture and efficiency, its biological and economic rhythms of growth, and its pathological destiny.

This extreme instance of nonnarrative assertion twists the kaleidoscope of the story to zero-thought, virtually demolishing the story, but it then returns, as it were, to its alternate, that moving forward by means of a concretized comparison, which keeps the hierarchy in place as "number" is more articulated. For example, after lexia 92, we are presented with the contrast of the nomads and the barbarians, the latter "almost fully civilized" (p. 76). The former, however, are hypersaturated by the archaic, the doomed, the nonfuture:

(93) it was *only* the Old World that experienced this extraordinary breed of humanity.
(94) These arid and abandoned lands formed an endless explosive fuse from the Atlantic to the waters of the Pacific.
(95) It burst into flames at the slightest spark
(96) and burned along its entire length.
(97) When . . . dispute . . . drought . . . population increase drove them out . . .
(98) they invaded their neighbors' lands.
(99) They represented speed and surprise at a period when everything moved slowly (p. 57).

> (100) The nomads, condemned to stay home, appeared in their true colors:
> (101) A poor species of mankind put in its place and destined to remain there.
> (102) . . . a long parasitical existence that came to an end once and for all (p. 60).

"Number," considered now as a narrative function, is organized according to a dramatic framing: once "outnumbered" by stable populations, the "nomads" lose their dramatic force and become what they were all along—a subhuman category ("parasitical"). Because they did not "enjoy" a future comparable to that of a civilization, they could never have; they could never have because they were never numerous enough; they were never numerically significant because they never inhabited territory according to the "rules" of civilization, and so on. "Number" meets *post hoc, ergo propter hoc* in explaining away the nomads. So the science of number is also a means of redramatizing and narrating: every time a "barbarian" people (Mongols, for example) collided with a civilized group, the "mass" of the latter triumphed. Nomads are dehistoricized because their structures were inefficiently historical. I can now say that the story within the paradigmatic is dominant; for while the story runs forward, its thought-form is the display of writing off those who lacked the condition of what the historian presupposes, the historical itself.

Number triumphs: the nomads prove the truth of number. And so does the discourse: lexia 101 saturates one's sense of history—"destined to" gives essence, role, image, marker, all at once. The story operation—the nomads as an illustration of the historical truth of the Old World—also generates a vicious syntagmatic contrast, that of past existents who are auxiliaries (or helpers) of negative progress, or nonprogress, those of the past who deserved no future, who could not cross over to the life of maturity.

The chapter closes with the motif of the conquest of space.

> (103) As a general rule, the civilizations played and won.

(104) They won their struggles against "cultures" and primitive peoples.

(105) Even better, they won their war against empty space.

(106) In this last case, everything had to be built up from scratch.

(107) And this was the Europeans' great good fortune in three-quarters of America. Russians . . . Siberia, . . . British in Australia . . . ,

(108) How lucky it would have been for the Whites in South Africa if the Boers and British had not been called

(109) upon to face Black pressure.

Lexias 103 through 109 no doubt satisfy that desire for "comprehension" Jameson (1972:9) speaks of when he suggests that "diachronic history" has "great elegance for the mind" insofar as it answers some puzzle and discards earlier interpretations. "Mere" groups ("cultures") were successively defeated by "civilizations," reduced to a "struggle" of zero interest by comparison to the superlative conflict, the "war" against "empty space." Filling up with numbers, the European civilizations did not succumb to later "overpopulation"; Europe managed to resolve its "space" problem (!). This narrative prolepsis, provided as a summary of what is to follow, gives the result first; how it occurred is almost an afterthought. Lexia 107 tells us the "lucky" spaces for these Europeans reached their temporal limit in Africa; the "would have been" introduces an "unreal condition" (see Joos 1968:124), the sense of "otherwise" concerning Africa; reversed, does it mean the Whites were "unlucky" because the Blacks were there? Perhaps this is an example of a counterfactual wish-statement. True, the narrator castigates the Jesuits in Latin America (p. 60) and the hunting of Indians; but this moral assessment is quickly overthrown in favor of completing the "unreal condition" by a topic switch that initiates a new recoding:

(110) The real issue was not conquest of men (they were annihilated) but of space.

(111) Thenceforth it was distance that had to be conquered (p. 61).

The "destruction of men" is recoded as a by-product of the conflict with "space." This valuation—dismissal of violence—is introduced by a distinction between civilizations and cultures, which, to my knowledge, has no parallel in any previous speculative notions of history. What is supposed to make lexia 110 acceptable is the narrator's overcoding of lexia 68 and the different "destinies" that intrinsically accompany a tropism toward the future. The "conquest of men" is a mere fact of mature civilizations, those that are already oriented toward the future, a case where historicality itself is thought of as a structure of survival:

(112) . . . Black Africa . . . Mexico and Peru . . . These immature civilizations, which were really cultures, collapsed in the face of a small number of men.

(113) A culture is a civilization that has not yet achieved maturity, its greatest potential, nor consolidated its growth.

(114) Meanwhile . . . adjacent civilizations exploit it in a thousand ways, which is natural if not particularly just (p. 63).

The model reader can think: it is mature to exploit, or those cultures that do not exploit are immature. The reversibility of the contrast is nevertheless subservient to the implied narrative trajectory: the future belongs to those civilizations that imperceptibly slide from "can exploit" to "must exploit," a sign that the historian has simply added cultural transcendence to those that in fact were successful as exploiters. The chrononym "maturity," the toponym "consolidated," and the anthroponym "exploited" (referring to a "natural" human orientation) are fused so as to produce a piece of historical instruction aimed at the reader: justice has no particular status in historical thought or within the forces that generate historicity. "History hurts," says Jameson. Indeed, this instructive scene is embedded in overcoding *simpliciter;* in a discussion of the "resistance" of "immature cultures," the narrator pauses over the Chinese exploitation of the Indian archipelago, its "colonial market," so as to isolate nothing less than a "law of exploitation":

(115) If China has remained so uninventive and so backward at the capitalist level . . .

(116) it is to the extent that this exploitation was so easy and widespread.

(117) The Chinese had things too easy (p. 64).

More equivalences: "hard exploitation" = a narrative test of a civilization's "maturity," all of which is the encoding of European "civilization" as equipped to do the job of exploitation. The image the reader forms of those civilizations that did not advance into the capitalist future may be that of a *sequence* that remained "vacant," to use Iser's (1978:195–199) phrase, but the law of the social at lexia 117 outstrips the reader's application of narrative categories.

The last thematic opposition in this "conquest of space" is the opposition between civilizations; the narrator engages in an entry of a *nonshifted past*, that is, setting up a context where the difference between past and now is made irrelevant by comparison to, we shall say, the temporal continuity of continuity itself (see Banfield 1982:104).

(118) When civilizations clash the consequences are dramatic.

(119) Today's world is still embroiled in them.

These lexias generate no shift between past/present; then this:

(120) . . . stormy conquests looked at retrospectively, through the eyes of men today, seem like episodes, *whatever their duration.*

(121) They came into being more or less suddenly, then collapsed one fine day like stage sets (p. 64, italics added).

Lexia 120 reminds one of Danto's prescription cited in chapter two: the historian organizes the then pointlessness of past present-tomorrows, considered as a spatial matrix, into temporal wholes. Who can say the "value" of violence is a mere "episode," a "stage set"? What semic markers connect "conquests" and "stage sets"? All of this is nothing more than an instance of disengaging from the story any strong comprehension of violence; unlike "disease," coded as superdramatic in past and zero-dramatizable today, "violence" is organized as undemonstrable, it points to nothing of significance ("like episodes"); it leads neither into story nor the reader into history by comparison to the nontheatrical predications of continuous processes (for example, "maturity").

If we focus on narrative-theory terms for a moment, we must stress once more that the story is organized virtually without action: population, disease, psychological reactions, and so on, are roles strictly controlled by their illustrative functions and their discursive embeddings, both *exempla* and omni-temporal processes identified as historical ones. It is not hard to see that "necessity and finality," those supreme signifieds, have here been recast as a linguistico-cognitive competence, the accepted series of presuppositions which the narrator announced at lexias 32 and 44, and which are nothing more than a new version of significations of mode—what could and could not happen. Nowhere does the narrator relinquish the authority that he has imputed to the implicit science of the discursive. Structuralism is that science, a modernist design of liberating objects in their functions (see Baudrillard 1981:194), and it is grafted onto narrating and story by overcoded acts of antiphrasis: the reader has to free himself from what Mandelbaum called "special histories" and relocate himself in the presence of the simultaneity of story and system. The consistent elimination of any discontinuous set is clearly an instance of "history from the top," where the narrated is formalized by a successive discounting of its information in favor of creating maximum comprehension, the latter "itself explicable only in terms of biology, geology, and finally cosmology" (Lévi-Strauss 1966:262). The undeletability of lexias 57 and 68, the coding of "recessions" as determined by "number," the forgiveness of lexias 85–88, the judgment ladled over the "nomads," are moments in the decoding of Structuralist theory so it can be recoded for the presentation of a new temporal system.

The narrator has activated the "time of the system," which does not parallel historiographical, sociological, formal, or material time, as one commentary on Braudel suggests (Santamaria and Bailey 1984:81–82). This can be established by paying attention to the kinds of time ejected from the story. Discontinuous temporality has no place in the time of the system. There is no room for an intercalation of trajectories that somehow do not feed the system. And as the narrator has explicitly accepted the voice of the future, this is reflected in an internal shift: the narrator stresses times that are all institutional ones, given over to reproduction—what we could call linearity, direction, and result saturated by the requirements of institutions. The intensity of the seventeenth-century "great confinement" is simply wiped out, the multiple violence of "confinement" reduced to a single fact of psychology. The story is itself "confined" by the non-narrative schema that unfolds its own space-time, what was initiated at lexias 44 and 45. In a world such as ours, where "becoming" is significant for those integrated to a continuum ("becoming" means more of the same, where institutionalizing subjects have futures, for example, "careers"), the turn to "spatial history" is homologous with a shift acutely denoted by Baudrillard:

one goes from a system of productive forces, exploitation and profit, as in the competitive system dominated in its logic by social labor time, to a gigantic operational game of question and answer, to a gigantic combinatory where all values commutate and are exchanged according to their operational sign (1975:127).

Capitalism and Material Life indexes this shift in its organization of distances: the reader is not released "in the past" so as to form there empathies, identities, connections of the traditional historical kind; the full meaning of this instance of global history is not, as the profession would have it, a "new organic logic" (see Kinser 1981:92), but rather the generalized displacement of critical thinking. This line has only one addressee, the reactive reader.

The system's time carries over to food production:

(122) Men's diet between 1500–1800 . . . essentially consisted of vegetable foods (p. 66).

The frame: consumption restricted to the same type. This is immediately grafted onto

(123) . . . food bears witness to his social status and his civilization or culture,

which allows the narrator to focus on change defined by binary sets, where the "rare" and the "innumerable" (meat versus bread/vegetable consumption) is, in turn, associated with an unspecified principle of transformation (the consumption of meat is cause/consequence of growth), and "meat consumption" is undercoded as part of the West's capacity to break out of its limits. After a long inventory of the difficult systems of crop production, the story summarizes the overall increase in food production with a genuine narrative pattern, that of decline:

(124) All too often these exertions were accomplished to the detriment of peasant life.

(125) The peasants were as much the slaves of corn as of the nobility.

Within an overall increase in cereal production for the period (p. 82), the reader can think of the "peasants" separate from the function "improvement," especially by comparison to the dilemmas of the system, which

(126) was incapable of providing for the supply of the enlarged towns . . . (p. 87).

In the absence of any sort of systematic market system (or allocation), the economic level makes its appearance here, interlaced with a growing population, especially in northern Europe, and where a strange sort of choice accompanies those who came into contact with money:

(127) The attraction in each case was ready cash.

(128) The rich always paid cash down in the corn trade.

(129) The poor succumbed to the temptation and, of course,

those who made the biggest profits were the middle-
men, like the merchants who speculated on corn in the
blade . . . (p. 84).

Where "number" was bluntly used to overcode nonchoice (lexia
76), the very introduction of the sememic unit "money" is conveyed by the equivalence: attraction—cash. Now one sees, for
example, that this "attraction" is detrimental to the "poor" ("succumbed"), which opens the sense, in Bremond's terms, that the
"poor" might not have "succumbed," which in turn opens a
primary choice: did the poor have to or not have to use cash to
purchase corn? Pursuing this topic would require the narrator
to desemanticize "attraction," its positivity suspended if any
sense of coercion in fact surrounded "cash." As usual, the narrator veers away from implicit social contradictions in favor of
a higher dramatic function, which cancels what lexia 129 inadvertently opened:

(130) This long distance trade holds endless fascination.

After which follows a summary of the "wonders" of trade
(p. 85), and then this narrative stop:

(131) Large scale systems of purchase, warehousing, and dis-
      tribution . . . did not appear until the eighteenth
      century
(132) In fact no concentration appeared in the corn trade until
      the nineteenth century

These summaries encode "economic incapacity," a theme then
made subservient to the main focus, "food as witness" (lexia
123). In China, rice fields were

(133) a factory,

much more efficient in calories than corn or livestock, and the
conclusion:

(134) The Far Eastern civilizations' preference for vegetarianism certainly does not spring from idealism (p. 103).

Then a philosophy:

(135) Perhaps we can venture the idea of a dietary choice by a civilization, a dominant taste, even a passion,
(136) of which the European has not the slightest understanding.
(137) The choice is the result of a conscious preference for what is best.
(138) To stop cultivating rice would be to lose caste (p. 103).

The evidence cited in support of such propositions is the report of a contemporary geographer, another metadiegetic past interpreter transposed by the narrator so as to "speak" a conclusion. This device presents the authority from "outside." In the East there is strict identity between consciousness and structure, whereas in the West there is at best a mixture of "attraction" and "slavery." To the encoded semi-chaos of Western agrarian production, which is also narratively its "openness," the East is hyperrational: a "factory" of "rice fields" results in dietary patterns of an unmediated order (lexia 134), which they lived out as an absolute rule of differentiation and hierarchy. The historian moves, without raising any problematic, from material life to the deepest recesses of psychic organization (lexia 138). Implied, as we shall see, is the idea that the specificity of Europe lies somewhere else than in material production.

The "contrasts" promised at lexia 32 which are supposed to yield knowledge of "mechanisms" (lexia 34) no doubt involve the reader in making textual "logic-likenesses," the next-read the completion of the read (Eco 1979:32), the chronological order a signifier of "proof" (correct order = truth-effect). So while in the West the peasants were subject to double slavery, and in the East to a "factory" (homogeneous structure), these differentiations really are illumined only by the system in Meso-America; because maize production was easy there,

(139) They were therefore free, too free.
(140) Maize . . . brought about theocratic totalitarian systems
    and all the leisure at the disposal of the countryside was
    used for immense Egyptian type public works.
(141) All this suffering, and for what?
(142) What is lacking is meat; meat is persistently absent.
(143) Their only resort is to chew coca leaves, which numb
(144) . . . dangerous drinks enabled these sad, weak popu-
    lations to escape from themselves in Goyaesque scenes
    of drunkenness (p. 111).

Meso-America offers the perfect contrast because, as described, it is the obliteration of contrast: Egypt and Goya or monumental waste and infinite dissolution encode the bestial; this narrative pause provides the story of Europe with *signifiers of undetermination* (Europe as undercoded by comparison to the East and Meso-America), because, after all, Europe was "unfree" ("slavery") and so "limited" but not overdetermined. Here too is a significant textual isotopy: one way or the other, life was always worse outside Europe, this isotopy now coded as a narrated connotation. Lexia 139 also indicates some trace of a purely cultural voice which, for now, we shall index only as that of a "cultural cop." Again, the European series is open by comparison to the non-European. Meso-America is now organized for another historian merely to fill in the contextual selection, actors and primary verbs. Its actantial role is Self-Destruction, which equals nonstory, no history, nothingness.

The narrator's final categorization of "daily bread" is an occasion for the narrator to plunge the reader into a suprahistorical mytheme, another instance of historicality from the top, where the real itself is erased:

(145) Maize was not a dominant plant . . . it largely involved
    primitive peasants.
(146) In fact these peasants were a category apart, like a sep-
    arate species of humanity.
(147) To consider their fate is to turn our attention away from
    the dominant plants—

(148) that is away from the civilizations that have been favored by history and so arrogate to themselves the front
of the stage.

(149) . . . a whole book on corn . . . would have been misleading. The fate of things grown is predominantly a
matter of the fate of their cultures.

(150) . . . It was the mainstream of history that passed manioc
by (p. 114).

The "full narration" of corn, its "totality" (recognized by the
narrator as a theoretical possibility), would degrade the narrative
of history: such is the position taken by the voice of the historian
who can now directly assign value prior even to that level of
engagement/disengagement we analyzed in chapter two. *Cursed
or favored* by history: the former is an instance of a story not
worth telling, the latter is an instance of an untold story (narrated
"correctly"), the binary choice ushered in by the *ab ovo* mainstream of history. The syntagmatization of lexias 145–150 looks
like this: the elementary semes are

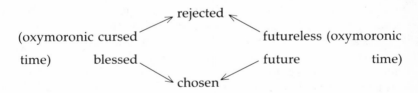

where the top row, complementary, gives rise to "rejected" as
its category of inclusion, and where the bottom row generates
"chosen" as its amalgamation (see Courtes 1976:59 on this syntagmatic square and its independence from the paradigmatic
square). To be "cursed and futureless" is to be "rejected" and
to be "blessed and futural" is to be "chosen," "rejected" the
complex term because it synthesizes by conjunction, "chosen"
the more neutral term because it is bound to the negation of
"not-blessed" and "no future," and so still semantically controlled by "rejected" (the negative is stronger than the positive
in setting out a syntagmatic arrangement). The implied conclu-

sion: both "rejected and chosen" are *semantic selections* of history. The mainstream of history that passed by selects: even nonselected cultures were first objects of rejection before their own time, "selected out" at the start, a Calvinism applied directly to the category "history." What *is* narrated in the future deserves to be narrated: such is the law not just of the successful (Hegel's conceit) nor of the victors (Carr's position) but of value itself. "History" writes out and is a writing out.

So once again we pass from narrating to hypertranscendence. And the reader passes through a zone where, at any given moment, what is narrated already has the status of deserving such narration. The enunciator tells us: "favored by history" is intrinsic to the historian who must then be in touch with history itself. After all, it is stated with the utmost sincerity, seriousness, and grace. Number is gone, absorbed, by the freeing of Europe as a narrative topic (lexia 130). The reader has to know by now that non-Europe is, at best, mere contrastable material, a duplication in textual form of its existential relation to Europe (and the United States), that of a supplier. The narrator thus continues the practice of reducing the non-West to regimes of bodies upon which the West has rights/writes. The narrating could now dispense with that program of comparing recurring features announced at lexia 34, although it does not.

Narrative speed, where the gearings of expansion, inclusion, distortion, contraction, roles, isotopies, and so on, systematically encode one another, perhaps as the signified takes its priority over the signifier, has only variable connections with types of actions, settings, and theorizing, on both the level of the fabula and discourse. Genette (1978:94–99) has argued, for instance, that summary has a variable tempo with what it recounts, every summary both a transition (between scenes) and an acceleration, a way of talking about what happened without stopping and doing so. One might note that summary is also comparable to what linguists call a downgraded sememe, like "doctor," where a stable denotation precludes expansion of its possible meanings (see Leech 1974:149–154). The narrator of *Capitalism and Material Life* summarizes the discursive telling (its organization) just as often as elements on the story line (fabula) are summarized, neutralizing the narrating in its duration, thereby promoting both a sense of scientific value on the level of the discourse and "significance" on the level of the story. But in effect, what narratists such as Genette point to as features of "telling" are also sign forms in Baudrillard's sense, devices where, for example, summary performs functions such as synthesis, axiomatizing, or defining (see especially lexia 110). The story is now speeded up by introducing topics closer to perception than "number" or "daily bread" were, reorganizing a complex series of connections with the previously told. For example, the economic pair

(151) Superfluity and bare necessity are constantly to be found side by side,

or, as "more than enough" and the "just enough," are manifestly semes that pertain to "excess and minimum" (pure quanta), pleasure and pain (a cultural code), length and proximity (the implied duration of "excess" subcoded as a "pleasurable time" and "proximity" pre-embedded in "mere consumption"), and are immediately joined to this sign form:

(152) . . . by comparing the condition of the majority—on food, houses, and clothing of the general run of men—

(153) with that of the minority, the privileged, those whose way of life we may call luxurious (p. 121).

So that "majority" = consumption at the limit of production, while "minority" = consumption beyond such a limit. Such designations are legitimized by the narrator's invocation of the agonistics of the historian:

(154) Distinguishing between the ordinary and the exceptional will involve us in a difficult and flexible procedure.

The economic is introduced through "material results," and so I note, again, the sliding of the signifier: the reader is shifted from a contrary (at lexia 151,) a full transcendent one (*without temporal periodizers*), to the contextual selection of "ordinary" and "exceptional," the last arrangement capable of being narrated (which lexia 151 is not) since "ordinary" = frequent, "exceptional" = infrequent, both at least possible actions. The reader has been guided to the question "how often?," a trivialization and desemanticizing of the very opposition set out at lexia 151, a pseudo-invitation to empathize with the "scientific historian."

The speaker does not want to perform the scientific task laid out by lexia 154 as much as try to narrativize "luxury":

(155) . . . luxury cannot be identified once and for all with the necessary precision.

"Luxury" is also not simply socialized forms of "superfluity":

(156) Luxury therefore has many facets, according to the period, country, or civilization in question.
(157) In contrast, the social drama, without beginning or end,
(158) with luxury as its prize and its theme,
(159) scarcely changes at all.
(160) A choice spectacle for the sociologist, psychoanalyst, economist, and historian (p. 122).

Stoianovich (1976:109–110) and other historians would view the predications of "luxury" as the result of a choice about mental structures, that "luxury" has the status of one of Foucault's epistemes, only here coded as a "cultureme." No doubt "luxury" can be interpreted as part of that generalized acceptance by the social sciences that "meaning structures" (language) have a status akin to Bourdieu's (1976:164–166) notion of "habitus," "structured structures capable of functioning as structuring structures," or axioms of cultural experience. But the succession of lexias about luxury has to be read as a sign form itself, these lexias constituting something like the intersection of a syntagmatic sequence (from object to subject, the reversal of stating/stated) and a paradigmatic contrast, naturalized to the point of pure stasis—the "social" is *always*, "luxury" *always-different*, a narrativized contrast. This is another story embedded within the paradigmatic, which here is: "the first sensibility arose as desire for luxury," "luxury" the precursor and fate of all of its subsequent futures. The origin of the telling proper is the story of Desire, this putative "center" a version of the myth of the cultural endowment of story itself, that it varies repetition, the dreaded antithesis of story (see the suggestive remarks by Barthes 1977:124). I stress that the social drama is completely embedded in the pure fictitious matter of history, which is driven by the "transcendence of the lack (of prize)." This is an essentially consumerist model, the desire to achieve the inessential ("superfluity"). One might say it is the subject's desire to become aestheticized, which I shall take up later. The sequence is completed with the mention of the "human sciences": they are not called "sciences of the spectacle" or "knowledges of the spectacle," a curious syncopation of Debord and the situationists.

The social classes are recoded:

(161) privileged and onlookers (p. 122),

or "elites and masses" are reciprocally linked by a "desire" traveling from the masses' "watching" of the elites and the elites' self-objectification, for both

(162) agree to a certain amount of connivance.

This recoding of contract theory is rendered now as a Law of the Social: the masses overvalue signifieds—

(163) social success, fascination, the dream that one day becomes reality for the poor . . . ,

which, however, endlessly dissolves into empty signifiers—

(164) and in so doing immediately loses its old glamour.

By the time the poor possess what the elites enjoyed, "too late" saturates the "poor" in the endless repetition of "desiring" that which cannot "satisfy," and so the process of "desire" is a permanent automatism:

> (165) The appetite becomes sated. The rich are thus doomed to prepare the future life of the poor.
> (166) It is, after all, their justification: they try out the pleasures that the masses will sooner or later grasp (p. 122).

Such is "fundamental history": founded on agreement, the permanent structure of desire necessitates that one think of history as a narrative schema, where history is the performance of acts with this structure:

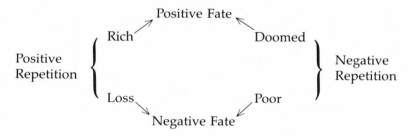

Only the poor in this schema are subjects of both desire and negation; the rich escape this contradiction, this Schopenhauerian dissolution, for they are defined as nothing other than the principle of "cultural production" itself: "doomed" is made positive, the happy repetition of elites. As *bricoleurs* of value, the rich are never too late: they are always on time in this historicist fable, this substratum of cultural existence, even though the "time" of the rich is marked by temporal relators of "wasted time": "futility, pretentiousness, and caprice" (p. 122). What connects these social planes is the time of luxury itself, another structural time:

> (167) every luxury dates and goes out of fashion.
> (168) But luxury is reborn from its own ashes and from its very defeats.
> (169) It is really the reflection of a difference in social levels that

(170) nothing can change and that every movement recreates.
An eternal "class struggle" (p. 123).

This textualization, which makes familiar a consumption model of historical transformation, thus completely psychologizes the historical in its very schema, a kind of perverse Kantian elaboration of the "transcendental a priori" of historical experience. "Man is a creature of desire and not a creature of need," says the narrator (p. 123), who, relying upon Mauss, Bachelard and Sombart, eternalizes all of history as a gigantic narrativization of a fake reciprocity ("connivance"). Lexias 169 and 170 recode lexias 161 and 162 in terms of pure structure, but with consent (lexia 162); the difference of "rich and poor" was always agreed to, that is, it happened at the same time the structure proper was established. As a semiotic process, "eternalization" is a seme that traces the very "stop" of all action, the point at which the discursive is simply the nondiscursive substratum. "Desire" comes before "before": but it always "came" with "agreement," and it "comes" as a combinatory, that in which each subject (individual or group) tries to close the "gap" opened by each successive failure of "luxury." And this long time of history is not a plot structure, not a logic, nor anything immanent to the social; such a "time" is bereft of all temporal marks, as satisfies signifiers of full presence:

(171) . . . an ineradicable and primordial mechanism is involved,
(172) even in present-day societies and in the face of rampant mass luxury (p. 123).

The "logic of desire"—this bulimia—is primordial because it determines the base of periodization, and as the condition of the continuousness of society, the reader is thus given the code of all historicity, the "in the past as today" (p. 123), the affirmation of an affirmation that cancels and annuls in advance, the negativity of "luxury" (lexia 168).

The modern consuming classes have found their historian. Here we see immediately the distortion effect of periodization, which validates the eternal even in condemning past-excess:

(173) . . . before the nineteenth century luxury was the unjust, unhealthy, brilliant, and anti-economic utilization
of any surplus produced in a given society.
(174) . . . luxury was more like the action of an engine often
running in neutral than an element of growth (p. 124).

Condemned as "limited and superficial," "luxury" is also acceptable as "rampant mass luxury": in the latter period—now—
economic growth confers the status of a more heroic quality to
"luxury," this taking place after the sociality of the peasant way
of life recedes in favor of the noncontestability of the bourgeois
period, its massification of "luxury." The "eternal time of luxury"
is more acceptable today; the proletariat is wealthy beyond the
dreams of the past-peasantry (!).

As is usual here with such discursive claims, the story then
undergoes a series of long comparisons and enumeration of
items, a superabundance of "motivated linear descriptions," to
use one historian's phrase (Streuver 1978:5, 1980:74). For those
interested, there was no "sophisticated cooking in Europe before
the fifteenth century," meat consumption declined after 1550,
meat was "rare in China," there are averages for the consumption of sheep in Istanbul, and so on—topoi of contrasts. Simultaneously dramatized and narrativized, these topoi are
extremely dense and informationally full, as well as integrated
with the voice of a conversationalist, periodically intervening to
invite the reader's question and render an answer, all of this a
tour de force of juxtaposed scenes. This is history told in a
painterly style, verbal copies of older, anterior codes of the real
(for example, long citations from travelers such as Montaigne).
Then summary:

(175) . . . a new code of behavior (p. 139)
(176) . . . the luxury of a room solely used for meals
(177) . . . all Europe, in the grip of an omnipresent luxury
. . .
(178) Hence Western travelers thought even less of the customs and habits of the wide world and looked down
on them more than ever.

Luxury and ethnocentrism—lexia 178 provides here an internal reason for dismissal of non-Europe. Another descent, this one into pepper:

(179) pepper . . . far from indispensable today
(180) Everything depended on it, even the dreams of the fifteenth-century explorers.
(181) As dear as pepper was a common saying (p. 152)

This confirms the monotony of diet in the period. One can say that Desire was frustrated in the consumptive chain; the "imbalance" of the period (lexia 173) is nothing other than this alternation between displacements:

(182) France fell madly in love with perfume
(183) It invaded stew, pastries, liquors, and sauces (p. 155).

When we turn to "drinks, stimulants, and drugs," however, the narrating strategy (or sign form) we earlier called the narrated story within the paradigmatic, the super-overcoded past used to "write away" non-Europe, also returns:

(184) Drunkenness increased everywhere in the sixteenth century
(185) . . . wine . . . had become a cheap food stuff.
(186) . . . a compensation . . . [for] purses emptied by high prices during famine periods
(187) Beer . . . was the object of legislation (p. 169).
(188) The great innovation, the revolution in Europe was the appearance of brandy . . . alcohol (p. 170).

And this is subsumed by the economic:

(189) Alcohol . . . succeeded . . . stimulants, a cheap source of calories . . . an easily accessible luxury with vicious consequences. And the watchful state soon found . . . profit (p. 175).

Europe: equilibrium. In non-Europe:

(190) It would really seem as if the civilization of the Mexican plateau, losing its ancient framework and taboos, abandoned itself to a temptation which wrought havoc with it after 1600 (p. 178).

The narrator recognizes the policy of Europe to saturate such peoples in "alcohol," but lexia 190 completes earlier mentions (for example, Europe did not "desecrate" Africa, the nomads as a "poor species"), closing off, in effect, non-Europe as a narrative subject. The classificatory function dominates which, again, duplicates the actual social relations of non-Europe to Western society (see Amin 1976:344–345).

In Europe, however, not "abandoned to," a verb simulating "internal collapse," but "compensation" registers the European capacity to integrate alcohol and stimulants, and move forward, as befits all "genuine" narrative schemas:

(191) Tobacco . . . conquered the whole world (p. 189).
(192) by pipes . . . later by cigars . . . later still in cigarettes.
(193) Cigarettes appeared in Spain . . . then reached France where they earned the approval of French youth.

"Temptation" in Mexico, "approval" in France: tobacco, a "compensation," indexes the destiny of "collapse" of Mexico but is a function of sequence in France, where "approval" obviously furthers a continuum of consumption. Again, Europe is awarded continuous semes, non-Europe dissolving ones.

The rejection of any phenomenological casting of action—focus on someone-to-someone interaction—and the irony expended on Marxism ("luxury" as "class struggle") might lead us back to the literary zone for bearings on *Capitalism and Material Life*. We could, for example, consider the excessive information given about tobacco, plants, and the like, to be part of a Menippean satire, including its use of past "scientific enthusiasts" who provide truth-citations for the narrator. To do so, however, would be erroneous: figures of literary genre do not generate a consideration of the history effects. The use of "luxury," for example, as precursor and fate, cannot be amalgamated to literary categories without, at best, reducing the specificity of this historical text. What I am suggesting is that we pursue, as far as possible, the text's driving "into signification" of an equivalent to Gay's sense of "loss" and Thompson's "defense of process," the "history effect" as it aims at the prefigurative "before and after" of the reader's thoughts, the text as a "fixation of past experience" and slowing down, if not stopping, the reader's critical thought on the present (see Lotman 1975:73). With "houses, clothes, and fashion,"

(194) luxury is more conspicuous
(195) to make comparisons between civilizations (p. 192).

Lexia 194 promises more visuality, focalization on cultural differences that made a difference, while lexia 195 aims at an aesthetic comparison between civilizations. It is important here to note, once again, that such characters ("civilizations") are not released by the historiographical apparatus to "say and do" more than the narrator allows (the latter bound to forms of omniscience, the unallowability of direct speech and thought, use of adjectival "determinations"; see Chatman 1978:219 ff.), and that character in this historical text is tantamount to subjectivization, what we have seen to be the narrativization of a European "desire" by comparison to non-Europe (see lexia 177). With "housing," there are

(196) . . . unchanging features . . . at least with slow evolutions (p. 192).
(197) A house is built or rebuilt according to traditional patterns.
(198) Here more than anywhere else the strength of precedent makes itself felt.
(199) The influence of customs and traditions is *always present* . . . ancient legacies that can never be discarded.
(200) Islamic houses are closed in on themselves . . . the nomad's tent has come down . . . without change
(201) . . . a "house," wherever it may be, was an enduring thing . . . perpetual witness to the slowness . . . (italics added)

As with the importing of "dialogue" into objects mentioned at lexia 123, one can now see how historiography is linked to "evidence": the "witness object" (house) has "spoken," "speaks," and is "speaking" now, a case of *ratio facilis* or preestablished interpretability (see Eco 1976:183–184); such is "good evidence," since it is unmarked by negation, by doubt, by pointlessness. As before, this materialist history requires of discursivity very stable signifiers and codes, signifieds of base. And as before, there is the same act of historicizing one side of a contrastable set by narrativizing the privileged side, precisely on account of its accumulation of a story line:

(202) . . . Indian villages never had stone houses.
(203) . . . straw . . . mats . . . cowdung . . . (p. 194).
(204) This picture is still true today. Nothing has changed.
(205) In the West . . . stone civilization took centuries to evolve . . .
(206) a human investment
(207) for centuries on end.

Then the analeptic recall of that history, followed by "rich and poor":

(208) . . . the advent of stone and tile
(209) . . . while the straw roof remained a sign of the past and of poverty (p. 195),

all of which prepares the release of the simultaneous motivation for a transformation and the intellectualization of change:

(210) When their numbers increased . . . the poor continued to be housed even more abominably than they are today, which is saying a great deal.
(211) Furnished rooms in Paris . . . were dirty . . . the police searched them remorselessly . . . Poverty was the rule on the sixth or seventh floors . . .
(212) Luxury . . . meant primarily the separation of the living habitats of the rich . . . the home . . . the house where the man worked (pp. 200–201).

If we provide motivation to these lexias, to the "rich" goes a continuation of what lexia 176 connoted as "separation" (the "rich" as the principle of differentiation, nothing more), and to the "poor," more undifferentiation, the signifiers "abominable" and "remorselessly" connoting ceaseless identity of the negative. Two psychologies: the first is that of the void (undifferentiation) of the poor, the second that of a lesser psychology, since "separation" indicates some degree of surplus in the "habitat" of the "rich," and, to that very extent, is relatively less psychological. This is followed by the narrativization of these "psychologemes," narrated, one might say, down:

(213) . . . universal poor . . . impoverished civilization . . . interiors barely changed.
(214) . . . Only the West is distinguished by uninterrupted change. Such is the ruler's privilege.
(215) The destitution of the poor goes without saying
(216) . . . almost complete deprivation
(217) All this is quite natural: poverty was everywhere (pp. 204–205).

Thus the European poor now belong to the same nonnarrative set as non-Europe: no narrative schema, no sense of a qualifying, decisioning, or glorifying *test* engulfs them as "historically significant." (Leftist historians have a lot to say about this "writing off" of the poor, but McLennan, Althusser, and others, have been quite polite with the Braudelian texts.) Here too the narrator finally has an opportunity to speculate on the case of China, which in earlier sections was mentioned with a mixture of awe and timidity—not written off, but a silence in the face of China's antiquity (see lexias 135–138). As to furniture there, the chair

(218) . . . was probably first used as a seat of honor
(219) but the important thing is the seated position that chair and stool imply, and therefore a way of life
(220) . . . seated and squatted life
(221) the latter domestic, the former official
(222) almost two different biologies

(223) the latter (squatting) is omnipresent except in the West
       . . .
(224) impossible or at best difficult for a European
(225) Everything is adapted to life at floor level (p. 210).

Once upon a time, lexia 222 was considered "vulgar materialism." One sees here, especially with lexia 219, an attempt to
stabilize the "chair" as an index, but the slide to "biology" collapses around a pure bio-program: past signs become one with
their context (and connected to the task announced at lexia 34).
Thus the difference between Europe and non-Europe is linked
to the capacity for story and narrative itself, the latter plane also
materialized. The stasis of China reflects that the telling can stop
and taxonomize, syllogize, and biologize in the presence of this
"way of life," but European "luxury"

(226) bore witness to a broad economic and cultural move-
       ment carrying Europe toward what it itself christened
       the Enlightenment, progress (p. 212).

The West, in short, has always been "historical." Burckhardt (1958:2)
called this the European "spirit," an "active humanity" before
which the "non-Caucasian races offer resistance, give way and
die out." As such propositions cannot be directly stated today,
they are obviously expressible as narrative ones. Before this "desire," variously recoded as "luxury" or nonsubjection to signs
(lexias 223–225), as liberation from the "iconicity" of China, Europe is storified according to a rigorous temporal program:

(227) Society—we might as well say vanity—was the arbiter
       in this matter of furniture
(228) Importance and then insignificance; in any event fash-
       ion was the winner
(229) fifteenth-century Italian interiors . . . a theatrical spec-
       tacle. Luxury . . . became a means of government
(230) Let us jump two hundred years (p. 223).
(231) In the seventeenth century the decoration of the house
       sacrificed everything to fashion, to social significance—

in France, England, and even the Catholic Netherlands
. . .

(232) Privacy was an eighteenth-century innovation
(233) . . . the individual was soon to have his revenge
(234) Housing and furniture changed because individuals wanted them to and because large towns favored their inclination (p. 224).

The trajectory, even though hundreds of years intervene, is nothing other than from "langue to parole," a temporalization of the relaxation of the system over subjects, an instance of "improvement" (lexias 24–25), the overall transformation a de-systematization of "fashion" toward its "subjectivization." Europe's history is attached to destructuration—the "causal" mechanism:

(235) In the rapidly growing towns . . . everything became more and more expensive, luxury unrestrained.
(236) . . . this dismantling of the home,
(237) . . . everyone thenceforth lived to some extent as he pleased (p. 224).

New needs, consumption, and the economic appear at once: they are linked by a bio-anthropological postulate, whereby "luxury, fashion, vanity" are productive in their own right, which raises history to the threshold of a coming-to-know-who-we-are, insofar as the historical is also attached to this bio-anthropological code:

(238) . . . the passion to move up in the world or the
(239) desire to wear those clothes which, in the West, symbolized the slightest social promotion (p. 226).

"Passion" to "move up" is thus encoded as a "historical" axiom, a figure of that tautomorphic "race" I mentioned earlier and, in the strong sense, is nothing other than the actant subject of its own destination, the materialist desire for status. This is again a historical paradigm for modern consumers who, like the poor of old, misidentify signs of value for value, and the professional classes who fear the self-dissolution into anachronism if they fail to set the criteria and agenda of what society can and should desire. It is boggling that such global history can overcode, from the inside as it were, such legitimation, but one should expect no less in a society where the academization process requires a nonarbitrary/transcendental signified of even its vulgarity. It is activated by a narrativized conjecture that fuses "passion," "up," "unknowing," which, in turn, replaces the "barely conscious" of lexia 6 and intersects with story (linearity) and reader (confirmed at the level of shared identity). Perhaps these "transtemporal" constants are derived from structural constants raised by Lévi-Strauss (incest, exogamy); but whatever their intellectual formation, they are recoded and subordinated to the traditional task of the historian: "passion" and "move up" are little more than a projection of an origin (the origin is constant, a constant origin) and semes of destination. Told as a story of the form/ motive of capitalism by a celebrant of the story of progress, the text thus maintains a meta-récit, cast in the form of meta-thinking, "desire" to "move up" now the transcendent content of history at the micro-subjective level.

(240) . . . fashionable whims . . .
(241) Even the most wretched looked on and encouraged them in their extravagance (p. 231).
(242) . . . fashion . . . barely enforced before 1700.
(243) . . . keeping up with the times
(244) If we go far back into the past we find unruffled times . . . India, China, and Islam.

Lexias 161–164 are returned in lexia 243 with the sense of some collective time of the "rich and poor," a continuous temporal chrononym, which is a rather pure subcode of hyper-familiarization: everyone knows what the referent is of such statements, the operation Jakobson isolated as the metalinguistic function, the checking up on and reaffirming of a coding. One must assume it is registered by the reader as "Yes, that is so," an absolute response of affirmation, which Barthes more acutely associated with the dissolve into mirroring, the affirmation of affirming, where subjectivity projects itself into all the spheres of its existence (see Jakobson 1960:345; Barthes 1972:151–152). Not-being-out-of-style is presence as it is suspended: how can it be both historical and ever present?

It is obvious that if the "time" and "fashion" of the "rich" were only a *singular* frequency (a cultural constant, what historiographers call a nomothetic rule), narration could not manifest such a phenomenon: without variation, discontinuity, or indeterminate completion, as Todorov puts it, only descriptions of scenes could be employed. Along the axis of "fashion," "luxury," and style, if 1700 and, say, 1800 remain uncontrastable, narration is reduced to zero-temporality, a textual state inconceivable in the historian's economy of the code of telling. One would expect, following lexia 244, a statement of "cultural determinism," another discursive synthesis of the "point," the launching of a comparison between East and West. Instead, as if the rules of the genre are preserved by variation, the narrator in fact introduces just the appropriate way of preventing such narrative self-destruction, an active time in the face of so much stasis. First, discontinuity:

(245) There were time lags, aberrations, gaps, delays (p. 232).

Then downgraded complements, the first giving the redundancy of the past, the second, the type of action:

(246) the immense inertia of the poor . . .
(247) local resistance, regional partitioning.
(248) The Valois court . . . was too near Germany and too original to follow the fashion of the French court.
(249) Italian women noticed . . . the profusion and wealth
(250) There is an account left by three young noble Venetian travelers (p. 233).

Lexia 250, the mention of the primary source, functions as the helper of this complementary time, the restoration of a descriptive scene/report. The evidence-report textualizes a totality: a synecdoche located in the evidence itself. At any rate, the poor are slowed down when they have to be (here, "inertia" = repetition, "no time"), while the mention of "otherness" (lexia 247) and its example (248–250) presents a kind of brake appropriate to the time of differential or rapid speed, the "competition" between elites, which establishes an instance of "perceptual realism" (lexia 249), although this is left unspecified.

There is another time, that of structures. When the narrator summarizes and poses to the reader the rhetorical question whether or not "fashion" is cause or effect, force or symbol, it is temporalized according to its compatibility with exchange:

(251) Its mechanism depends on the rules governing cultural transfers. And all diffusion of this type is by nature slow . . . (p. 234).

But "slow diffusion," in turn, is of lesser interest than the narrator's affirmation that "diffusion" and "transfer" can only be brought about by Europe. For the next lexias are a piece of "historical ground zero": after first a long citation from Mercier, an eighteenth-century "wit," cited as "testimony" about the speed of "fashion," and then a complaint reported by the sailor Vivero (one of the first Europeans to have contact with Japanese elites in the seventeenth century) that the Japanese thought Europeans "inconstant," the citation/report stops, and absolutely so:

(252) The conversation is revealing.
(253) Costume is a language.
(254) It is no more misleading than the graph drawn by demographers and price historians . . . each generation can repudiate its immediate predecessor and distinguish itself from it . . . inventing . . . of pushing out obsolete languages (p. 236).
(255) In fact the future belonged to societies which were trifling enough,

(256) but also rich and inventive enough to bother about changing colors, material, and style of costume . . .

The nonnarrative "costume is a language," which resonates and careens off lexias 165–171, means costume is a materialization of the differentiation of the elite from the masses, rich from poor, and so on. And this is derived from the sign form "thus it has always been so." How is "future" generated as a "process"? How could one derive time from such nontime? Lexia 255 starts the renarrativization going: its propositional force can be reduced to an axiom of Desire, something like "the West left nothing alone." The "trifling" of "fashion" (lexia 256) is then part of and identical with some temporal-machine, the positive side of lexias 165 and 168. For in the next series, we read: The narrating makes "language" temporal, its negative markings that of an exclusion/identity (from others, of oneself/class), part of a social primary process, so that European "progress" is specified by more than just the "liberation from iconicity" I mentioned earlier. The "generational timing" (lexia 254) is obviously subservient to the sense of a historical principle of differentiation, which is now characterized as nothing other than a signification process. The nonnarrative lexias which so often veer toward "shutdown" of the story, once more shift the reader back to the discursive, recoded now as discontinuity contained by linguistico-temporal continuity, for as the notion that elites determine (they "think," they "desire," etc.) is here grafted onto a recoding of the Structuralist model, change is introduced into the social by the silly tag that invention is the motor of the historical process, a celebration of the existential moment of the system. The narrator affirms past "speech"—"pushing out"—which is also the closest he gets to the negative process of history, quite different from the negativity practiced against the non-West and groups like the poor. A grammatical shift makes this clear:

(257) I have always thought that fashion resulted to a large extent from the desire of the privileged to distinguish themselves *whatever the cost*

(258) from the masses who followed them; to set up a barrier (p. 236, italics added).

"Fashion" = Code, the latter signifying both discrimination ("barrier") and distinction. What the historian has done is take the linguistic model of Structuralism and simultaneously necessitate it by narrativizing it: we are back at the plateau of non-disengagement from history. We could put it this way: the introjection of an identity between "linguistics" as model and the marking by elites under the psychology of needing victims (lexia 257, and see lexias 43, 48) is affirmed as a structure of the historical process, the latter now rendered as the motivation of transformation and directionality. This is the deep psychology of the historical process, the desire to distinguish made eternally present in the composition of elites, as is the history that results: the aestheticization of the elite's existential self-temporalization.

(259) Pressure from followers and imitators obviously made for a lively race (p. 236).

This is the moment of the "original scene" of past-present (see lexia 17). Everyone is present. The historical is offered as the progress of structure; and in order to ensure that such structures and the history entailed are transcendent (narration and discourse joined to atemporal thought), the aesthetics glimpsed at lexia 254, where "inventing" *can* push out "obsolete languages" (significations), should be reinterpreted to mean that "distinguishing" and "discrediting" are mere moments, aspects really, of the social primary, the pricelessness of culture (lexia 257). To occupy these posts in the realm of culture means the price of admission is nothing less than perpetuation of a genuine narrative process, reproduction of the marking of barriers between "rich and poor" and the nonstoppability of this process ("whatever the cost"). Such is the semantics of history rendered directly to the sectors of cultural management, those who maintain culture, "whatever the cost."

We should pause over the density of such textual relations, which began in earnest at lexia 194, before showing how all of this is further readjusted by more telling. The most important point is that the narrator has actually succeeded in a thorough recasting of the Structuralist enterprise and salvaged a systematic narrative, stopping, as it were, the fragmentation of the collage effect of historical writing, the indeterminacy of floating narratives that never add up, and so restoring the cultural conditions for the integrative-identity functions of *general* history. This goes beyond recognizing that among some Annalistes "narrative history" is seen as an ideological representation (White 1984:9–10). If one reads, for example, Braudel's own commentary on writing history, only a specific sort of "narrative history" is challenged (1980:9, 11, 200–202, where he alternates between rejection and acceptance of narrative, only to privilege more fully the acceptance). But *Capitalism and Material Life* takes all the components of Western culture—number, food, housing, and so on—and rewrites the singulative ("history happened once") yet all-embracing narrative. As rewashed in the used waters of Structuralism by means of the devices we have noted—for example, the barring of authenticity to cultures without "number" (India), narrativizing away (lexias 87–88), narrativized paradigms (see sections on the nomads), and, especially, the reserving for Europe of the *lie of historicality*—this general history is the Utopia of the professional classes, namely their release from society. Its blend of common history, common language, and common psychology is the suppression of nonacademic versions of the past, for who is to nod in agreement at the connection between lexias 252 and 258 unless it is the reader foreseen as having some right to change yet stay the same (boards of directors, for example)?

(260) We are not only in the realm of things but really of "things and words."

(261) Our concern is with terminologies, with languages, with all that man brings to them

(262) and insinuates into them as in the course of his everyday life

(263) he makes himself their unconscious prisoner (p. 243).

Lexia 263 returns the reader to what was raised at lexia 45, the status of the modal establishing both an event and a historiographical theory. Left blank at lexia 45, asserted only as "was," now it is affirmed as a "doing." This is a hermeneutic threshold, coming as it does as a conclusion to the first four chapters. All the previous mentions of an "unconscious" are now recuperated—the biological unconscious ("famine" as balance), the psychological unconscious ("rationality" of the seventeenth century), the cultural unconscious (all that has to do with "luxury"-competition)—so as to constitute a particular form or set of the past. The renaming of lexia 260 also cites Foucault (and Praz) as intellectual support but, more importantly, it reestablishes one of the pure ambitions of historiography, the restoration of the stability of "context." Today it can be thought by historians and readers alike that the "unconscious" of "structures" is somehow a given "context" both historiographically and as a fact of history.

(264) to see these commodities and these languages in their context . . .

(265) If luxury is not a good way of supporting or promoting an economy, it is

(266) a means of holding, of fascinating a society.

(267) Civilizations—strange collections of commodities, symbols, illusions, phantasms, and intellectual models—work in this way.

(268) An order becomes established that operates down to the very depths of material life.

(269) It is inevitably self-complicating, being influenced by propensities, the unconscious pressures, and all that is implicit in economies, societies, and civilizations (p. 243).

Lexias 264–269 suggest that the narrator does not glimpse the distances in semic value between commodity and language; such categorical issues are reduced with lexia 266, where "luxury" is raised to an intellectualized actant-mechanism (subject of story/ condition of story), both the container and point of "luxury." Doing and causality are herewith reduced to the nonthinkable in favor of a line directed to the reader, signaled in the grammar of a certain kind of presence—the reader can now suppose ("if," "in this way") that he or she is in contact with the secret of continuity itself, the maximum collapse of "why" and "what." Every "civilization" is the same in regard to what one can learn about them, why they are what they are, for their "order" = their "luxury." The "idealism" of lexia 267—"strange collections"—is irrelevant by comparison to this eternalization of the ideological, where necessity is made to parallel invisibility, and narration is then projected as a primary revisualization of such secrets and order itself.

We shall highly condense the next two chapters, on technology, drawing out only those lexias that pertain to the movement of story-forward and the devices on which we have thus far focused as determinative of both the telling and the site of the model reader. The new topic, technology, is introduced in the same way as number, food, luxury—that is to say, as the strategy of historicality welded to the narrativization of the paradigmatic and the upward movement of progress.

> (270) Everything is technology . . . brisk changes . . . and innumerable actions . . . the fruit of accumulated knowledge
> (271) . . . society in the broadest sense . . .
> (272) . . . a slow, muted, and complicated history;
> (273) a memory that obstinately repeats known solutions, that avoids the difficulty and the danger of thinking up something else (p. 245).

The encoding suggests, beyond its positivity of uninterrupted progress ("fruit of accumulated . . ."), that technology is closer to the series earlier marked by an internal historicism, a system where memory served as the stable ingredient of a "hearer-oriented type of culture," to use Lotman's (1975:66) phrase. Lexia 273 is an intradiegetic recoding of the earlier sense of "inertia," memory being here its counterforce, now to be transcended. The interesting aspect would be whether or not memory was actually organized as a kind of cultural reciprocity (in Baudrillard's sense of antiproduction, the refusal to exchange nonequivalents), but here it is linked to the narrative schema of the conservatism of the past and tradition. This "inward memory" is then juxtaposed to possibility and a limit which, when crossed, renders the technological as

> (274) the technical breach becomes the point of departure for a rapid acceleration (p. 246).

Diachrony ("point of departure") must negate memory in order to proceed. Historiographically, lexia 274 raises the issue of how the West could "take off" (the question of Rostow, among others). Rejecting both the historiography of "internalist" change and pure "linear progress" (p. 244), the narrator begins anew supercomparisons, once more dramatizing until a narrative line is established. Manpower, animal power, wood, water wheels, sails, and coal each take their turn in an inventory of power sources; horses are superidealized (p. 250)—Cosimo de Medici was "ruined" by the cost of provisioning 2000 horsemen, the monopoly on horses by the rulers called forth smuggling (p. 256, its first mention), and so on, establishing, however, this same device:

> (275) Indian oxen were ill-fed and never stabled.
> (276) too many highly efficient coolies in China (p. 249)
> (277) Well distributed . . . wild horses in Europe
> (278) were, therefore old Europeans (p. 253).

This gives the reader a very clear sense of the compartization—

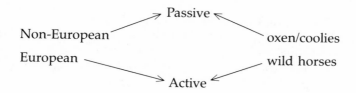

and becomes, by assuming the equivalence of oxen/coolies as "abused" and the "ancestry/identity" of European horses (lexia 278), a privileging of the latter couples' narrative role— "centuries-old contact helped to bring about the gradual improvement in harnessing . . . thenceforth they played a very large part in harrowing, tilling, and transport" (p. 253). Again, negation of the non-West = narrative positivity of the West. A consideration of all the available sources of power leads to this series:

(279) . . . the economy was trapped in the old inflexible solutions,

(280) and it was this that hampered the development of

(281) mechanization most of all,

(282) not any delay in the inventive urge

(283) . . . what was lacking . . . was a surplus of easily mobilized power.

(284) Came steam and everything was, as if by magic, speeded up (pp. 274–275).

Technology then is slowed down, subject to what Genette calls "reach," an anachrony through which a narrator can present the anteriority and futurity of a topic, enabling a narrator to link unfamiliar temporal semes (speeds, rhythms, cadences); but here the results of such descriptions amount to little more than a kind of historiographical stress upon the extent of the slowness of technological transformations:

(285) The great technological "revolutions" . . . were artillery, printing, and ocean navigation.

(286) But to speak of "revolution" here is to use a figure of speech.

(287) Nothing took place at breakneck speed.

(288) And only ocean navigation ended by creating any upheaval or "asymmetry" in the world.

(289) The usual result was for everything to become widespread (p. 285).

Uninterrupted continuity marks the development of cannon (p. 288); it spread to ships (p. 289). This weapon resulted in the structure of "siege and defense" used in the capture of towns, ending only with "the strategy of Frederick II and Napoleon,"

(290) because they were no longer concerned with taking towns but with destroying enemy manpower (p. 288).

What retards the "speed" of technological accumulation and breakthrough is the nonintegration of (military) technology, which, in effect, keeps technology in the status of a great historical potentiality, neutralized, until aligned with another series that severs the cultural memory of lexia 273. There is little of the "romance of the technique" (Axelos 1976:309) here, the narrator instead "deautonomizing" technology from the historiographical versions of both positivist and romantic stories (see pp. 293, 298). An entirely idealist position maintains that the printing press allowed Europe to reinstate Greek mathematics (p. 299). In general, the continuity of artillery is accomplished by the undercoding of the emergence of the state (Frederick, Napoleon), while printing is inserted in the context of its control by monopolies (see pp. 291, 299). This control over the story line of technology is maintained by lexia 273 until a narrative function is introduced with "ocean navigation."

(291) . . . Europe's explosion onto all the seas of the world
(292) . . . all the maritime civilizations . . . could all have entered into competition. But Europe alone remained in the race (p. 300).

"Race" recalls the "lively race" of lexia 259 and is a scene-setting function, placing actors ("maritime nations") in the set of competition. At first stasis encodes this commonality, a common lack of history:

(293) . . . the maritime frontiers of the civilizations were as rigid as their continental frontiers.
(294) Everybody kept to their own territory at sea as well as on land (p. 301).

The Arabs and Chinese drop out of the race when it comes to exploring the Atlantic, and there is little of the erasure of these civilizations regarding the maritime. However, in the face of the European move to dominate the oceans, the reader is presented with an encoding of the psychological complementary to lexia 214:

(295) . . . the greatest difficulty was to brave the venture and take the plunge.

(296) The courage required for such an unwonted feat has been forgotten—

(297) as probably our grandchildren will know nothing about the bravery of astronauts today (p. 306).

Following this, the narrator again asks why the absence of "technical" difficulties in fact resulted in the Europeans' domination of the oceans, and the withdrawal of the non-West; the answer is rendered this way:

(298) . . . the merit of the West, confined as it was on its narrow "Cape of Asia"

(299) *was to have needed the world,* to have needed to venture outside its own front door.

(300) Nothing would have been possible . . . without the growth of the capitalist towns of the West at that time.

(301) They were the driving force. Without them technology would have been impotent (pp. 308–309, italics added).

We have to ask immediately: what kind of complex transformation is involved with lexias 298–301, in Todorov's sense of a complex transformation providing for one predicate interpreting another. (For example, how are "merit" and "need" linked to transformation? See Todorov 1977:225 ff.) The answer is that lexia 299 once again appears eminently narrative, as the answer to a question, but in fact is marked by nonnarrative semes: (1) "Merit" is the declaration of a judgment of attitude, a result, the "merit" in this case established by the prior condition of Europe, "confined," this negative condition also a sufficient "reason." (2) One shifts from establishing "confined" as a condition to get out of to the hyperpsychologized "need," semantically registered (lexia 299) as a story that had to be lived,

enacted, carried out—the psychologization of a narrative structure and the narrativization within an imaginary psychology
imputed to the Europeans. (3) Towns as a "driving force" asserts
an absent cause, in Jameson's sense of the term, but in textual
terms is here a proleptic anticipation of another topic. (4) The
vagueness between such a "driving force" and "need" will have
to be connected, since the specter is raised that the "need" for
"the world" would be "empty" but for the towns. Introduced
as a narrative topic, the towns are given this disclaimer:

(302) This does not mean that it was money, capital that was
responsible for ocean navigation (p. 309).

No one is to think that! Once in this realm of psychologization,
there is no way out, it seems, except to intensify the predicates.
Completing the historiographical disengagement of the story
from all nonpsychological versions but that of an indescribable
"need," we read:

(303) What historians have called a lust for gold or a lust for
the world or a lust for spices
(304) was in the technical sphere accompanied by a constant
search for new utilitarian inventions and applications—
(305) utilitarian in the sense that they would be in the service
of man, to ensure both the lightening and the greater
efficiency of his labor (p. 309).

This is melodramatic inoculation: what lexia 303 says is that
"need" is not lust—"need" reappears in lexia 304 as a "search,"
a displacing; the inoculatory function begins as soon as "technical sphere" is recoded from "breach," a violence (lexia 274),
and joined to a subcoded connotator of "beneficence": the "capitalist towns" were not part of a "breach" but the site where
Utilitarianism (the postulate of a happy equilibrium between
fractionalization of labor-power and the "right to consume") was
first successful, permeating, one supposes, such towns in a homogeneous system of value ("service to man" = psychology of
city). The narrator employs the voice of eighteenth-century Util-

itarianism in order to justify such a context, the speaking requiring, however, that the narrator (lexia 305) momentarily
assume the role of a homodiegetic narrator: nothing has inter-
vened between then and now to cancel or annul the "voice of
the Utilitarians" of the eighteenth century. This is an instance
of the political economy of the "happiness principle" of history:
a celebratory annihilation of negativity, "lust" evaporating before the Positive whose own nonviolence on thought is expunged. Note how lexia 305 codes away the violence of the
economic.

Narration establishes proportions, said Lukacs (1970:127),
when he was not completely bent on autonomizing history, and
so it does, for all that belongs to the "technical" is systematically
detached from Capital, making the "lightening and greater efficiency of labor" the positive line of a story told from the positive
perspective of a late idealization of an origin (Utilitarianism).
The historian introduces Capitalism through semes of "progress" restricted to the imagination of labor seen through the
coding of labor's ultimate transcendent use-value—given
enough "time," Capitalism promises a Utopia of nonlabor, or
Capitalism is the "history" of the future necessitated by labor's
realization of itself.

The charge made by some leftists that Braudel's work gets rid
of linear, teleological history and relies upon an inert unconscious (D'Amico 1973:83–84) misses the point: by means of its
absolute model of linearity and teleology the reader is screened
from the nonlinearity of Capital. For with the introduction of
"world conquest," town, technology, and Capital, the narrating
ceases taking up strong paradigmatic exposures of "mechanisms" and "structures," especially when it comes to money and
labor. By comparison to a generalized beneficial history, *money
and labor are shut out from the realm of narrativity*, not "history" as
many leftists protest. Surplus value no longer haunts the historicality of this academic narrative, neither at the level of a
primary "motivation" (lexia 299) nor as a developmental structure: lexia 305 is targeted as the name of desire motivated by
the question, "do you wish to say there has not been progress
in the lightening and efficiency of labor?", the question de-

manding a counternarrative, a version of antihistory no member of the elite would ask today. One can see why leftists have hardly contested narration: it forces one to employ first a counterversion of history, this because one still believes that "past" is not yet closed (what Benjamin called "fanning the spark of hope in the past"). Later we shall take up the impact of lexias 303–305.

The sections on technology close with a return to the barriers obstructing the future. Renarrativized,

(306) Thousands of factors obstructed progress.

(307) What could be done with a labor force threatened with unemployment?

(308) Finally there remains a matter of the greatest interest to the capitalist—the question of costs.

(309) Even when the industrial revolution in cotton was well advanced . . . domestic production was sufficient to supply the weaving looms at much lower cost.

(310) The tempo of demand had to increase immeasurably before the use of mechanical spinning became general, well after its invention (p. 324).

Technology—society—could not go forward; its existential force was spent and exhausted on a surplus of invention and a paucity of applications. Lexia 309 initiates propositions that set back, in Ryan's (1979:146) phraseology, the "narrative clock" of technology so that the simultaneity ("greatest interest") of another topic can be braided with it and supply more complete knowledge about the "limits" (lexias 307–310) of the technical, as well as providing a principle of action which illustrates the form of desire that pulls story into forward. We see as well that the example selected to illustrate "obstructions" downgrades Capitalism to a question of costs and demand: "progress" was suspended or unrealizable (imperfective, nonresulting in terms of temporal aspect) until some subjective factor or mechanism overturns the stalling of society—the positivity of lexias 255–258 will have to be specified rather soon.

Now the introduction of "money" in story-time supplies the answer to the "limits" of the technical, so there must be semic links whereby the simultaneity of money and technology can be made conecessary, and in such a way that Utilitarianism and "costs" are as well shown to contribute to the story without displacing any of these story-existents (see Mink 1978:142). Money is presented, as one would expect, with utter positivity:

(311) . . . tool, a "structure," a deep-seated regular feature of all slightly accelerated commercial life.

(312) Above all money is never an isolated reality . . . it influences all economic and social relationships.

(313) This makes it a wonderful indicator: a fairly reliable assessment can be made of all human activities down to the most humble level from the tempo of its circulation, or the way it becomes complicated or scarce.

(314) It is an important source of illumination for us (p. 325).

All of which say: "money" is a good sign, a stable signifier, appropriate, in its very form, for academic denotations, its everpresence a true use-value for discourse. Opposed to these metalinguistic predications are the manifestations of "money" at the level of its social relations:

(315) . . . an ancient fact of life

(316) an ancient technique . . . never ceases to surprise humanity.

(317) . . . mysterious and disturbing.

(318) . . . complicated in itself.

A "naturally" reified object-relation, one might say: the "never cease" encapsulates "money" in a perpetual repetition, a narrativization endowing "money" with the status of a transtemporal objectification, and so annulling any definition of "money" in all its capitalistic shapes. As before, "money" perfectly serves the purposes of narration, as the narrator immediately recognizes that stressing "money" either directly as an index of transformation (sign value) or as transhistorical (an integral sign) must give way to calibrating "money" and story. Here the first denotation is:

(319) . . . money was nowhere fully developed . . . in a country like France . . . even in the nineteenth [century].

(320) It was a novelty more because of what it brought with it than what it was itself.

(321) What did it actually bring? Sharp variations in prices of essential foodstuffs;

(322) incomprehensible relationships in which man no longer recognized either himself, his customs, or his ancient values.

(323) His work became a commodity, himself a thing (p. 325).

A whole battery of strange lexias, but their order of presentation is not a random feature, for the very piling up of the differing semes and their connotators simultaneously contrasts and narrativizes. Lexia 317 is the start of which lexia 323 is the obvious stop. "Mysterious and disturbing" to "humanity" once again smashes, pulverizes, any analytic but that of "money" as an unnameable "it is what it is," identical to itself in all contexts (subcode: thing-in-itself of the social). Platonized in this way, erected as a transcendent presence, when the narrating temporalizes and hence activates "money," suddenly (lexia 321) it is all effect ("variations"), and with lexia 322 it is functionalized as an "effacing intruder" who plunges subjects into cultural vertigo (like the Arabs in Camus' *Stranger*). The absurdity: "money" is affirmed as identity and atemporality, but its force ("no longer") negates a history that could not have existed ("customs") if "money" is always as lexia 317 said it was. When did "money" not shock and disturb? Just as lexias 155–160 established this precursor and fate matrix, so too here, but the echo of Marx with lexia 323 must be reread as a kind of cliché, since "money" has already been established as part of eternal commodification ("never ceases to"). In other words, this textual nod to Marx is rendered sentimental after it has been eternalized, thereby embedding "money" in the context of a dramatized index (for-the-historian) and an eternal story that dimly points toward the negative "in history."

But "money" disappears as a problem; with Marxism acknowledged and dismissed, the real work of the narrating can proceed. The narrator establishes another universal psychological law where the "whole" is encoded as a transtemporal "structure" where

(324) Actually every society that is based on an ancient structure and opens its doors to money sooner or later loses its acquired equilibria and

(325) liberates forces thenceforth inadequately controlled. The new form of interchange jumbles things up, favors a few rare individuals and rejects the others

(326) Every society has to turn over a new leaf under the impact (p. 326).

Lexia 33 already told the reader the sense of these lexias which here aim at establishing a law at the level of the historical itself; recast, it reads: "money" = disequilibrium, of which the narrative effect = inequality, and where money, as with lexia 150, is awarded the power to select. Money is an actant, another subject of itself, autonomous. "It" accomplishes acts through its power to cause inclusive-disjunctions: for its beneficiaries, money is a gift, while to the rest it duplicates the nonnarrative program of lexias 146–160. Intellectually, the reader can draw the conclusion that one should never expect from money anything more than its form to be identical with its content; it is mysterious, disturbing, complicated, because it is "money," its class connections irrelevant, its basis (labor) nonexistent. Devoid of contextual (social/cultural) markers, which is to say of a particular coded social formation, money is thus restored, obscenely, to a fetishistic organization:

(327) We can get a good picture of these basic processes . . . Black Africa . . . in over 60% or 70% of exchanges money is not used.

(328) Man can still live there for a time outside the market economy . . .

(329) But he is a condemned man on temporary reprieve.

(330) History shows us an endless procession of these condemned men—men destined not to escape their fate (p. 326).

And so the reader passes back into a full-blown metaphysic neither of money nor history, but of a philosophy of history which is one with a metaphysic of inescapable hierarchies of money, which, as with lexias 77 and 273, dissolves any discursive form, any critique operating at a lower level of signification (for example, analysis of money functions or institutions). An affirmative fate, "boomrattling from burst to past," as Joyce put it in *Finnegans Wake*, money is parallel to luxury and fashion in terms of manifesting both a narrativized hierarchy ("few") and a hierarchical eternal contrast for consciousness to recognize as its own, thus autonomized and transcendent. Now the reader shifts to the level of events, existents, the enumeration of characters (State, tax collector, merchant) where reengagement with story-forward saturates one in more eternalizing relations:

(331) Their net stretched everywhere . . . And naturally . . . did not arouse sympathy, like their equivalents today.
(332) The faces of financiers look down on us from the museum . . . the painter has conveyed the ordinary man's hatred and mistrust.
(333) But ultimately the course of events was scarcely diverted by such feelings . . . (p. 327).

So much for a history of such social control—told, in advance, its omni-temporality, the reader is especially enmeshed by the "net" of lexia 331, and "money" can now appear as the actant-dynamo of the question in lexia 50. After writing off "art history" as an index of the logic of the social, the historiographical narrator yet again leaps into, as with lexias 87–88, the absolutism of a frame where anthropology, need, history, and rationality all intersect; not historicality and future (as in the erasure of the nomads) but now a symmetry between story and telling:

(334) It is often said that money is "only a veil."
(335) In fact it only comes into being where men need it and can bear its cost (p. 328).

All traces of negativity concerning "money" thus evaporate: in the face of lexia 335 what reader is going to object (see lexia

299)? So far is the reader led out of and away from "money" as a concrete problematic ("money" as a signifier of exchange-value, exchange-value a signifier of commodity production, commodity production a signifier of labor-power, labor-power the signified of all "money") and into another recoding of Structuralism, that "money" is at last encoded as a nonnarrative but historicizing formation:

(336) For money is a language . . .
(337) it calls for and makes possible dialogues and conversations; it exists as a function of these conversations (p. 328).

Once again, a narrativized nonnarrative set-rule-code (lexia 336) issues forth in a wholly positived temporalization, contemporary historiography once more embracing and recasting the arche-form of "dialogue," encoding it now as a property of past conditions. It is plausible to that model reader whose thinking can decode the message as something like "money is just like facilitation of exchange, like the circulation of words." Lexia 260, where this particular line started, is now completed: "words and things" are, for the historian, an unproblematical way of "talking" (modeling) the past. Gone is all disturbance and problematic of "progress," any strong meaning of "money," banished, at best, to another telling.

It would be no good to protest the fact that the masses of the planet actually pay for the writing of such class self-subjectivization. Lefebvre (1976:114) has called recoding of process the "theorization of the *fait accompli*," and it is; however, it is signified not as a theoretical discourse but as a historicization, whereby to be "condemned" (lexia 329) to this dialogue is offered as a progressive sequence, the latter now a sign form of the very shape of history itself. Indeed, the accessibility of this past world and the reader's present is guaranteed now: there is no unfamiliarity, even as a residue, which obstructs the reader's passage from present-now to past-then:

(338) When you talk to someone you are forced to find a common language, some common ground.

(339) The merit of long-distance trade, of large-scale commercial capitalism,

(340) was its ability to speak the language of world-trade.

(341) Long-distance trade was the source of all rapid accumulation of money

(342) If Europe finally perfected its money, it was because it had to overthrow the domination of the Muslim world . . . linked to its urban progress . . . the growth of a "real middle-class civilization" in privileged towns.

(343) Everything is connected (p. 329).

Thus academic historicization completes itself; first level: the identity of language and money; second level: the identity between an existent ("long-distance trade") and the first level ("trade" = language); third level, and the only properly narrative one, the process of perfection of Europe and negation of non-Europe, all of this accomplished by the significations of a "long-distance trade"—its ability-to-speak—encoded as the only competent subject of time (lexia 340). This is history at maximum intelligibility. It is so intelligible in fact that it even accounts for exploitation (p. 330) by means of a pure achronicity:

(344) there has always been a Third World,

so that for the masses of the eighteenth century, it was only their

(345) regular mistake . . . to agree to the terms of a dialogue which was always unfavorable to it. But it was often forced to (p. 330).

This is another nod to the nonhistoricality of the past (Third World = nonparticipants) and the fate of the masses, and another specification of lexias 112–114 and the historicality of "mature" civilizations who really knew how to exploit, especially their own members.

Money, then, is a full narrative character and function, synchronic in its own field of contact and diachronic in terms of serving as that "vanguard" of the economic life of the past mentioned at lexia 43. The entire story has managed to unbolt Europe from nonnarrative relations: the program asserted at lexia 214 is fulfilled by the insertion of "money" into a narrative trajectory. And as before, "historical necessity" is the form of meaning of this story, so long as we recognize that historical necessity is not just assigned by the narrating but placed by the narrator in the very structure of European existence. So here I shall say that historicality is *the* semantic investment made by the historian in terms of describing, classifying, taxonomizing, and so on, and "historical necessity" is the thought-product achieved by the reader insofar as the past is opened to the reader-now as a continuous meaning with the reader's present.

After a good deal of comparison among the different media that served as money—and where non-Europe is redundantly deprived of semes of future-forward—the narrator returns to a focus upon Europe framed by this lexia:

(346) Europe was beginning to devour, to digest the world (p. 344).

Story-now is restarted by an inventory of European metallics, at which point the narrator pauses to consider, from the perspective of the capitalist, why metallic money was a terminal patient of a self-inflicted disease (which is not possible, but no matter; see pp. 348–350). Context setting is closed when the narrator disappears and the voice of a narrating economist takes over with these lexias:

(347) European monetary stocks . . . had to confront a series of tasks . . . to supply . . . to swell the reserves of the money-hoarders, above all to provide the raw material necessary for the transactions of the European economy and make good the follies of monetary policy.

(348) The same answers came up every time: increase production and speed up circulation (p. 351).

Who provided these answers? In other words, what continuous subject wanted rationality, speed, circulation, production, and so on, all at once? The answer to this question would yield the appearance of what classical historiography has termed Humanism, where, as Collingwood put it, "the human point of view is final. What God thinks about the Italian language is a question which [the historian] need not ask, and which he knows he could not answer" (1948:66). In narrative terms, one of the already narrated existents—what Barthes (1974:151) calls the nominalized entity, the indicator of both story and telling—or one yet to be introduced, must emerge to articulate the very resolution called for in the answer required by lexia 348. Since the narrator speaks, as it were, from the angles of the capitalist, the economist, and others (the positivized actors), we can expect the identification to be redundant.

Here, I think, the constitutive authoritarianism of telling, as opposed to, say, intensity of argument, comes back upon itself in terms of exposing its own false positivizations. As the narrating recodes itself, the requirement to specify a complex transformation becomes all the more apparent. The techniques raised at lexias 306–310 concerned lowering costs (the Capitalist's condition for competition) and raising demand (the Capitalist's condition for realization), and are recoded at lexia 348. Intellectually, the reader is poised at the threshold of that enormous historical question, the transition from "feudalism to capitalism" which Marx saw concomitant with the "divorce of labor from its external conditions" or the capitalists' speculation on the labor of others (see Althusser and Balibar 1977:279–280; Cohen 1978:299–302). "Increase production . . . speed up circulation" specifies to the reader that Europe's needs (see lexia 342) show that the condition at lexia 341 resulted in, now, a subject who produces a state of change, a doing, such a specification performing the function of transformation, and cognitively absorbing the differing senses of discursive and narrative structures.

The narrator renders an inventory of past money forms and their velocity, ranking them as to their efficiency for velocity and speed, the ability "to dialogue." The coexistence of money and credit is introduced (p. 357) simultaneously with the coexistence in the period of barter and other past common practices. Credit was well known in places like Greece and Egypt, and so was only a rediscovery of an old technique (p. 359). This scriptural money "shows" that credit was really a form of writing (!), encoded analogously to the speech act of promising (p. 358). The introduction of an issuing bank (of England) was only an innovation, the most systematic instance of a generalized process:

> (349) Every time there was a breakdown in metallic money anything was pressed into service and paper money flowed in or was invented (p. 361).
> (350) . . . In fact it soon involved the artificial manufacture of money, of ersatz money, or if you like a manipulated and "manipulable" money . . . (p. 362)
> (351) a sensational discovery and a huge temptation.
> (352) And what a revelation to us!
> (353) It was the slowness of the heavy metallic money that created the necessary profession of the banker from the very dawn of economic life.
> (354) He was the man who repaired or tried to repair the mechanical breakdown (p. 362).

This *rapport des forces* (historical conjunction of nonsynchronous temporalities) is narrativized with the introduction of the "banker," released as the isotopic signifier of the actorial trajectory, and the answer to lexia 348. Specifically: given the feature at lexia 353, "metallic money," the signified of an impasse—the story could not proceed. This is overcome by the banker modeled as the *bricoleur* of the machine, for this subjectivity provides both equilibrium (to exchange) and temporality (to the realization of exchange), and so is the textual manifestation of a narrativized actor, a subject whose complete encoding is isomorphic with the Utilitarian story. The banker is no element, no structure, no role except as the need-completer whose appearance within the story is synchronous with the avoidance of the breakdown of long-distance trade and the disposal of the accumulation which has, somehow, already happened. The banker appears on time in every sense of the concept. And, I might add, the Marxist objection to such narrating (see Mandel 1975:510) is less interesting than Nietzsche's, which at least foresaw the intellectual mystification of the narrating organization, "given sufficient time, anything can evolve out of anything else . . . traced back to pressure and stress" (1968:332). Can we say the banker is thus a protogram of the academic mentality, since it never ceases to valorize the forward of all that "can be" story, as well as the narrating that assures us of "necessity"? Like the academic requirement that knowledge-production always arrives in the time of postponing and deferring "breakdowns," the banker glows in the darkness, providing a "service" ripped out of a violent and contradictory scene (surplus-value *is* ugly).

Qualifications are presented: the increase in scale (the return of number), acceleration was restricted to a "few market places, a few nations, a few groups" (p. 370). There are summaries: "Berlin had become a city rotten with speculation by the end of Frederick's reign" (p. 371). Russia is compared to the West and found to be non-European. All of this is then gathered into a temporalized scene:

(355) . . . coexistent worlds, modern or very modern, backward or very backward . . . an economic symbiosis . . .

(356) . . . the impetus of modern centuries also carried the rudimentary economies themselves along in its momentum . . . sometimes a painful process for the more backward regions

(357) who were forced to progress as best they could,

(358) but progress at all costs (p. 371).

This recodes the granting of selection/choice (subjective function) to the elite in lexias 256–258 and now takes that voicing and applies it to the process as a whole. This expands the role of the reader, now shifted from agreeing to the signifiers of "determination" (lexias 140–144) of non-Europe and embedded in pure historicism; there is no alternate future for the non-European "third world" and no going back for the whole series of "traditions" that made up the past's presence in Europe. This is made final, as well, in the most solemn and corny of macro-narrative propositions, an *exemplum maiorum* of historicity itself:

(359) . . . the natural economy benefits from a general impetus (p. 371).

Althusser's brand of Structuralism, in getting rid of the notion of "expressive causality," where the specificity of each "structure" (for example, Family, School, State) defeats any Hegelian projection of an "essential section" or underlying unity of the "whole" (see Gordy 1983:7), calls into question the possibility of signifiers of a continuous process, or even complexes of processes. The historian has, of course, rejected nonsubjectifying Structuralism (Althusser, for one) in favor of singling out some "subject" who continues to "live" in a future not-told but accessible to the reader. Accordingly, here I want to focus on the redundancy of the narrating in shaping new motifs (adjusting the story) and the sign forms directed to the reader's pragmatic performance, stressing what Ryan (1979:150) has called the turn of a "tellable narration" into a "successful" one, or what Lotman has called the correlation of a "secondary modeling system" ("historical narration") and everyday discourse, or what I would call, with Barthes, the suturing of "necessary historicality" to thought so that not a cultural doubt remains as to the reality of history.

Towns are introduced with signifiers of controlled disequilibria:

(360) . . . electric transformers . . .
(361) . . . increase tension . . . accelerate the rhythm of exchange and ceaselessly stir up men's lives.
(362) . . . oppressive and parasitical formations . . .
(363) embodied the intelligence, risk, progress, and modernity towards which the world was slowly moving.
(364) . . . accelerators of all historical time (p. 373).

Dialectically framed by the *loci communes* of a historiographical tradition in which the decline of the city prompted Xenophon to wash his hands of "collective history" or Marx to embed the city in the "third period of private property," the rise of productive forces (see Chatelet 1962:304–305; Marx 1977:78–79), the mention of towns moves the reader closer to the zone of actions and happenings. Saying "accelerators" is the same as saying that some form of immediate causality belonged to the towns. After once more stressing the universality of the language model,

> (365) . . . a town is a town wherever it is . . . one basic language for all the cities of the world . . .
> (366) . . . to dominate an empire, however tiny, in order to exist (p. 374),

the town is given a narrative trajectory indistinguishable from its very definition: the "conquest" of lexia 110. The town is a complex isotopy, referring the reader to previous textual states, trajectories, and providing closure to the overall syntagmatic axis. That this is so is clear from the next set. After restoring the determination of "number" and the permanent "quarrel" between town and country (a recoding of lexia 171), we read:

> (367) . . . the urban problem consists in separating out certain activities in a partnership that was originally a joint one . . .
> (368) Economists would call it
> (369) detaching
> (370) the specialized "secondary" sectors from a primary sector incorporating the whole (p. 376).

This embeds earlier semes of social differentiation squarely in the division of labor, downgraded to the status of an "elementary rationalization" (sufficient condition) for growth. And if the town were to grow as such,

> (371) it could not do so by itself.
> (372) . . . it left the lowly tasks to new arrivals.
> (373) Like our over-pressurized economies today, it needed North Africans and Puerto Ricans in its service,
> (374) a proletariat which it quickly used up and had quickly to renew.

(375) The existence of this wretched and lowly proletariat is a feature of any large town (p. 381).

The economist's discourse and the "town planner's" voice are synchronized with the paradigmatic and syntagmatic axes: to be a town = exploitation, and growth = exploitation, the "town" now fulfilling the narrative program of lexias 46–48, the proletariat lodged in the role of "victim" as it is reduced to an eternal singularity ("like our . . . ") and so also a feature of the very "ordinariness" of history itself (see lexia 145). Exploitation is also thinkable as simultaneous with "mature" civilizations—it is an ever-present and always developing phenomenon of "growth." This is the realization-truth of the narrator switching to the voices of the economist and planner, as well as providing for the reader a conceptualization of exploitation identical to that of "luxury" (see lexias 167–170). The "time" that figures-forth the proletariat is *still-time,* as they are redundant to themselves (lexia 374) and so barely less erased than the non-Western peoples of the Third World (see lexias 141–144).

After more description and scene setting, focusing on the differences between relay towns, market towns, suburbs, and so on, the narrator returns with the promise of connecting the "vanguard" of capitalism (lexia 43) to the "history" of European cities. As the vanguard, capitalism is presented within lexias where the city is, in story-now, a pure result:

(376) The West was, as it were, the luxury of the world.
(377) . . . towns there had been brought to a standard hardly found anywhere else.
(378) . . . autonomous worlds . . . outwitted the territorial state . . . ruled their fields autocratically . . . economic policy of their own . . . (p. 396).

The Western cities had achieved this state because of the influx of money,

(379) Money is the same as saying towns (p. 397),

so that whatever strong connections there are between capital-ism and the city (not yet specified), we can only presume that it is the very historicity of the city which made possible in the first place the success of the division of labor, the expression of "luxury," the "digestion of the world." An analepsis moves the reader to an *aspectualization* in which the cities of Europe are made relays of continuity, marked by signifiers of "progress":

(380) . . . the miracle in the West was not so much that every-thing sprang up again from the eleventh century . . .

(381) [but that] the town won entirely.

(382) It was able to try the experiment . . . a completely sep-arate life . . . This was a colossal event . . . (p. 398).

(383) . . . They were able to follow fairly rare political, social, and economic experiments right through to the end.

The cities alone perform action, and so are awarded the status of a narrative subject who could cause:

(384) They invented public loans . . . reinvented gold money . . . organized industry and the crafts . . . reinvented long distance trade, bills of exchange . . . accountancy.

(385) They also quickly set in motion their class struggles (p. 399).

Framed by the "miracle" of lexia 380, which absorbs the semes of "favored by history" (lexia 150), the city is where the "main-stream of history" did continuously *stop* (which answers why the cities were "blessed"). As the subject of doing, the city is traced in its modernity right to the "state of mind" of the capitalist:

(386) A new state of mind was established . . . an early, still faltering, Western capitalism—

(387) a collection of rules, possibilities, calculations, the art both of getting rich and of living. And also gambling and risk (p. 400).

The capitalist is the accelerator: as marked out above, the capitalist persona here completes the social process of "innovation" (see lexia 254), the "progress of the past" culminating in the continuous attributes of the capitalist. The "art" referred to in lexia 387 intellectually stresses and fetishizes what the capitalist desired, suspending the attributes of the utilitarian "system" introduced at lexia 308. One may well ask: how is it possible to conjoin the capitalist to an "art" of "getting" and simultaneously speak of the "lightening and efficiency" of production (lexia 305)? The semantic disjunction between "getting rich" and Utilitarianism or the intellectual disparity of such differential messages is left suspended, as two more "historisemes" complete this "historicity of continuity":

(388) The merchant was economical . . . calculated . . . his investments according to their yield.
(389) The hourglass had turned back the right way (p. 400).

Lexia 388 instantiates what we can call the linearization of the rate of profit, "later" *literally* the progressive accumulation of the "past," while lexia 389 overcodes to the reader the message that lexia 26 has now been achieved: the "right road" of lexia 26 is now the "right way" of the capitalist, capitalism the means of progress; this, in turn, immediately ties the status of the capitalist's "mind" to the condition for the next sequence of progress:

(390) the state . . . heir to their institutions and way of thinking . . . (p. 400),

so that the State too is saturated in all this positivity.

Drawing identifications between capitalism and historicity is not a new cultural phenomenon. Marx is filled with comments about their mutual coding and decoding, and Lévi-Strauss is too, with his notion that capitalism belongs to an excessively overheated system of generalized displacement, and which Deleuze (1977:230–232) reminds us never ceases deterritorializing ("liberating") every conceivable zone and arena through which surplus is both the means and end of an immanent series of investment "times." Our question here is related: how does the recoding of Structuralism for-the-historian promote a historicization of capitalism consonant with what is sometimes called "historical assessment," where the historicality of the story (here, "progress") and the historicality of the telling (here, the language of structure, the voice(s) of the economist, planner, and others) are realized by a model reader as a necessary judgment? To answer this, let us consider these lexias.

The European states "caught up" with the cities, these new "classical Romes" and "luxuries of the East," the cities made into "privileged" capitals (p. 411) through the transformation of the states, a recoding of lexias 157–160. The cities are now treated as internalizations of dynamic change:

(391) Which would have the first pavements . . . lamps . . . numbered houses

(392) The town that did not grasp this opportunity was necessarily left behind.

(393) The more its old shell remained behind, the greater its chance of becoming empty (p. 411).

The capital town's historical function, the production of the modern state and the national markets (p. 414), is modeled on the case of London,

(394) an enormous demanding central nervous system, which caused everything to move to its own rhythm, overturned everything and quelled everything (p. 414).

The narrator ranks the cities according to the degree that their respective modernizations (construction) was in harmony or not with their own past. Amsterdam is "admirable," London a "disappointment," Paris, Madrid, Berlin, and Naples an "unhealthy situation" (p. 316), Naples focalized as a case of the "sordid and beautiful, abjectly poor and very rich," the poor (one in five) erased by this judgment:

(395) The fault lay in their excessive numbers. Naples drew

them but could not feed them all. They barely survived (p. 417).

The city survived precisely because of the very negative historicity of the traditional classes:

> (396) . . . peasants, shepherds, sailors, miners, craftsmen, and carriers *inured to hardship* (p. 418, italics added).

Lexia 48 is confirmed: the "infinite number of victims" is completed in the growth of the capital towns, once again "growth" complemented by the unnarratability of the consciousness of the masses, their primary predicate that of a permanent (unspecified) form of the "connivance" at lexia 162, their very "sense of history" determined by their "massification" (see lexia 77), proletarianization, one might say, having its own historical vision:

> (397) The London drama—its festering criminality, its underworld, its difficult biological life—
> (398) can truly be understood from this worm's-eye view of the poor (p. 436).

Thus the theoretical program of lexia 92 is fulfilled as well in terms of the "masses." The reader can automatically think: negative semes entail nonnarration—"inured to hardship" ensures zero-degree temporality, time so familiar that only a perpetual present is given to the masses as their mode of temporality. And the reader can judge why what could not have happened had to happen.

However, there is a "collective destiny" to the towns, a positive form of historicity. Here is its intellectual articulation:

> (399) The enormous towns had their faults and their virtues.
> (400) They created, let us repeat, the modern state, as much as they were created by it. National markets expanded under their impetus as did the nations themselves and modern civilization.
> (401) . . . a prodigious test of the evolution of Europe and the other continents.

> (402) . . . a disequilibrium, asymmetrical growth, and irrational and unproductive investment . . . (p. 439).

This combination of positive and negative temporal markers is then, in turn, resequenced: the towns were more "past" than "future," their story of creativity closing in favor of a new extradiegetic role, their reduction to story tellers. As "subjects of the story" the cities of the ancien régime are forced to give up their own historicity, for as they cease to be involved in their own story as autodiegetic (self-directed) actors, they become, at best, possible narrators:

> (403) The obvious fact was that the capital cities would be present at the forthcoming industrial revolution in the role of spectators (p. 440).

And what would they tell? The prophetic narrator of lexia 403 says that the merchant alive in London in 1830 who could no longer compete with the rate of speed and transformation of the economic has become the *told* who can also tell, as spectator (observer), his story, this capacity a function of the loss of historical competence, the subject no-longer favored by history. Historical actors lose primary historicity all the better to acquire—for the historian—the sign status of potential tellers of stories, which, as told, yield their meaning to the historian. The positive judgment: past necessity in whatever form becomes evidence, the tellable, the recountable. Positive history slams the doors of the mind shut against potential loss (of meaning, significance, value).

The narrator of *Capitalism and Material Life* closes the text with a micro-masterpiece of positive historicity, initiating the next phase of the story in a suspension of before and after:

> (404) Capitalism is protean, a hydra with 100 heads.

What is the intellectual sense of this lexia if not literally for a last time granting to capitalism a narrative base in the very act of displaying predicates about it? This lexia instances the suppression of an argument or premise about what capitalism is. What capitalism can be known as—its "is-ness"—must wait for the historian to tell its story. One cannot complete one's thoughts about capitalism until the historian has sentenced the past. The "time of capitalism," as "protean," recodes Schumpeter's notion of "creative destruction," this reperformed now by the mythic figure of Hydra, which goes to the reader as the narrativized myth of capitalism, as an adventure story. Hydra is the figure who made possible Hercules, who is the condensation of subjectivity and "humanity," whose very story is the determination of and by a test. The reader can thus easily think of capitalism as an ongoing test ("with 100 heads") that is necessary for the reader, precoded all along as someone who had passed certain tests of capitalist society, the main one being the ability to read this history and affirm its "essential truth" of the society of the reader. With *Capitalism and Material Life*, the recoding of "historical thought" *affirms* disintellection, which is the very point of historical narration.

Conclusion

I cannot conclusively judge whether the sentence of narration, as Banfield (1982:263) puts it, is "linguistically free of the taint of subjectivity, of interpretation and evaluation," because I do not share the linguist's framework. It is questionable whether a model of narrative sentences can yield a model valid for a text of narration. What does seem clear to me, however, is that narrative effects are circulated when their product, the told, can be detached from the telling and, as retold or inventoried for telling (as image, example, proposition, metaphysic, and so on), are released for the cultural function of banishing critical thought to marginalia. Whatever grammatical, syntactical, and logical analyses say about "historical narration," the told and the telling are both a dimension of that strange linguistico-cognitive and cultural category, the shifter. In this mode the told can be thought of as part of the autonomy of "necessity," and when this occurs, the telling unleashes "history" from its nonnarrative basis in some discursive system. Such is frozen thought, for the impact of narrative history results in the affirmation and "positivity" of the nonnarrated, and not in any sense of transformation. The transcendence given to "unpolitical subjects" in Gay's "Weimar," the institutionalization of history as "dialogic business," or "historicality" made a semic nucleus of "genuine desire," wherein the narrator of Braudel's *Capitalism* perpetuates the sign form of "inauthenticity" as the story-reality of the non-

West and proletariat—these are nonnarrative meanings. Such tellings are primordially nonnarrative insofar as they can only refer to how thought is put together. So far as I can determine, no "historical" text supposes a reader of disconfirmation, argument, theory, or critique. "History" texts can be disentangled by a reader already subjectivized by other versions (but each text presents itself as nonversion) or by a reader who systematically refuses the signifier as it is made part of such distorting and deintellectualizing sign forms.

Historians object: "that is not what we do." And therein is an index of the subjectivization of the discipline as a whole, its denial of its materialized thoughts, semantics, thinking. In fact, the reception of the historian's texts by a public really certifies what the profession, and little else, has validated as "necessary" forms of the presence of history. The historian decodes a discourse and recodes it for story telling, a cultural practice that projects "finding history" as itself the "center" of past-present-future, this "finding" the kernel of intellectual distortion generated by historians as their singular sign form. Historians promote the historical in accordance with academic requirements that have never been decided upon by a free discourse, one without all the restraints thrown up by the division of labor within thinking, a "muck of thought" which outstrips any image of the past. Who else culturally defines subjects as "historical" insofar as they internalize "unpolitical subjectivity" or eternalize "muddles" or essentialize the banker as a "repairman," if not the historian? Such narrative definitions—narrativizations—enable the told to be thought of as that which provides subjectivity with its cultural obligations—to overvalue elites (Gay), to rise to moral judgment (Thompson), to celebrate capitalism (Braudel), acts that allow subjects to imagine the transcendence of their own actual social and intellectual operations.

Just as the telling is organized as unstatable, readers can reproduce ideations and forms of the necessary, the common, the general, the limit, the referent, and other coded abstractions. It is the form of story that allows this to happen. The semantic construction of an if-clause can be recoded into nonhypothetical thought when situated as a description, so that "fate" or "structural flaws" (of "Weimar") can be made familiarly conclusive—necessary—to a reader's thoughts. An assumption is recast as an assertion so placed in a story that it appears to be part of the very fabric of the story: the "banker" is made not critical, but narrative, not a function, but a need, not suitable for analysis, but comprehensible as narrativized. The historian who writes that today "the subject has less interiority than formerly," as I pointed out in chapter one, provides finality when this thought is made an ending to a story, but how is such a nonnarrative thought true? The narrator never relinquishes control over these linearized precritical thoughts and their reproduction as utterances of the reader's parole. As I see it, the very forms of historical narrative presented in chapters three through five are preintellectual, simulations of history that exclude, as Baudrillard (1975:179) puts it, the "reciprocity and antagonism of interlocutors, in the ambivalence of their exchange" in favor of the aestheticized and moralized intellect of academe. Historical narratives evade the nonauthoritarian form "What do you mean by . . . ?" (What is capitalism? What is a "disciplined procedure"? What is the "shamelessness" of the masses?) as they recode these questions into modalized/narrativized answers. Obligative thought, a form of cultural terror, appears through story telling as "realistic" because semantics itself is pulverized by narrating into yielding to the smoothness of resolution.

At the close of *Metahistory*, White suggests that historians could link up with the "Golden Age" of history by opening their telling to nonironic tropes and plot structures; his work supports the increased novelization of the discipline by promoting the autonomy of imagination. He suggests that the "crisis" of historiography is resolvable by the individual will of historians if they would call forth suppression of the excessive negative imagination of irony. Metaphor, metonymy, and synecdoche (romance, tragedy, comedy) could be recombined for the "positive imagination" of authentic telling, in which thinking and aesthetic style coemerge released from skepticism, irony, positivism, and so on. White would reexistentialize the historical profession through a decoding of literature and recoding it as the means of "historical" presentation. Opposed to this ideal, others assert "scientized" strategies based upon the appropriation of what is accepted in some scientific community as stable significations, so that narrative form is supposedly neutralized as an apparatus. Each position always includes components of the other.

What I have argued is that when historians synthesize so that their narrations are readable by an "ordinary educated public," such syntheses restabilize semanticized, logicized, and especially cognized markers and sign forms of discourse already riddled with semantic contraries, status, ideology, modals, symmetry, "appropriate" contradictions, disthought. Historians work over significations—discourse—already achieved, already ideologized, their collective acts determined by the maintenance of the historian's privilege: that the form of story is compatible with every mode of intellection, yet transcendent to critical thought. Such a privilege generates "history," "historicality," and "historicity" as signifieds raised to the plane of transcendence: "history is what hurts," or "historicality" is the equation between unfulfilled promise and present negativity (Adorno's conceit), or "historicity" is a primary predicate, a purely positive signified of the real, as in the scenodrama of *Capitalism*, where "historicality" is used to define Europe's legitimation and is found "in" the story line.

In all cases, academic codings persist. It is hardly coincidental that the values of linearity, continuity, career, and accumulation—strategic exchange values of social reproduction—are the sign forms of both academic culture and capitalist economy, both of which are in advance of all possible contents, all possible relations, all possible transformations insofar as the category of "possibles" is embedded in narrations. Critical thinking cannot stem from such defensive positions, nor from the strangeness that affirms that "historicity" is agent and cause and that past is intrinsically present. Present-thought alone performs such reactive affirmations, enacts the repetition of the belief that "history" is an obligation for one's access to "reality," that all present results are realizations of "history." In this sense, "historical narration's" consequence of issuing forth versions of reactive subjectivity may be only the result of its aggression against the present, a function at one with the plenitude of capitalism's promotion of thought forms that make the present as something that matters all but inaccessible.

Glossary

This glossary is offered for those unfamiliar with basic semiotic and critical categories as applied to the plane of historiographical and cultural meanings.

Academic discourse: refers to texts that build in defensive significations, such as "unalterable" binary oppositions, "irresolvable" contradictions, or archaic dramatic modes. This type of discourse is accomplished by the superimposition of positivized signifiers upon the ambiguity and contention of meanings and forms. It is realized when the thought content of semantics is accepted as inherently defining (closure).

Actantial/actant: refers to the complex exchange between what a "historical" narration allows to be the subject of doing (for example, capitalism treated as the actant of innovation or capitalism presented as the subject of dialectical transformations) and the reader's ability (generally) to acknowledge primary roles of action as necessary to a culture.

Bourgeois-academic: is a discursive and systematic function that favors the recoding of economic surplus, usually founded on "need," and intellectual passivity (the reduction of the intellect of the reader to desire for integration). Academia recodes this function by the reproduction of a "code of last resort": the obligative modality, which is set against critical thinking.

Code: involves the isolation of the ways in which semantic materials are linked. Includes physical units (sounds), ideation (concepts), pragmatic responses of readers, and the rules that generate acceptable and unacceptable syntactic combinations. Codes ensure that states (of mind), qualities (of value, predication), and responses (what one thinks) are simultaneously generated. The act of *encoding* is inferred from textual effects, and its isolation yields new knowledge; analysis of the transmission of messages passes through multiple *subcodes*, partial constructions (devices) that convey information about prior codings and present to the reader unforeseen arrangements; *undercoding* pertains to textual sections that are ambiguously connected to stronger (syntactic) codes; *overcoding* refers to predications where new information is reduced by subsumption to the already said, already known; and *recoding*, which dominates in the academic system, suggests the proliferation of ways in which meaning is recalibrated to favor the Same, the elimination of the untimely from meaning and thought. In all cases, coding is radically opposed to intellectual states of apertinence, asyntacticality, and semanticism: these latter categories are intolerable to bourgeois-academia since they scramble the production of continuous meanings.

Communication: is an event of speaking, which cannot occur between readers and texts or traces of texts and present readers. The term denotes the copresence of speakers in disruptive exchange and nonagreement, activities that are unstable yet do not preclude consensus. The texts of historians are noncommunicative, although such texts simulate communication.

Culture: is the ensemble of ways in which sign systems, gestures, and behavior are promoted to favored positions or, conversely, relegated to the status of negative examples. For example, the act of literary criticism as defining cultural integration occurs when such criticism is said to reveal, disclose, and model the nonliterary. "Historical culture" is defined by what it encodes, implicitly, as the "nonhistorical," actions or meanings that cannot be calibrated and recoded for narrativization. When it is believed that capitalism is a form of culture *and* that anti-capitalism is anti-historical, capitalism is positivized—made valued, defining, and necessary.

Disengagement: a textualization (of propositions, statements, meanings) made in such a way that readers are positioned to accept the autonomy of content and dismiss its mode of presentation. Significations—descriptive, theoretical, or explanatory—are released from their articulation and read as objectifications. In "historical narrations" devices like the performative onset require the reader to shift from a critical decoding of the text to accepting the stability of the encoded. The term *nondisengagement* characterizes the historiographic subcode where the reader is positioned to react to the loss of his or her present roles unless a nonreciprocal contact is made with "history."

Disintellection: is a textual property of narrativization. It is the act of organizing semantic units that block thinking-out nonnarrative constructions. The markings of presupposition, entropic associations, axioms, and category relations are unstated in favor of having the reader occupy the position of thinking about disengaged meanings. Includes the distance between the reader's critical thinking and the story, this distance an index of a "historical narration's" maintenance of the ease of reading.

Distransitivity: refers to present meanings and contradictions held to be chaotic, irrational, senseless, and unnameable until brought into line with the "seamless" text of "history" itself. It is the belief that the present is unclear and unreadable until it is thought of under the categories of the Same and Different.

Enthymeme: is the mixture of logic and distortion. It is used here to include relations between textual levels—actant, narrative trajectory, and causality—where an unstatable meaning is later realized as a logical/chronological completion of sense and the termination of thought about some topic or problem.

History: is a concept of last resort, a floating signifier, the alibi of an alignment with obligatory values. It pertains to no signified at all; depending on how the past is positioned, it can preclude confusion of temporal coordinates, preserve the imaginary idea of collective relations, substitute when for where, or dismiss present intensities. "History" must be radically severed from "past": the former is always calibrated with cultural contradictions, whereas the latter is much more fluid a notion. "Past" is involved with both active and involuntary memory, but "history" can only project the simulation of the remembered.

Imaginary: refers to what a reader is to think. Involves the distribution of oppositions and contradictions presented to thought as valid, normal, necessary, and pragmatic. In regard to historiography, this term covers irreversible/transcending temporal processes (for example, "later" answers "earlier"), the belief that to be "historical" makes the present significant, and that to become actantial, one must fulfill some obligation which has been "historically" transmitted.

Isotopy: refers to narrated topics that convey hierarchically determining meanings. It pertains to meanings that traverse specific presentation; for example, when the classemes of the Nazis (murder, illegality, horror, madness) are recognized by the reader as the story of the Nazis' role of introducing negation and disjunction, the reader can identify and inventory the Nazis under the category of judgment. The same isotopies can be attached to more than one narrative program.

Narrativization: is the organization of signifiers so as to display transformations whereby subjects, actions, and sanctions install modalities of "history" in the form of a story. The term refers to the ways in which that which cannot be directly stated—an axiological projection, for example—is nevertheless manifested as a narrative answer. Includes the effects of the reader's pragmatic response, which is to not engage in the act of semantic contention against the narrated. The reduction of meanings to stories.

Psychologeme: is the presentation of universal forms of desire and need as they are "found" in "history" by the narrating and as they are given to readers as acceptable codings of present experience.

Semic: refers to metalinguistic categories named in textual analysis as the elementary relations (opposition, contradiction, exclusion, and the like) that purportedly are immanent in existence. For example, linear/nonlinear gives rise to distinctions between anteriority and possibility, repetition and individuality, meanings invested with political, psychological, and intellectual values.

Shifter: in linguistic usage pertains to expressions of context (*here/there*) and ambiguities of speaking (for example, when saying *I* refers to *he/then*). Here it refers to narrativized senses that straddle impersonal and personal frames, whereby what must be thought not only appears disengaged from thinking but also excuses the historian from presenting the activities of intellectual construction.

Sign: is the result of underlying semantic operations. It is the unit of signification that enables isotopies, actants, motivations, and the like to stand for and as meanings. I use the term *sign form*, borrowed from Baudrillard, to specify the recoding by historians of hierarchical meanings that establish both the past and the reader in relations of differentiation and privilege in which actions are thought of as necessary. An instance of this is the historian's use of an example to define a model of "historical" process which is also used to suggest the "need" for certain kinds of research, the promotion of ideals, or the directionality of thinking.

Stabilization: refers to standardized, homogenized, and centralized acts of signification. It is the domination of a sign form over heteronymous meanings and interpretations, whereby expression, criticism, desire, and the like are prevented from manifesting excessive signification. A term borrowed from Deleuze.

Symbolic: refers to the Imaginary raised to the second power—the freezing, by narrativization, of signification *and* existential actions by stressing "what has to be." It describes any act of narrativization that invests the reader's thinking with the function of legitimizing contradictions.

Transcendence: is the use of a cultural form as the interpretant of another where the interpreting form contains the interpreted. This generates the belief that such forms ("historical thought," for example) are obligative for understanding so that what is missing (from knowledge, for example) will thus answer, satisfy, and resolve contradictions and antinomies on the plane of immanence. In signification, it is the release of sign forms from their composition so as to function as interpretants which provide access to cultural positions.

References

Narrative Theory, Linguistics, Cultural Criticism

Althusser, L., and Balibar, E. *Reading Capital*. London: New Left Books, 1977.

Bakhtin, M. M. *The Dialogic Imagination: Four Essays*. Austin: University of Texas Press, 1982.

Banfield, A. "Where Epistemology, Style and Grammar Meet Literary History." *New Literary History* 9 (1978):415–454.

————. *Unspeakable Sentences*. Boston: Routledge and Kegan Paul, 1982.

Barthes, R. *Writing Degree Zero*. New York: Hill and Wang, 1967*a*.

————. *Elements of Semiology*. Boston: Beacon, 1967*b*.

————. "L'effet de réel." *Communications* 11 (1968):84–89.

————. "Historical Discourse." In *An Introduction to Structuralism*, edited by M. Lane. New York: Basic Books, 1970.

————. *Mythologies*. New York: Hill and Wang, 1972.

————. *S/Z*. New York: Hill and Wang, 1974.

————. "Change the Object Itself." In *Image, Music, Text*. New York: Hill and Wang, 1977.

Baudrillard, J. *The Mirror of Production*. St. Louis, Mo.: Telos, 1975.

————. *For a Critique of the Political Economy of the Sign*. St. Louis, Mo.: Telos, 1981.

————. *In the Shadow of the Silent Majorities*. New York: Semiotexte, 1983*a*.

_____ . *Simulations*. New York: Semiotexte, 1983*b*.

_____ . "The Ecstasy of Communication." In *The Anti-Aesthetic,* edited by H. Foster. Port Townsend, Wash.: Bay Press, 1983*c*.

Benveniste, E. *Indo-European Language and Society*. Coral Gables: University of Miami Press, 1973.

Blanchard, M. E. *Description: Self, Sign, Desire*. New York: Mouton, 1980.

Blanchot, M. *The Gaze of Orpheus and Other Literary Essays*. Raleigh, N.C.: Station Hill, 1981.

Bremond, C. *Logique du récit*. Paris: Seuil, 1973.

Bruss, E. *Beautiful Theories*. Baltimore: Johns Hopkins University Press, 1982.

Chatman, S. *Story and Discourse*. Ithaca, N.Y.: Cornell University Press, 1978.

Clastres, P. *La société contre L'Etat*. Paris: Minuit, 1974.

Cohen, S. "Structuralism and the Writing of Intellectual History." *History and Theory* 18 (1978):175–206.

Comrie, B. *Aspect*. Cambridge: Cambridge University Press, 1976.

Courtes, J. *Introduction à la sémiotique narrative et discursive*. Paris: Hachette, 1976.

Culler, J. *On Deconstruction*. Ithaca, N.Y.: Cornell University Press, 1982.

Damisch, H. "Semiotics and Iconography." In *The Tell-Tale Sign,* edited by T. Sebeok. Lisse/Netherlands: de Ridder, 1975.

Debord, G. *Society of the Spectacle*. Detroit: Black and Red, 1977.

Deleuze, G. *Nietzsche et la philosophie*. Paris: PUF, 1962.

_____ . "Nomadic Thought." In *The New Nietzsche,* edited by D. Allison. New York: Dell, 1977.

Deleuze, G., and Guattari, F. *Anti-Oedipus*. New York: Viking, 1977.

_____ . *Mille Plateau*. Paris: Minuit, 1980.

_____ . *On the Line*. New York: Semiotexte, 1983.

Derrida, J. *Of Grammatology*. Baltimore: Johns Hopkins University Press, 1976.

_____ . "From Restricted to General Economy." In *Writing and Difference*. Chicago: University of Chicago Press, 1978.

Eco, U. *A Theory of Semiotic.* Bloomington: Indiana University Press, 1976.

——— .*The Role of the Reader.* Bloomington: Indiana University Press, 1979.

——— .*Semiotics and the Philosophy of Language.* Bloomington: Indiana University Press, 1984.

Faye, J. P. *Langages totalitaires.* Paris: Hermann, 1973.

Feyerabend, P. "Consolations for the Specialist." In *Criticism and the Growth of Knowledge,* edited by I. Lakatos and A. Musgrave. London: Cambridge University Press, 1970.

Foucault, M. *L'archéologie du savoir.* Paris: Gallimard, 1969.

Freud, S. *The Ego and the Id.* New York: Norton, 1962.

Genette, G. *Narrative Discourse.* Ithaca, N.Y.: Cornell University Press, 1980.

——— . *Figures of Literary Discourse.* New York: Columbia University Press, 1982.

Gossman, L. "History and Literature: Reproduction or Signification." In *The Writing of History,* edited by R. Canary and H. Kozicki. Madison: University of Wisconsin Press, 1978.

Greimas, A. J. *Du Sens.* Paris: Seuil, 1970.

——— . *Sémiotiques et sciences sociales.* Paris: Seuil, 1976.

——— . *Structural Semantics.* Lincoln: University of Nebraska, 1984.

Greimas, A. J., and Courtes, J. *Semiotics and Language: An Analytical Dictionary.* Bloomington: Indiana University Press, 1982.

Group μ. *A General Rhetoric.* Baltimore: Johns Hopkins University Press, 1981.

Guirard, P. *La Sémiologie.* Paris: Presses Universitaire de France, 1971.

Heidegger, M. *Being and Time.* New York: Harper & Row, 1962.

Hervey, S. *Semiotic Perspectives.* London: Allen & Unwin, 1982.

Hjelmslev, L. *Prolegomena to a Theory of Language.* Madison: University of Wisconsin Press, 1969.

Holloway, J. *Narrative and Structure: Exploratory Essays.* London: Cambridge University Press, 1979.

Iser, W. *The Act of Reading.* Baltimore: Johns Hopkins University Press, 1978.

Jakobson, R. "Closing Statement: Linguistics and Poetry." In *Style in Language,* edited by T. Sebeok. Cambridge: M.I.T. Press, 1960.

Jones, M. R. "Only Time Can Tell: On the Topology of Mental Space and Time." *Critical Inquiry* 7 (Spring 1981):557–576.

Joos, M. *The English Verb.* Madison: University of Wisconsin Press, 1968.

Kress, G., and Hodge, G. *Language As Ideology.* London: Routledge and Kegan Paul, 1979.

Kristeva, J. "The System and the Speaking Subject." In *The Tell-Tale Sign,* edited by T. Sebeok. Lisse/Netherlands: de Ridder, 1975.

———. "Psychoanalysis and the Polis." *Critical Inquiry* 9 (September 1982):77–92.

Labov, W. *Language in the Inner City.* University Park: University of Pennsylvania Press, 1972.

Lacan, J. *Ecrits.* New York: Norton, 1977.

Lanser, S. S. *The Narrative Act.* Princeton, N.J.: Princeton University Press, 1981.

Leech, G. *Semantics.* Baltimore: Penguin, 1974.

Lévi-Strauss, C. *Le Cru et le Cuit.* Paris: Plon, 1964.

———. *The Savage Mind.* Chicago: University of Chicago Press, 1966.

Lotman, J. *The Structure of the Artistic Text.* Ann Arbor: University of Michigan Press, 1977.

Lotman, J., et al. "Theses on the Semiotic Study of Cultures (As Applied to Slavic Texts)." In *The Tell-Tale Sign,* edited by T. Sebeok. Lisse/Netherlands: de Ridder, 1975.

Lotman, J., and Pjatigorsky, A. "Text and Function." In *Soviet Semiotics: An Anthology,* edited by D. P. Lucid. Baltimore: Johns Hopkins University Press, 1981.

Lyotard, J. F. *Instructions païennes.* Paris: Editions Galilée, 1977.

———. *Driftworks.* New York: Semiotexte, 1984*a*.

———. *The Post-Modern Condition: A Report on Knowledge.* Minneapolis: University of Minnesota Press, 1984*b*.

Martinet, A. *A Functional View of Language.* Oxford: Clarendon Press, 1972.

Marx, K. *The German Ideology.* New York: International Publishers, 1977.

Metz, C. *Film Language.* London: Oxford University Press, 1974.

Michaels, W. B. "The Interpreter's Self: Peirce on the Cartesian Subject." In *Reader-Response Criticism,* edited by J. Tompkins. Baltimore: Johns Hopkins University Press, 1980.

Mink, L. "Narrative Form As a Cognitive Instrument." In *The Writing of History,* edited by R. Canary and H. Kozicki. Madison: University of Wisconsin Press, 1978.

Moles, A. *Esthetic Perception and Information Theory.* Urbana: University of Illinois Press, 1968.

Nietzsche, F. *The Genealogy of Morals.* London: Foulis, 1913.

———. *Beyond Good and Evil.* New York: Modern Library, 1954.

———. *The Use and Abuse of History.* New York: Bobbs Merrill, 1957.

———. *The Will to Power.* New York: Vintage, 1968.

Perelman, C., and Olbrechts-Tyteca, L. *The New Rhetoric.* Notre Dame, Ind.: University of Notre Dame, 1969.

Ransdell, J. "Semiotics and Linguistics." In *The Signifying Animal,* edited by I. Rauch and G. Carr. Bloomington: Indiana University Press, 1980.

Ryan, M. L. "Linguistic Models in Narratology: From Structuralism to Generative Semantics." *Semiotica* 28.5 (1979): 127–155.

Segre, C. *Structures and Time: Narration, Poetry, Models.* Chicago: University of Chicago Press, 1979.

Sollers, P. "Niveaux sémantiques d'un texte moderne." In *Theorie d'Ensemble.* Paris: Seuil, 1968.

Sperber, D. *Rethinking Symbolism.* Cambridge: Cambridge University Press, 1977.

Todorov, T. "On Linguistic Symbolism." *New Literary History* 6 (Autumn 1974):111–134.

———. *The Poetics of Prose.* Ithaca, N.Y.: Cornell University Press, 1977.

———. *Symbolism and Interpretation.* Ithaca, N.Y.: Cornell University Press, 1982.

Tomashevsky, B. "Thematics." In *Russian Formalist Criticism,* edited by L. Lemon and M. Reis. Lincoln: University of Nebraska Press, 1965.

Van Dijk, T. *Text and Context*. New York: Longman's, 1977.

Virilio, P., and Lotringer, S. *Pure War*. New York: Semiotexte, 1983.

Wojcik, T. "The Praxiological Model of Language." In *Sign, Language, Culture*, edited by C. Van Schooneveld. Paris: Mouton, 1970.

Historiographical Texts, Texts Analyzed, and General

Adorno, T. *Prisms*. London: Spearman, 1967.

———. *Negative Dialectics*. New York: Seabury, 1973.

Amin, S. *Unequal Development*. New York: Monthly Review Press, 1976.

Anchor, R. "Realism and Ideology." *History and Theory* 22 (1983):107–119.

Arendt, H. *Between Past and Future*. New York: Meridian, 1963.

Aron, R. *The Dawn of Universal History*. New York: Praeger, 1961.

Axelos, K. *Alienation, Praxis and Techne in the Thought of Karl Marx*. Austin: University of Texas Press, 1976.

Bailyn, B. "The Challenge of Modern Historiography." *American Historical Review* 87 (1982):1–24.

Barraclough, G. *Main Trends in History*. New York: Holmes and Meier, 1978.

Beard, C. A. "Grounds for a Reconsideration of Historiography." In *Theory and Practice in Historical Study: A Report on the Committee on Historiography*. New York: Social Science Research Council, 1946.

Benjamin, W. *Illuminations*. New York: Schocken, 1969.

Bergson, H. *Creative Evolution*. New York: Random House, 1944.

Berlin, I. *Historical Inevitability*. London: Oxford University Press, 1954.

Boccioni, U., Carra, C., Russolo, L., et al. "Futurist Painting: Technical Manifesto, 1910." In *Futurist Manifestos*, edited by V. Apollonio. London: Thames and Hudson, 1973.

Bourdieu, P. *Entwurf einer Theorie der Praxis*. Frankfurt: Suhr-kamp, 1976.

Braudel, F. *Capitalism and Material Life 1400–1800*. New York: Harper & Row, 1973.

————. *On History*. Chicago: University of Chicago Press, 1980.

Burckhardt, J. *On History and Historians*. New York: Harper & Row, 1958.

Butterfield, H. *The Origins of History*. New York: Basic Books, 1981.

Carr, E. H. *What is History?* New York: Knopf, 1967.

Carroll, D. "The Alterity of Discourse: Form, History, and the Question of the Political in M. M. Bakhtin." *Diacritics* (Summer 1983):65–83.

Castoriadis, C. *Crossroads in the Labyrinth*. Cambridge: M.I.T. Press, 1984.

de Certeau, M. *L'écriture de l'histoire*. Paris: Gallimard, 1975.

Chatelet, F. *La Naissance de l'histoire*. Paris: Minuit, 1962.

Chesneaux, J. *Pasts and Future or What is History For?* London: Thames and Hudson, 1978.

Clark, T. J. "Preliminaries to a Possible Treatment of 'Olympia' in 1865." *Screen* (Fall 1980):18–41.

Cochran, T. C. *Frontiers of Change*. London: Oxford University Press, 1981.

Cohen, G. A. *Karl Marx's Theory of History*. Princeton, N.J.: Princeton University Press, 1978.

Collingwood, R. G. *The Idea of History*. Oxford: Clarendon Press, 1948.

————. *The Idea of Nature*. Oxford: Clarendon Press, 1967.

Coward, R., and Ellis, J. *Language and Materialism*. London: Routledge and Kegan Paul, 1977.

Craig, G. *Germany: 1866–1945*. New York: Oxford University Press, 1980.

D'Amico, R. "The Contours and Coupures of Structuralism Theory." *Telos* (Fall 1973):70–97.

Danto, A. *Analytic Philosophy of History*. London: Cambridge University Press, 1965.

Eagleton, T. *Criticism and Ideology*. London: New Left Books, 1976.

_____ . *Literary Theory: An Introduction*. Minneapolis: University of Minnesota Press, 1983.

Elias, N. *The History of Manners: The Civilizing Process*. New York: Pantheon, 1978.

Fernandez, J. "The Performance of Ritual Metaphors." In *The Social Use of Metaphor*, edited by J. Sapir and J. Crocker. Philadelphia: University of Pennsylvania Press, 1977.

Foucault, M. *The Order of Things*. New York: Pantheon, 1970.

Gadamer, H. G. *Truth and Method*. New York: Seabury, 1975.

Gallie, W. B. *Philosophy and the Historical Understanding*. New York: Schocken, 1964.

Gardiner, P. *The Nature of Historical Explanation*. New York: Oxford University Press, 1961.

Gay, P. "A Short Political History of the Weimar Republic." In *Weimar Culture*. New York: Harper & Row, 1968.

_____ . *Style in History*. New York: McGraw-Hill, 1974.

Gellner, E. *Legitimation of Belief*. London: Cambridge University Press, 1974.

Genovese, E. D., and Genovese, E. F. "The Political Crisis of Social History." *Journal of Social History* 10 (Winter 1976): 205–220.

Gordy, M. "Time and the Social Whole: Reading Althusser." *History and Theory* 22 (1983):1–21.

Habermas, J. *Legitimation Crisis*. Boston: Beacon, 1975.

_____ . *Communication and the Evolution of Society*. Boston: Beacon, 1979.

Hartman, G. *Beyond Formalism*. New Haven: Yale University Press, 1970.

Henretta, J. "Social History As Lived and Written." *American Historical Review* 84 (December 1979):1293–1322.

Hexter, J. H. *Reappraisals in History*. New York: Harper & Row, 1961.

Hoffman, R. "Asking the Wrong Question: Of What Use Are the Humanities?" *Academe* 68 (1982):25–27.

Horkheimer, M. *Critical Theory*. New York: Herder and Herder, 1972.

Jacoby, R. *The Dialectic of Defeat*. Cambridge: Cambridge University Press, 1981.

Jameson, F. *Marxism and Form*. Princeton, N.J.: Princeton University Press, 1971.

———. *The Prison-House of Language*. Princeton, N.J.: Princeton University Press, 1972.

———. *The Political Unconscious*. Ithaca, N.Y.: Cornell University Press, 1981.

———. "Radicalizing the 60's." In *The Sixties, Without Apology*, edited by S. Sayres. Minneapolis: University of Minnesota Press, 1984.

Jauss, H. R. "The Alterity and Modernity of Medieval Literature." *New Literary History* 10 (Winter 1979):181–227.

Kelley, D. R. "Vico's Road: From Philosophy to Jurisprudence and Back." In G. *Vico's Science of Humanity*, edited by G. Tagliacozzo and D. R. Verene. Baltimore: Johns Hopkins University Press, 1976.

Kellner, H. "Disorderly Conduct: Braudel's Mediterranean Satire." *History and Theory* 18 (1979):197–222.

Kermode, F. *The Genesis of Secrecy*. Boston: Harvard University Press, 1979.

Kinser, S. "Annaliste Paradigm? The Geohistorical Structure of Fernand Braudel." *American Historical Review* 86 (February 1981):63–105.

Kracauer, S. *History*. New York: Oxford University Press, 1969.

Krieger, L. *Ranke: The Meaning of History*. Chicago: University of Chicago Press, 1977.

Kuzminski, A. "Defending Historical Realism." *History and Theory* 18 (1979):316–349.

LaCapra, D. "Rethinking Intellectual History and Reading Texts." *History and Theory* 19 (1980):245–276.

———. "Is Everyone a *Mentalité* Case? Transference and the 'Culture' Concept." *History and Theory* 23 (1984):296–311.

Lasch, C. *The Culture of Narcissism*. New York: Warners, 1979.

———. "The Prospects for Social Democracy." *Democracy*, July 1982.

Lefebvre, H. *Everyday Life in the Modern World*. New York: Harper & Row, 1971.

———. *The Survival of Capitalism*. London: Allison and Busby, 1976.

Le Goff, J. "The Historian and the Common Man." In *The Historian between the Ethnologist and the Futurologist,* edited by J. Dumoulin and D. Moisi. Paris: Mouton, 1973.

Louch, A. R. "History as Narrative." *History and Theory* 8 (1969):54–70.

Lowe, D. M. *History of Bourgeois Perception.* Chicago: University of Chicago Press, 1982.

Lowith, K. *Meaning and History.* Chicago: University of Chicago Press, 1964*a*.

————. *From Hegel to Nietzsche.* New York: Holt, Rinehart and Winston, 1964*b*.

Lukacs, G. "Narrate or Describe?" In *Writer and Critic.* New York: Grosset & Dunlap, 1970.

————. "The Historical Novel of Democratic Humanism." In *Marxism and Art,* edited by B. Lang and F. Williams. New York: McKay, 1972.

Macheray, P. *A Theory of Literary Production.* London: Routledge and Kegan Paul, 1978.

de Man, P. *Allegories of Reading.* New Haven: Yale University Press, 1979.

McLennan, G. *Marxism and the Methodologies of History.* London: Verso, 1981.

Mandel, E. *Late Capitalism.* London: Verso, 1975.

————. *The Second Slump.* London: Verso, 1980.

Mandelbaum, M. *The Anatomy of Historical Knowledge.* Baltimore: Johns Hopkins University Press, 1977.

Marcuse, H. *Eros and Civilization.* New York: Vintage, 1955.

————. *Negations.* Boston: Beacon, 1969.

Mink, L. "The Autonomy of Historical Understanding." *History and Theory* 5 (1965):24–47.

Moore, B. *The Social Origins of Dictatorship and Democracy.* Boston: Beacon, 1966.

Munz, P. *The Shape of Time.* Middletown, Conn. Wesleyan University Press, 1977.

Nadel, G. H. "Philosophy of History Before Historicism." *History and Theory* 3 (1964):291–317.

Nield, K. "A Symptomatic Dispute? Notes on the Relation between Marxian Theory and Historical Practice in Britain." *Social Research* 47 (Autumn 1980):479–506.

Olafson, F. "Narrative History and the Concept of Action." *History and Theory* 9 (1970):265–289.

Pettit, P. *The Concept of Structuralism*. Los Angeles: University of California Press, 1975.

Ricoeur, P. "The Model of the Text: Meaningful Action Considered As a Text." *Social Science* 38 (Autumn 1971):529–562.

———. "Narrative Time." *Critical Inquiry* 7 (Autumn 1980): 169–190.

Rüsen, J. "Die vier Typen des historischen Erzählens." In *Theorie der Geschichte*. Beiträge zur Historik, Band 4. Munich: Deutscher Taschenbuch Verlag, 1982.

Said, E. *Beginnings: Intention and Method*. New York: Basic Books, 1978.

———. "Opponents, Audiences, Constituencies and Communities." In *The Anti-Aesthetic*, edited by H. Foster. Port Townsend, Wash.: Bay Press, 1983.

Santamaria, U., and Bailey, A. "A Note on Braudel's Structure As Duration." *History and Theory* 23 (1984):78–83.

Sartre, J. P. *Search for a Method*. New York: Random House, 1968.

Scholes, R. *Structuralism in Literature*. New Haven: Yale University Press, 1974.

Shklar, J. "Let Us Not Be Hypocritical." *Daedalus* 108 (Summer 1979):1–25.

Skinner, Q. "Meaning and Understanding in the History of Ideas." *History and Theory* 8 (1969):3–53.

———. "'Social Meaning' and the Explanation of Social Action." In *Philosophy of History*, edited by P. Gardiner. London: Oxford University Press, 1974.

Stoianovich, T. *French Historical Methods*. Ithaca, N.Y.: Cornell University Press, 1976.

Stone, L. "The Revival of Narrative: Reflections on an Old New History." *Past and Present* 5 (November 1979):3–24.

Streuver, N. "Historical Rhetoric." Paper presented at conference on White's *Metahistory* (1978), p. 5; published as "Topics in History." *History and Theory* 19 (1980):66–79.

Tholfsen, T. R. *Historical Thinking.* New York: Harper & Row, 1967.

Thompson, E. P. *The Poverty of Theory.* London: Merlin, 1978.

Tilly, C., Tilly, L., and Tilly, R. *The Rebellious Century.* Cambridge: Harvard University Press, 1975.

Ulmer, G. "On A Parodic Tone Recently Adopted in Criticism." *New Literary History,* Fall 1983.

Vico, G. *The New Science.* Ithaca, N.Y.: Cornell University Press, 1970.

————. *Practice of the New Science.* In G. *Vico's Science of Humanity,* edited by G. Tagliacozzo and D. R. Verene. Baltimore: Johns Hopkins University Press, 1976.

White, H. *Metahistory.* Baltimore: Johns Hopkins University Press, 1973.

————. Review of L. Pompa's *Vico: A Study of the New Science. History and Theory* 15 (1976):186–201.

————. "The Historical Text As Literary Artifact." In *The Writing of History,* edited by T. Canary and H. Kozicki. Madison: University of Wisconsin Press, 1978.

————. Review essay of J. G. Droysen, *Historik. History and Theory* 19 (1980):73–92.

————. "The Politics of Historical Interpretation: Discipline and De-Sublimation." *Critical Inquiry* 9 (September 1982): 113–138.

————. "The Question of Narrative in Contemporary Historical Theory." *History and Theory* 23 (1984):1–33.

Wilden, A. *System and Structure.* London: Tavistock, 1972.

Windelband, W. "History and Natural Science." *History and Theory* 19 (1980):165–185.

Yeager, M. "Trade Protection As an International Commodity: The Case of Steel." *Journal of Economic History* 11 (March 1980):33–42.

Name Index

Subject Index

Designer:	U. C. Press Staff
Compositor:	Publisher's Typography
Printer:	Braun-Brumfield, Inc.
Binder:	Braun-Brumfield, Inc.
Text:	10/12 Palatino
Display:	Optima